Literary Olympians II

Linda Brown Michelson
General Editor, Editor of Fiction

Elizabeth Bartlett
Editor of Poetry

Associate Editors: Rich Ives
 Judith Neeld
Contributing Editor: Samuel Hazo

D1712172

Crosscurrents
Anthologies

Crosscurrents
A Quarterly

Westlake Village, California

First Edition 1987

Crosscurrents
Anthologies

Crosscurrents
A Quarterly

Westlake Village, California

ISBN: 0-9619332-9-1

Foreword

With our thoughts turning to Olympiad XXIV, we present this first edition of *Literary Olympians II*, an anthology whose purpose is to mark the celebration with a memorable collection of contemporary literature. During our four years of gathering material for this collection, we limited our selections to the poetry and short fiction of leading, living writers. We asked that all short fiction and all poetry in English be previously unpublished; also, we decided to offer many of the poems in original language text, as well as in English translation.

In *Literary Olympians II*, we are especially pleased to feature photographs of museum art. We are fortunate to include reproductions of paintings, prints, lithographs, photographs, sculpture and woodcarvings. The historical span of these pieces ranges from Greece in the sixth century, B.C., through the Old Silla dynasty of Korea, the nineteenth and early twentieth century work of artists such as Toulouse-Lautrec, Picasso and Jawlensky, to the recent work of Ansel Adams and Elliot Erwitt. In short, we have complemented today's literature with art from varying periods.

We consider it important that these masterworks touch the span of centuries, for their purpose here is more than ornamental. By accompanying our literary art, the pictures add a visual dimension to it, and certainly they grace our pages. But they also remind us of a considered principle underlying this collection, specifically, our respect for the continuity of literary culture. For just as the artistic treasures of antiquity inspired the growth and evolution of art, so will the writings of today's fine authors add to our literary heritage.

As publisher, *Crosscurrents'* habit has been to include professional biographical information about our contributors. In tribute to the distinguished guests on our pages, we have continued this practice in the Contributors' Notes of *Literary Olympians II*.

Linda Brown Michelson

CONTENTS

12   *Contents*

16   *Contents*

Front cover photograph, *Mars with Cupid,* by Marcellini. Courtesy of Hearst Castle. Photograph by Cara Moore.

Back cover photograph, *The Three Graces,* by Boyer. Courtesy of Hearst Castle. Photograph by Cara Moore.

Greetings from Mr. Seh Jik Park
President, Seoul Olympic Organizing Committee

The Olympic Games is a celebration of the Heart, Mind and Body. In many ways, these three elements are more important than Gold, Silver and Bronze. The Olympics is more than just the world's premier athletic event—It is a rare opportunity for the world to come together in a spirit of harmony and progress and to demonstrate the most admirable of abilities and talents.

We are extremely pleased that while Korea will honor leading athletes from throughout the world when it is host to the Olympics in 1988, Crosscurrents publication of Literary Olympians II will offer a tribute to leading writers worldwide. We are gratified that just as the nations of the world have selected Seoul for Olympiad XXIV, Crosscurrents will include in its anthology our distinguished poets, and these two events will continue to show the way for a better world.

In ancient Olympia, the Hellenic Greeks enjoyed the arts and culture festival as much as they did the sport. That tradition has flourished in the modern Olympics, and Olympiad XXIV in Seoul will be no exception. Indeed, it is our desire to further the artistic and cultural aspects of the Olympics with a spectacular program which represents the coming together of people united in an Olympic Spirit and transcending race, religion, culture and ideology.

The phrase, "The world to Seoul—Seoul to the World" is therefore appropriate not only in the sporting context but also in art and culture. Individuals from all spectrums of artistic and cultural spheres have been invited to come to Seoul to participate in the Olympic-related programs. They will include sculptors, musicians, dancers, painters, poets, writers, lecturers, actors and more. They will come from all over the world, from East and West, from North and South.

It is the Olympics that brings them together. It is the Olympics that, for sixteen days at the very least, will bring the whole world together in peace, harmony and friendship.

Park Seh-jik
President
Seoul Olympic Organizing Committee

Introduction to Literary Olympians II

It is with great pride and pleasure that we bring this book into existence, a collection of work by leading, living writers around the world, by way of paying tribute to literature on the occasion of the Olympics. The goal was conceived of four years ago, beginning with Olympiad XXIII in Los Angeles, when *Crosscurrents* brought out *Literary Olympians: 1984*, which contained work representing nine countries. For this second gathering, we have received work from some forty countries, surely a major step toward achieving that goal. We feel honored by the recognition granted our efforts by Olympiad XXIV's host country as part of the celebration in Seoul. In doing so, Korea has revived the cultural character of the Olympic Games as they were observed in ancient Greece, where they originated some 2,700 years ago.

It is fitting that we remind ourselves how the Greeks regarded the festival they celebrated every four years. Olympia, an important religious center, was chosen as the site of the festival. There, a temple created by the Athenian sculptor Phidias, contained a gold and ivory statue of Zeus, a forty foot statue towering seventeen times higher than human mortal. Clearly, the people loved their gods. Also, they loved sports and were eager to cheer the champions whose strength, endurance, skills and superior ability outperformed all competitors. How important the gods and athletes were, we learn from

Pindar, the greatest poet of his age (502 B.C.–452 B.C.), whose "Odes to Victory" greeted the victors and were sung in choral processions.

Although the gods have faded with "the glory that was Greece and the grandeur that was Rome," the love of sports as the majestic expression of the body, and the love of literature as the supreme expression of the spirit remain. So we thank Olympia not only for the flame lit by the sun's rays and carried by torch to the 1988 site in Seoul, but for the magnificent example set by those competing in the Games and for the inspiration provided by today's great poets and writers.

The five rings which symbolize the intercontinental reach of the Olympics serve *Crosscurrents* as well, as we reach across all currents and borders for an international presentation of world thought and feeling. Through the ages, people have been able to communicate across language barriers by means of music and art, but it is by means of translation that we have been able to communicate verbally. Despite attempts made to develop a universal language, only translations have succeeded in spreading the Gospel, the works of Plato, Shakespeare, and other immortals. As Professor Enrique Anderson Imbert of Harvard University explains, there are 2,796 living languages; from these, an international committee of linguists would be expected to put together a universal language to satisfy a billion Chinese, 60 million English, 275 million Russian, 100 million Spanish, 60 million French, and many million each of German, Arabs, Bengalis, Hindus, Italians and Japanese. What kind of literature would evolve: poetry, stories, drama, biographies? As daring a problem for the imagination as that confronting astronomers in their labs and observatories. Quite recently, such a challenge was ardently taken up by some six thousand followers of Ludovic Zamenhof, the Polish founder of Esperanto, who met in Warsaw to celebrate his 100th birthday. To his credit, let it be said that some 8 million are reported to speak Esperanto today.

For the literary translator, however, the problem remains how to turn words in an alien tongue into one's own so that it achieves a perfect metaphrase of sound and sense. This requires both renovation and innovation, based on practical skill, comparative judgment, and artistic finesse. Obviously, more than a dictionary is involved in the process, for words are related to time, place, tradition, semantic resonances and grammatical peculiarities. It is these relationships and associations that change mere words into a language.

So we are grateful for the translators whose competence has made it possible for *Crosscurrents* to present so much excellent work from other languages into beautiful English. We are grateful for the assistance provided by our associate and contributing editors, who brought us important work from Turkey, Armenia, the Near East . . . from writers we might otherwise have missed. We extend our thanks to the many helping hands of friends, like Nancy Schapiro of the *Webster Review*, Victor H. Brown in England, and John Vanderby, the librarian in charge of literature at the San Diego Central Library. Above all, we are grateful to the Olympics Committee in Seoul for the opportunity of reintroducing literature as a part of the world's contribution to our international festival.

It is our hope that many more writers and many more countries will answer our call for celebrating literature on each Olympiad. We welcome them and the translators who can magically bring their languages to us. Neither religious nor political by intent or design, our movement has already attracted a great number of distinguished poets and prose writers, as this anthology confirms, including several Nobel Laureates. Who knows, but our roster may contain a modern Sappho, Corinna, Hypatia . . . another kind of Aeschylus, Euripides, Sophocles . . . ? We go forward with the symbolic flame to a worthy future.

Elizabeth Bartlett

Courtesy of Los Angeles County Museum of Art

22   *Elihu Vedder*

Eugenio de Andrade

SEPTEMBER SEA

It was all luminous:
sky, lips, sand.
The sea was near,
trembling with froth.
Bodies or waves:
to and fro, to and fro,
sweet, light—just
rhythm and whiteness.
Happy, they sing;
calm, they sleep;
awakened, they love,
swelling the silence.
It was all luminous,
young, with wings.
The sea was near,
golden, and utterly pure.

—Translated from the Portugese by Alexis Levitin

Etelvina Astrada

From SUDDEN DEATH
A SEQUENCE OF FIVE POEMS

Para la búsqueda
        necesitamos tiempo,
para cicatrizar las haridas
        necesitamos tiempo,
para una deducción
        necesitamos tiempo,
para reparar la injusticia
        necesitamos tiempo,
para horadar con alma el silencio .
        necesitatmos tiempo,
para fecundar la contradicción
        necesitamos tiempo,
para escuhar el rumor de la revolución
        necesitamos tiempo,
para recoger el fruto maduro
        necesitamos tiempo,
para reflexionar
        necesitamos tiempo,
para fertilizar el vientre
        necesitamos tiempo,
y apenas para todo o nada,
se nos permite un hoy.
Mañana tal vez.

Etelvina Astrada

From SUDDEN DEATH
A SEQUENCE OF FIVE POEMS

To search
       we need time,
To heal wounds
       we need time,
To make a deduction
       we need time,
To check injustice
       we need time,
To pierce the silence with soul   ·
       we need time,
To foster contradiction
       we need time,   ·
To hear the strains of revolution
       we need time,
To harvest ripe fruit
       we need time,
To reflect
       we need time,
To make life in a womb
       we need time,
yet for everything or nothing
we hardly get a day.
At best tomorrow.

—Translated from the Spanish by Zoe Anglesey

Sin duda la ciencia está confusa,
esquizofrénica,
hamletiana.
Nos juegan a ser o no ser.
Esa es la cuestión.
El mundo,
se ha venido a menos.
Es una burbuja
que se bambolea
y nadie puede abarajar.

Etelvina Astrada

Without doubt, scientists are confused,
schizophrenic,
hamletic.
They play on us to be or not to be.
That is the question.
The world
has come to a brink.
It's a bubble
that totters
and no one can dodge the blockbuster.

—*Translated from the Spanish by Zoe Anglesey*

Etelvina Astrada

El mundo es una jaula
de universal tamaño.
Nadie se quedará sin su sitio.
Para esta único espectáculo,
todos estaremos juntos,
blancos, negros, amarillos,
cobardes y valientes,
trabajadores y ociosos,
occidentales y orientales,
católicos, budistas y ateos,
onanistas y eróticos,
confusos y lúcidos,
ignorantes y sabios,
pobres y ricos,
todos juntos,
al azar, contemporáneos,
casi fraternos,
dispuestos a soportarnos por última vez.
Cuando se levante el telón,
sin lugar a dudas,
será una obra en un solo acto,
demasiado breve,
sin epílogo,
y nada para recordar.

Etelvina Astrada

The world is a cage
of universal size.
No one can take its place.
For this single performance
we'll all be together,
white, black, yellow,
cowards and valiant,
workers and loafers,
easterners and westerners,
catholic, buddhist and atheists,
onanistic and erotic,
confused and lucid,
ignorant and wise,
poor and rich,
all together,
by chance, contemporaries,
almost kin,
willing to tolerate each other one last chance.
You can be sure
when the curtain rises,
there will be a one-act play,
all too brief,
without epilogue
or anything to remember.

—Translated from the Spanish by Zoe Anglesey

«Yo no creo que Dios juegue a los dados
con el universo»,
—claro que no—
señor Einstein.
Sólo al hombre se le. es permitido
arrojar el cubilete
y de una sola jugada
tirar por la borda el mundo.

Etelvina Astrada

"I do not believe that God plays dice
with the universe"—
Certainly not
Mr. Einstein.
Only man is permitted
to roll the dice
and in a single toss
turn the world on its ear.

—Translated from the Spanish by Zoe Anglesey

Un saber universal cargamos sobre las gibas.
Son las edades, las dinastías,
los crepúsculos, las leyendas,
las lujuriosas botánicas,
la sorprendente arqueología,
todas las nervaduras fluviales,
terrestres y lácteas
prendidas en la retina,
en el ojo de la memoria.
pegadas al seso,
y siempre removiendo la lumbre del saber.
¿Cómo preservarnos de este exceso,
y de esta ciencia en el poder,
que a ciencia cierta
echa la suerte del mundo
en los laboratorios funerarios?

Etelvina Astrada

We carry on our stooped backs
a quantum sum of knowledge—
epochs, dynasties,
twilights, legends,
botanical lushness,
astonishing archeology,
every fluvial rivulet,
terrestrial and lactate
inset in the retina
of memory's eye.
Time's cranial cobwebs
laced to the brain
yet always sweeping away the spark of insight.
How do we protect ourselves from this excess
and this science within power,
a science for certain
putting the world's fate
in the funereal laboratories?

—*Translated from the Spanish by Zoe Anglesey*

34   *Pablo Picasso*

Petros Glezos

THE TWO HUNDRED

Those were the first days following the Asia Minor catastrophe in August of 1922. Waves of refugees broke onto the shores of "Old Greece." Enormous masses arrived terrified, almost frantic, naked and hungry, into the large harbors of Piraeus and Thessaloniki. For a few days, they stayed on the streets wherever there was cover to shelter them from the cold and rain. The homeless even burrowed in the dressing rooms and balconies of the theaters, and the cabins of the seashore baths in the two suburbs of Phalero in Athens. The whole country grieved over their misfortune and pain. Why should we hide it? Although some did so, from sheer indisposition.

A ship also found its way to our island. The islanders received these refugees with heartfelt patience. Since they were few in number, we made them comfortable in empty houses, in partially completed buildings, even in homes where there was an extra room. Our Mayor begged our family to shelter a woman in our old tower house.

We lived high in the *kastro* or walled city; our tower house dominated the island. From our balconies you could see the gracious forms of islanders below, then down to the open sea. Sometimes, when the night was streaming with stars, you could see lights flickering. Dimly, dimly in the distance, mother once guessed she saw Tinos, island of miracles, where worshippers made their cross to the Virgin Mary, full of grace, in prayer for us and for the whole world.

The limits of our tower house stretched to the old huge fortress gate which was now left open day and night. We had no fear of anyone threatening us. The pirates, corsairs, Turks, Franks, were far from us now. The rooms in our tower house were large, high-ceilinged with heavy doors and strong oak windows, and the floors were made of indestructible hard wood. Only the large room was covered with pure white marble. King Otho and Queen Amalia had danced in this room!

When the Mayor escorted the woman to our tower house, we first reckoned that she was an official. But she was simply a lovely, still relatively young woman.

I remember her as if she were before me this very moment. She was "light brown"—this is how they describe women on our island who are not very dark-complexioned—resolute, with large sparking eyes that sweetened when she smiled, with lovely teeth and dark chestnut hair which spilled in charming disorder on her broad shoulders. Her whole carriage seemed infused with strength and generosity. And the refugee predicament seemed almost not to touch her; rather, it gave her the joy that lovely women feel when they have a need for pleasant warmth, for protection.

Kyria Myrsine Kleanthous—this is how the Mayor introduced her to us. Her Christian name and surname made an impression on me. I don't recall if it was then or considerably later that I again encountered such a name. It also belonged to another lady, a teacher; she too was a lady of substance; I met her in Athens years later. Most certainly it wasn't she. I was also impressed by her apellation "Kyria"—Madam. This young woman didn't look very much like a Kyria—she was simply a lovely young woman, rather one of the common people. With a somewhat forceful motion, she set down her small bundle in a corner of our room, while admiring its size. She extended her hand to mother. Mother embraced her and kissed her.

And Myrsine, surprised over the warm reception, dissolved into sobs.

"For the time being, I have lost both my husband and my mother. Now I am all alone and wretched. I hope to God that I will find them again. I thank you, Kyria, I thank you . . ."

We settled Myrsine in an empty room of our tower house. She made the rounds of the room, dismayed, as if she still sensed that some sudden danger could threaten her. Mother reassured her.

"As you see," Mother said laughing, "here we have great security. Our tower house even has a fortress gate . . ."

Myrsine also laughed. She was very pretty when she laughed.

Myrsine remained with us some three or four months. She was unobtrusive, and we almost did not feel her presence. She helped mother with household chores. Now and then she went out to visit other refugee families, expecting and hoping to learn something about her own relations. She would return home, sometimes in tears, sometimes exuding pleasure. She was now like a member of our family. Finally she received a message from Athens; someone had said that her mother was alive; she too cast about somewhere in Thessaloniki and Volos.

And Myrsine left. My brothers, sisters and I escorted her to the boat. My mother waved goodbye to her with her handkerchief from the balcony of our tower house. It felt as if one of our very own family had departed. She wrote us two or three times.

The years passed. When we settled in Athens, we searched for Myrsine. After considerable difficulty we found her. Like other refugees, she had been knocked about on the fringes of the city, in improvised or badly built apartment houses; refugee settlements had sprouted one after the other in 1922: Byron, New Ionia, New Philadelphia—the Philadelphians now renamed it the poor man's New Smyrna.

The tormented people rooted themselves in the new land. Little by little they made themselves comfortable; nostalgia whipped the elderly, but younger people threw themselves with aplomb into life's struggles, kneaded themselves into the place, and sang, although their songs were full of pain and melancholia.

Myrsine never did find her people, but she always kept expecting to. This is why she never remarried. No man suited her as a mate. She worked as a "supervising buttonhole maker," in a large handicraft shop, one of those that manufacture ready-made suits. She had grown older, gotten heavier, and her lovely hair had started to grey. This is how we saw her the last time at mother's funeral. And then we lost her.

We lived through the horrible slave days of World War II. The Germans and Italians had devastated our land, they had sucked its every vitality. The masses were hungry, they roamed about on the streets in despair like hungry dogs. All day you could hear the macabre voice of hunger throughout the city.

The apartment where we lived now was on the ground floor; passersby could look in the windows. Thus, frightened eyes of little children leaned over and kept staring at us; they would stretch out their hands, holding a small tray for a bit of food, a small tin for a bit of oil. Almost every noon we heard the same wild pained voice of some adult.

"I am hungry, dear ladies, I am hungry. . . ! Dear ladies, give me a bit of bread. Give me a bit of bread."

One noon we felt heartstricken when our dear young doctor came to our house, holding a small cup, to ask timidly, very timidly, for a bit of oil.

"Mother is swollen," he said. "She has suffered from a lack of vitamins."

We too were hungry. But we managed to go on living, with the help of God. We remained closely knit both in our hunger and in the little food that we managed to find. This is how we were able to prepare another small plate of boiled wheat offered at memorial services, to mother's memory, and to make the trip to the Third Cemetery in Kokkinias, a large quarter settlement in Attica, where thousands of poor residents of the city and also foreign sojourners are sleeping eternally.

Well, one morning, as we were coming out of the Cemetery, we saw a skinny, sallow looking young man leaving it, dragging an old ill-shaped wheelbarrow. When we looked more closely inside the wheelbarrow, we saw to our horror, a middle-aged dead woman, folded almost in two. She was a skeleton, her lovely white hair spilled outside the wheelbarrow, and her wasted arms, hanging outside, struck the metal wheels of the wheelbarrow; they were dark.

We were terrified. A German soldier was taking a picture of the spectacle.

"Where are you taking the dead woman, my boy?" we asked in amazement.

"I'm leaving," he said. "They won't accept her here. She lived," he added, "in a district in Aiyaleo, at the foot of Aiyaleo mountain. It's far from the center of Athens. They are not entitled to bury their dead here."

We were horrified. We approached the wheelbarrow and . . . with great difficulty we recognized her. It was Myrsine Kleanthous!

"Yes, Myrsine Kleanthous, they called her," the young man assured us.

We made him turn the wheelbarrow back towards the Cemetery. Almost beside ourselves, we protested to the man in charge. He was embarrassed, perhaps he was afraid, and turning towards the gravedigger, who followed the scene indifferently, he commanded him.

"To The Two Hundred."

We followed the wheelbarrow. A large grave, into which they had dumped other corpses, received Myrsine. The gravedigger threw a little earth, barely covering her face.

"In the afternoon, the priest will sing hymns to all of them together," he told us indifferently, accepting the gratuity we offered him. "And we cover the grave with lime and sand."

We stood a short while over the "Two Hundred." We

crossed ourselves many times for Myrsine and for all those who had preceded her into the large grave.

This is how she remained and will remain in our memory for the rest of our lives. Myrsine Kleanthous, a vigorous young woman in our idyllic island, where she had spent the first hours of her refugee life, near us, and now wretchedly dead in the cemetery of Kokkinias. There we wished her a good journey, where she is sleeping eternally, with the other one hundred ninety-nine. And so she traveled, from the prolific earth of Ionic Greece, from the refreshing island of the Cyclades, into the scorched earth of Attica.

—*Translated from the Greek by Rae Dalven*

Petros Glezos

THE COAT

That year the winter was very severe. The snow had blank-
eted the mountains of Attica, and for several days, uninter-
ruptedly, a wanton wind swept the streets of Athens. And it
was still only December. It was so cold that I felt not only the
frost stiffening my whole body, I also felt the shame of having
people see me walking about on the streets without a coat. I
was aware that people looked surprised; a number of them
who must have felt my situation was owing to poverty, looked
at me with sympathy and pity. It was as if I would hear them
saying:

"The unfortunate, brave young man!"

This shame pierced me much more than the cold, and I kept
thinking that all passersby cast piteous glances at me. So I
pulled my body erect, used all my forces to conquer huddling
myself. My body, with its natural tendency to be less of a target
to the north wind, tried to crouch, to bend. All my limbs
wanted to bind themselves together, to give a little warmth to
each other. And I reacted by stretching my body, as if I were
straining upright on a Procrustean bed. I walked on the street
almost like a wooden person. I recall that the north wind kept
blowing out of sheer obstinacy. Suddenly at street corners, it
would dash recklessly at me, slapping me right and left, then
it would beat my whole body with a switch; worse, it con-

tinued to sweep up from the road pieces of discarded old paper and stick them on my face. It was as if it had a mind and the human north wind was becoming stubborn, like a merchant's agent who sells coats and insists:

"Sir, you cannot roam about on the streets without a coat! You must definitely get a coat!"

That afternoon the cold had subsided somewhat. We had already entered the first days of January, we were approaching Epiphany, so assurance and happiness of expected kindness flooded my soul.

"Look, in a little while, the blessing of the waters, the plunging of the Holy Cross in the waters, cannot but sweeten the time, the winds will reduce their rage a little, the first messages of spring will blossom on the dry twigs of the trees."

Oh! Vain consolation! The brief spell of fine weather filled my heart with hope, made it forget that we still had before us all of January, February and March; when that March of Athens decided to act wild, it was truly frightful and terrifying.

But on that afternoon the weather had softened a little, one could walk without a coat, if he were very brave, or if he wasn't used to wearing a coat, the way several eccentric rich people, unsubdued by the winter, go up and down the streets wearing beautiful expensive leather gloves on their hands but without a coat. Thus, things came to me somewhat conveniently: I too could attend Kanelli's tea.

We were some ten boys, most of them rich boys, already in the last class in the Gymnasium, who had sifted our friendship from the finest sieve of the time, already truly elite, and all of us had pledged to knead life sweetly together. We were all soon to appear in the community as "academic citizens," "the active," "distinguish ourselves," "serve ideally." Besides, we were already "fighters," we devoted our first battles to the "language struggle." So our bond was holy in our dazzled young eyes.

Of course, as always, we spoke about language at Kanelli's tea, but we would also enjoy the lovely pastries that Mrs.

Kanelli did not mind preparing for the gatherings of her only son. She would bring them along with the tea, all deposited on a large tray, leave them in Kanelli's study, and disappear. She would leave us to ourselves, to eat freely, not to be shy in her presence. And the great combustion stove in the hall, which was always kept well supplied with the black shining stoker, sent out its pleasant warmth up to the study as if it too had a soul, as if it were our friend. It was a large beautiful stove, a work of art, with its green enamel adorned with embellishments in relief, and playful forms. The hospitality Mrs. Kanelli showed us was certainly an indication that the gracious lady spoke *demotic* or vernacular Greek in her house, so we felt free, not only to eat, but to speak out, to recite the language of poetry in the verses of Kostes Palamas, to read the works of John Psicharis, all written in a strictly demotic language, the juicy demotic pamphlets of Photis Photiades. On occasion we also read a bit of mathematics, which for most of us was our pathological fear and terror, so much so that we marvelled at Kanelli who was regarded as a mathematical talent.

Whenever I went to Kanelli's house, I used to stop at Phountouklis's house, and take him along with me as my companion. I would wait at the entrance of his house; Phountouklis would come down immediately and we would leave. He too was a rich boy. He lived in a large private four-story house; his father was one of the best known merchants in Athens; a distinguished person, but a little strict with us because of our "language." He was an adherent of *katharevousa* or purist Greek. Thus, I always went up those countless steps to their house with some diffidence; I preferred to wait for Phountouklis downstairs at the entrance.

Well, I also waited at the entrance on that afternoon. As always, I heard the heavy door of their apartment—they lived on the top floor—closing behind him. Then I heard the usual creaking of the steps, as he came down, not very impetuously that day, and at the last turn of the staircase, I saw him appearing, wearing his coat, but also carrying on his arm another coat. I didn't have time to reflect that it isn't possible for a young person to wear two coats, and certainly not during the afternoon, when the cold was less severe, when Phountouklis held out his coat towards me, and silently, with a slight blush on his cheeks, gave it to me. I understood at once that my good friend was offering me a gift of a coat.

I stood a little undecided. I saw Phountouklis as a good angel, who suddenly landed at this entrance here, to offer a poor devil a little warmth. Then, a painful feeling of dignity, the remains of some extinguished home breeding, some happy former freedom of want, started to boil within me, to bring forth denial to my lips.

"Thank you. Do you think I don't wear a coat because I don't have one? I don't wear one because I am not used to it, because I am not cold."

But he said nothing. All was determined in a moment, my hand played a bit nervously, then instinctively, I extended it toward the coat. The garment was folded on my arm and remained there.

"Won't you wear it?" Phountouklis asked timorously.

"Later . . . I . . ." I answered, and we went.

With a touching, gracious strength, my friend did not even cast a glance on the garment. It was as if he had forgotten, as if the coat had been mine for years, and I kept it on my arm out of habit. And when we reached *Omonia,* a central square in Athens, I left him for a few moments, went into a coffee-house, and returned without the coat. He said nothing, he showed no curiosity, no surprise.

I did not tell Phountouklis, I was ashamed to tell him, that I went into the coffeehouse and left the coat at the bar.

"May I please leave this coat here, till the evening?"

The bartender looked at me in surprise. Then his eyes became a little mistrustful, searching; he must have thought, "surely this young man has stolen the coat, and he is looking for a way to get rid of it." Then his eyes softened, thinking, "perhaps it is for sale, if it were stolen, why would the young man have brought it here?" Finally, his eyes showed indifference: "Never mind, people leave so many things here," and he extended his hand, took the coat, and hung it on the clothes hanger in the back, near the wire net with the unclaimed correspondence of vagrant customers who use the address of the coffeehouse.

As the bartender hung the coat, I could see with some comfort for the first time that it was a black straight coat, a rather fine overcoat with a velvet collar. It was an important man's coat. It must surely have belonged to Phountouklis's father. So then the good man did not want to see a *malliaros,* an extreme demoticist, die of the chill, and he consented to offer an old coat of his to that young devil who, since he *was* an extreme demoticist, could also have been an atheist, or an agent of the Slavs. Happy epoch! The people divided by their ideas, did not dog-eat each other, but each had the bigness of heart to offer a little warmth to the other.

I had a feeling of deliverance when I left the coat somewhere temporarily. I sensed that I could not appear in Kanelli's house wearing the coat. I thought that all the boys would immediately cast their eyes on it; they would ask: "where did you find the coat?" If they did not ask, they would wonder, and poor Phountouklis who could not dissemble indifference would betray himself, all would understand that he had given me the coat, and would feel sorry for me, they would be pained for me, they would be disconcerted because they themselves had not managed to offer me one of their old coats.

Now till nightfall, I had "credit time" as they say, even this credit is sometimes valuable, like some credits that Banks offer their depositors. So, I would feel the cold a little longer! In any case, I had endured it patiently for so long that the proud strain of my body could endure it a little longer.

In the evening, the same bartender was not there; he had changed shift with another. I had not thought of this. The new bartender looked at me more mistrustfully; he did not want to give me the coat:

"How do I know it is yours, my young man?" That is to say, he had cursed me. He almost let it be felt that I might even have been a thief. And how could I defend myself, how could I have the strength to claim the coat, who did not yet feel that it was truly my own? And had he asked me for the name of the tailor who had sewn it, the kind of lining it had, how many pockets, what could I have answered him? Fortunately, a kind old man, a customer who had been there during the afternoon, assured the bartender that I was the one who had left the coat. It appears that the matter had made an impression on the old man. He was a wrinkled old man, with many cross-etched wrinkles, with blue childlike eyes, and with a bump on his head like those that happen to children when they fall and hit themselves. I will never forget that old man who defended my honesty, who helped me retrieve my coat! My coat! Well, did I too now have a coat for that winter? When I reached the square, and as soon as I found myself a little beyond the lights, I put it on. I could have had the strength to walk into my house holding the coat on my arm, but I thought some policeman might see me and consider me suspect:

"How is it possible in such cold, for someone to hold a coat on his arm and not wear it, when it belongs to him?"

So I put it on. A sweet warmth something like the tender embrace of my mother enveloped my body to my knees, on my back, my armpits, my chest; when I took hold of the lapels and brought them together with my hands below the neck, the warmth was so perceptible that I thought a tender hand caressed me, a velvety cheek leaned over me.

You would think that now the north wind was scorning me, as if it wanted malevolently to deny me the joy of defending myself. It had died down completely. One of those sweet January evenings with a clear sky, a fine serene evening had spread over the city. The frost was always perceptible, only now I sensed that while it made my body feel the cold, it did not pierce my body with pins and needles. The coat protected me sweetly—sweetly; for me, it was now a loving obedient protector, whose protection I would feel still more when the wintry north wind would start again to shave the streets of Athens.

I put my hands in the pockets, in the still strange pockets. On my fingers I felt a few bits of tobacco. And the whole coat had a very faint, pleasant smell of tobacco. It was still someone else's garment until yesterday—the day before that Mr. Phountouklis must have worn it. As of tomorrow I would be wearing it, so little by little it would follow the line of my body, the smell of our house, little by little it would get old, fray the buttonholes and the pockets that were slightly frayed even then, thinned slightly by its use.

My mother was abashed when she saw me entering. Later she understood.

"Bless you," she told me, quite satisfied with me, for, as she looked at things of course, my good relations and worth were the reasons for this offering, which saved her from the expenditure, painful for us, of buying a coat. Sometime before that, my mother had laid her hand gently, very gently, on the ill-shaped, dusty, ready-made clothes on tailors' dummies that wore clothes ostentatiously on the streets of Athens. They smiled complacently, with a fixed, wretched smile, as if they wanted to influence the customer, that these soulless objects were also warmed by wearing the coats. Mother would stretch her hand, try the thickness of the material, would stop short; the clerk would rush to the sidewalk to surprise her, to captivate her.

"Please come in, madam, please come in and see. Only take a look, madam!" But my mother then left discreetly with a "thank you, another time," and looked at me with tearful eyes as I stood silently beside her, as I, a man now, expected from her, only from her, the blessing and the dignity of the little warmth of a ready-made coat of the street of Athens, hanging on her decision, which was not forthcoming.

"Bless you!"

She inspected the coat, she turned me here, she turned me

there, with her hand she straightened the garment a little on the back.

"And it fits you as if it were made to order."

Her assurance quieted me. So I would not appear ridiculous wearing Phountouklis's coat. At most, whoever saw me would think that I was more serious than was necessary for a young man, to be wearing a coat with a velvet collar. Besides, city people make such pretences of seriousness when they are young, and again when they are old, they chase the colorful, the "arty," the "sporty."

Little by little I got used to the coat. With use it became mine. I also managed with this coat the first winter at the small charming seashore town where I was first appointed as an employee. And on, until the coat frayed much more, the velvet collar lost its sheen and wore out. Then I could have a coat of my own made, a coat truly my own. And I had it made. But I did not dare offer this old coat with my own hands to some poor person of the town. My housekeeper undertook this, and I owe her my gratitude for this task among many others. I gave the coat to a poor old man, a transient from another island. Thus, he did not mind if it had worn out completely on a young body. And further, it wasn't so I would see it on the street, in the same city, completely worn out, covering a third body, trying to warm an old man.

Since then I have had many coats made. Now I have two, and I also have a trench coat. But there is no question, so it appears, that I will feel again the warmth of that first coat. It was a warmth flooded not with money, but with a kind of pain, with a light traumatism of a young heart, a proud heart, and this covering is very heavy.

—Translated from the Greek by Rae Dalven

Yu Kuang-chung

Pine Seeds on Empty Mountain

One pine seed falls
Without a sign.
Who is sent to greet it?
Pine needles or roots covering the ground?
The moonlight, the riotous stones overrunning the slopes?
Or the wind passing its way?
    Sooner said
    Than done
One pine seed falls
Greeted by an empty mountain.

—Translated from the Chinese by Julia C. Lin and
Tan A. Lin

Yu Kuang-chung

SUMMER IN SHAT'IEN: NIGHT DEEP AS WELL

Night deep as well,
The rope goes down far as it goes, but
Where is the sound of water struck by the rope?
A crowd of stars, like silkworms
Climb the mossed walls,
Oh how slowly, and
Not yet half way through
The well cries dawn.

*—Translated from the Chinese by Julia C. Lin and
Tan A. Lin*

Yu Kuang-chung

MOUNTAIN RAIN

The fog gathers, gathering, grows into rain,
The man walks farther, and enters deeper into the Minan
        Palace,
The road going dark, darkens with dusk,
Ink dots dotting an ink-black landscape.
And mist after mist rises from the floor of the valley.
Tell me, is this mountain in the rain,
Or is the rain in the mountain?
What explanation does a small pavilion make?
Listen!
One bird's call comes out from the tall shadows
Of the woods,
Four walls of empty mountain changed
Into a line of Zen.

—Translated from the Chinese by Julia C. Lin and
Tan A. Lin

52   *Ansel Adams*

Werner Aspenström

TREES

Trees have a lot to tell:
they mumble like bedouins at prayertime,
they lean together, murmuring and making music,
bickering with the magpie that snatches sticks.

Many trees are eminent thinkers,
especially the fir with the signified down-curving branches
and the maple shadowing the courtyards.
Even mere conversations are memorable
between the oak-crowns and the haymaking meadow
     creek—
many riddles are revealed there.

Some find meaning in the storm,
others love the cloister-still night
when only the fixed stars tremble.
Some stand their whole life and call
with scrubby arms.

The fate of a tree is to stand and perish;
man dies often far away,
in churchyards, near the horizon.

—Translated from the Swedish by D. L. Emblen

Werner Aspenström

FÖREBUD

Jag märker att min misstro växer,
som rosten växer, som en skugga växer.
Spindeln i taket, bringar den lycka?
Åt sol eller måne, men ej åt sitt offer.

Jag litar inte på den döda fågeln.
Jag ser nog glimten i hans döda ögon!
Ormen i flaskan får min hand att darra.
Två gånger väcktes jag i natt av väsande tungor.

Jag reste mig upp från min dröm eller vaka.
Mitt rum var förbytt och ändå tröstlöst detsamma.
Kniven jag sökte vilade blytung i slidan.
Den nyutslagna rosen hade redan vissnat.

Ord har jag samlat och skuggor, skuggor.
Allt i min närhet har uppsagt mig sin lydnad.
Den gamla guitarren spelar med falska strängar.
Hanfullt betraktar mig den gamla spegeln.

Werner Aspenström   .

PORTENTS

I notice that my disbelief grows,
as rust grows, as a shadow grows.
The spider on the ceiling, does it bring happiness?
To sun or moon, maybe, but not his victim.

I do not need to read dead birds,
I see enough of a glint in their dead eyes!
The snake in the bottle makes my hand tremble.
Twice I have been awakened in the night by hissing
    tongues.

I arise from my dream or my vigil,
my room transformed, yet hopelessly the same.
The knife I looked for rests leaden in the sheath,
the recent blossoms already withered.

Words I have gathered and shadows—shadows!
Everything near me has cancelled its loyalty:
the old guitar plays with wrong strings,
scornfully the old mirror observes me.

Jag byggde mitt hus på det föreskrivna sättet
med dörrar och riglar och varnande klockor.
Man har sagt mig att staden är kransad av murar.
Likväl tränger oupphörligt främlingar in.

Spindeln i taket spinner och spinner sin galge.
Någonting fullbordas under en lismande himmel.
Frågor och upprörda röster når mig från gatan.
Jag känner röken från brinnande kyrkor.

I built my house in the prescribed way
with doors and bolts and warning bells.
Someone has told me that the town is ringed with walls.
Nevertheless, foreigners keep pressing in.

The spider on the ceiling spins and spins his gibbet.
Something is completed under a wheedling sky.
Questions and disturbed voices reach me from the street.
I smell the smoke of burning churches.

—Translated from the Swedish by D. L. Emblen

Werner Aspenström

BARNET FRÅGAR OM SOLEN

Ljusets vita vattenfall
genom molnen, genom löven
och på barnets fragekvarn:
varför och varför?
Världens enkelheter går ej
att förklara. Inte gräset,
inte ljusets vattenfall, det vita,
ohörbara.

Werner Aspenström

THE CHILD ASKS ABOUT THE SUN

The white waterfall of light
through the clouds, through the leaves,
onto the child's question machine:
why? and why?
The simplicity of the world
is not to be explained.
Not the grass, not the waterfall of light,
that white—
inaudible.

—Translated from the Swedish by D. L. Emblen

Veno Taufer

V OKO

je ne v penah za ladjo ki jo zanese
skoz zvezdnati plankton je ko puhne
v nosnice suša in pesek pod vsem
mogočim kar ima glas
škripcev ne v vosku ne v znamenjih
na križpotjih je ne ko je prašno
mesto pred nogami in med kužnimi vrati
ni najti prahu na pragu je
ne ko iščeš okoli in znotraj je
v pišu ki ti zanese trepalnico v oko

Veno Taufer

INTO YOUR EYE

it is not in the foam beyond the ship adrift
through starry plankton it is when
drought and sand blow into the nostrils it is under every
possible thing which has the voice
.of pulleys it is not in wax nor in signs
at the crossroads it is not when the dusty
city lies underfoot and at the pestilent door
no dust can be found on the threshold it is
not when you look around and within it is
in the gust of wind sweeping a lash into your eye.

—*Translated from the Yugoslavian by James Ragan*

Courtesy of Norton Simon Foundation

62   Edgar Degas

John V. Hicks

DANCE SCRIABIN

Screen congeals, delivers up
round moon rising from behind
bare hill of October's clearing, a
setting for silhouettes of memory.

Two dancers hurry on
from side and side, discover
each and each, pause, begin
to sway, rehearse varying motions.

They dance Scriabin on that cold
stage, dance Scriabin in that cold
light, dance Scriabin to what cold
memory?
            "Where, when?" (The spirit.)

Moon completes its rise, slips
mooring; dancers touch,
interlock, break, twine, are
one. Semi-substance of dark invades

that sanctity; they are gone
without cue, without curtain, (strain
to whisper or footfall as you will).
Moon has carried its lamp

away, sifted shed of light and sound
away, drifted stage and barely step
away, lifted impotent grasp of memory
away.

John V. Hicks

THE ALDER TREE

Those million years ago I'll swear
there was no sensate thing
could pluck nine stones from here and there
and range them in a ring.
It remained for you and me
to set them round the alder tree.

Those million years ago the blood,
an elevating drum,
throbbed out the pulse of flower and flood,
puff pollen and bee's hum.
Underneath the alder tree
nothing has changed but you and me.

M. J. Roberts

FORGIVENESS

   Molly hadn't seen the man she'd married for thirty years, nor had she heard from him. But his letter had come that morning and something had to be done about it.

   She sat beneath the old redwood listening to a pair of blue jays squabble, her knobby old feet cooling in the stream. She had walked eight miles since morning and the arthritis she pretended didn't exist called out from every joint like the ache his words had roused: "I'm dying," he'd written. "Please come." It was a feeble scrawl written by a shaking hand, but his, unmistakably his.

   How that hand had once warmed her, she thought, turned her body into a singing wire. Now it was old. Her fingers curled over a clump of dried needles, so brown and brittle they snapped against her palm. Soon they would be earth, like her, like him, and what lay between them wouldn't matter anymore.

   Still, he wanted to see her. Why now? So much time had passed. So much change. So much pain. The last time they'd met was at the cemetery, their daughter's funeral, she alone, he with his second wife, a fashion model, far too dazzling for the day, like the sun, too bright when all the world should have been shrouded in darkness. She had hated him then, certain he could have saved the child, forbidden the bike ride through traffic-snarled streets, if only he'd been vigilant, if only he'd taken the time from his law briefs, his incessant tinkering about the house, from his private plane and his fashion model. But the child moved into his life on weekends, rode through the days unheeded, and then out again. Out . . .

He had cried at the funeral. She had turned her back on his outstretched hand.

Thirty years. She knew nothing of what time had wrought on his face or heart, what losses he'd sustained since then. She had left all vestiges of that life, knowing she couldn't listen to the school bus coming home in the afternoon, the children laughing at the beach, their parents hushing as she passed, their eyes turning from her in pity, toward their own children in fear. No, she had had to leave. Only for a while, she had told herself then.

Thirty years. She sighed as she pulled her feet from the stream and rested them on a sun-baked rock. The heat penetrated her soles and ran like liquid up her legs. She smiled. Loss had taught her about the simple things, about the song of water rushing over rocks, the soothing fingers of sunlight on her aching joints, the enticing tang of needle-dust in her palm, the comforting jacket of bark against her back. She knew how to still her mind and let her senses breathe, but the familiar quiet didn't last. His letter pulled her back, further than she wanted to go, back to the time when they'd been a family caught in the flux of beginnings, Molly on sabbatical, taking a year off to mother, Katie learning to walk and talk, Will new at his law firm, coming home late at night, his feet creaking against the loose floorboards in Katie's room as he kissed her good-night, then padded to bed, his long, slim body, more familiar than the comforter she'd had since childhood, curling along her back, her anger at his lateness dissolving in the warm cocoon of his arms . . .

Her toes tightened so her heels dug into the stone's sharp edge, the pressure a momentary relief, as if she could use physical pain to fend off this other, the deeper kind that came from the scenes rising in her mind—Katie with a fever, whimpering against Will's shoulder as he paced the living room, into the patch of moonlight, then out of it, over and over again, soothing the child and the child in the mother, ragged from a day of fear; all three of them at a beach party, Katie roasting her first marshmallow over the coals, her face glowing as the sugar blazed up into a blue flame, luminous as a halo, then darkened into a crusty lump that fell with a plop into the fire, Katie lunging for it, her small fingers only an inch from the red coals when Molly caught them, her motherly vigilance slackening only for a moment but long enough for danger to creep in; danger: Will standing in the doorway, a suitcase in one hand, briefcase in the other, his eyes bloodshot, brow creased, grey suit rumpled from flying all night (was it from Paris? London?). Wherever, one thing was clear—who he'd been with, that single bit of information enough to turn the earth beneath Molly's feet to liquid.

"How could you do it, Will?"

"It's not like I had a choice. I didn't want to. I mean, why would I choose to fall in love with someone else?"

"You did choose it. You bought the plane tickets. You left me and Katie here. You took her with you."

"That's the surface. What I did, not why."

"Then, why? Why, Will? Why did you do it?" Her voice was shrill, almost a scream.

"Molly, I'm sorry." He took a step back, out of the glare of the hall light, into the shadows on the front stoop. "I love her, Molly. That's why. I'm sorry."

She hadn't seen him leave. She just knew he was gone. In six months they were divorced. A year later Katie was gone. The cocoon was broken. Nowhere she looked was there comfort. She sold their house, took all her savings and wandered into the Santa Cruz Mountains where she found an abandoned cabin crumbling by a stream. It was in an isolated spot, far from the suburbs, miles from the nearest town. She bought it and, like an injured cat, went there alone to lick her wounds or to die. Her mind in a fog, her body acting with a purpose she didn't feel, she shored up the house as best she could, planted vegetables, drew water from the stream, chopped fallen branches into firewood. Days of clearing rocks and hammering slats over leaks, digging, hoeing, chopping, and hauling left her little time to think. She fell into bed at dusk as spent in body as in spirit. She ate little, challenging her legs and arms to go on without fuel, her heart to go on without will. A splash of water on her cheeks or the scent of coffee on a brisk morning would sometimes shock her into remembering that other life. Hard work, hand-bloodying work was her only weapon against those fisted moments that knocked the breath from her chest. Late at night, when thoughts of Will or Katie rose unbidden and she couldn't chop or dig or saw, she lit candles against the dark and drew the haunted shapes of her mind in pencil on odd scraps of paper. In the light of dawn, they glowed strangely beautiful, as if they were messages from another world. Her hands began to fight the ache of toil, seeking out pencils and paper at odd times of the day. A fawn would make her drop her axe and draw its eyes, wide and frightened, peering out of the wood at her own. She started to buy paints and canvas, charcoal and sketch pads. She knew nothing of art but painted the way a child paints. Around her grew a primitive world of color and texture, light and shadow, a world of mystery.

When her money was almost spent, she drove to town with a painting. Her blond hair streaming past her shoulders, her blue eyes edged with doubt, she headed for the General Store where she hoped Ben Strand, its owner, would listen to her odd proposal. He was a garrulous sort, a middle-aged widower who was always friendly to her even though their conversations were more often than not one-sided. Her isolation had made her shy and words no longer came easily to her. In fact, they often seemed like messages from a familiar, but long-forgotten planet, sounds that required a conscious decoding. Still, on this particular day, she knew she would need words, and a measure of luck.

She hesitated at the door, her painting tucked behind her back. It was small, frameless, and, suddenly, she was certain, without any value whatsoever. She wavered, tempted to run, but the smells of plenty—peaches and leather, onions and soap, herbs and turpentine—held her still long enough for Ben to notice her arrival.

He peered up at her, over his granny glasses, and marking a page in his book with his finger, smiled broadly as if he were genuinely glad to see her. "And what can I do for you young lady?"

Molly felt the embarrassment of a blush filling her cheeks. She wasn't young, thirty-seven, almost thirty-eight, but her unease made her feel childlike. "I'm not . . . I . . . You'll probably think I'm crazy, but . . ." She paused, unsure how to do this. Even in that other life, the one before where things were bought and sold, she'd been a teacher, a mother, not a barterer.

"You may be a bit of a loner," Ben said, "but I wouldn't call you crazy." He set his book down on the polished oak counter and studied her a moment, his eyes following the slope of her arms to where they disappeared behind her back. She shifted her weight from one foot to the other, then looked past his left shoulder to a rack of spices. He tilted his head into her line of vision and winked playfully. "If you don't show me what you're hiding, I might just have to leap over the counter and spin you around."

Steeling her courage, Molly took a deep breath, loosened one hand from a corner of the painting, and stepped forward till she was only a few feet from the counter.

"It's something I've done," she said. "Painted, I mean. I thought maybe . . . Well, I'm kind of out of supplies and . . ." She left the thought dangling, and then, not wanting to appear too needy, went on. "It's not that I haven't got anything important. I mean my vegetables are doing fine and the roof's all patched, but . . ."

"I guess you're going to force me to leap," he said and set

his big hands on the counter as if to hurl himself past the cash register. Despite herself, Molly laughed.

Ben's lively grey eyes grew wide. "Well, if that doesn't beat all. I thought you'd forgotten how to do that."

Her laughter dissolved as his words threw her back to a time when she had done "that," and, instead of her own voice, she heard Katie's, Will's, the two of them in the backyard, Katie on the swing, Will pushing her, a pair of shiny, red shoes and lacey, white socks drawing an arc in the air. The picture was sharp as a knife and it cut just as deep.

She looked down at the floor, traced a slat of wood with the heel of her moccasin, then slowly lifted the painting from her side and set it on the counter by his hands. A long moment passed. She couldn't look up, couldn't bear to see any contempt in his eyes. She wanted to flee, but if she left now, the sound of that other laughter would haunt her. Drawing had become the only sure way to silence. She saw her charcoal worn to a sliver, her paint tubes empty, her pads and canvases filled.

Finally, he spoke. "Redwoods, " he said. "Nice stand of redwoods you've got up at your place. Used to hike there when I was a kid. Camp by that stream. Kind of eerie. Haunting, I guess you'd say."

Molly looked up and saw his eyes serious for once, his brow creased in concentration.

"Now don't get me wrong. I'm no judge of art and I don't imagine this has any value. 'Cept to you maybe."

She felt hope drain away.

"Thing is, though, I kind of like it. It's something I could look at, you know?"

She met his eyes and found no pity or scorn written there. Just honest appreciation. It made her bold. "Would you take the painting in exchange for some new supplies?"

He scratched his cheek, the rasp of his nail against that bush of black whiskers the only sound in the store. Then he cocked his head and considered her a long moment, appraising her as if she were the thing being bartered. His glance gave her a hot-cold feeling, like dry-ice running through her veins. It had been a long time since a man had looked at her that way.

"How much are you thinking?" he finally said.

She shrugged. "I'll take whatever you say it's worth."

He drew himself up to his full height, some two or three inches over six feet, and, after a moment, nodded. "How about this," he said. "I'll give you whatever supplies you need now and you bring me a bunch of your paintings to put on the walls here. We've got tourists coming through every weekend. If they see 'em hanging up, who knows, you might just make some money."

Molly felt a strange ambivalence at this suggestion. It was exciting to think that people, strangers, might like her work, but it was jarring too. With only deer and birds for company, her paintings had become familiar, homey, almost like family.

"It's hard to let go of them," she finally said.

Ben nodded. "Well, think on it. Just get the supplies you want and next time you come in, tell me what you decide."

It didn't take Molly long to return once she realized that, ambivalent or not, she needed to paint more than she needed the paintings themselves, and finances dictated she choose one or the other. Fortunately, and much to her surprise, her paintings began to sell, thanks, at least partly, to Ben's natural talent as a storyteller. When tourists stopped by for cold drinks and snacks on hot afternoons, he would draw their attention to this painting or that by weaving tall tales about their creator, a hermit artist, he said, who talked to the owls and sang honey from the bees. According to him, she was a magical woman who lived far up in the mountains, painted with sap and thistle brushes, slept on a bed of bear fur, and lived on fish she caught with her bare hands. No doubt his elaborations were for Molly's entertainment, and his own, but they resulted in tourists buying her work as a folksy momento of their journey to the woods.

Molly called Ben an old fox, pitting his imagination against the gullibility of naive materialists, but she never begrudged him his fun. Neither of them imagined that the tales would seep into New York society where primitive art had become stylish, nor did they imagine that her paintings and sketches would be bought and sold by the Beverly Hills' chic. But by then, neither of them particularly cared. Ben had taught Molly to laugh again and she had returned his appraising glance with one of her own. A quick, sideways smile told her he hadn't missed its message and the bed in her tilted house had begun holding two through the long winter nights.

Molly sighed. The sun had passed its nadir and was slipping behind the redwood branches on the other side of the stream. It was time to go back to him—Ben, friend and lover for more than two decades, longer than she had been married, longer than Katie had lived, the closest person in the world to her and yet he knew almost nothing about that other life. He hadn't probed, forced her to tell, but with his gentle eye, she was sure he had sensed the unspoken pain peeking out of her paintings, a pair of soft blue eyes deep in a forest, a splash of red, a small shadow falling through a broken window pane. The child was there, always a presence, now a presence in the houses of the rich, in art galleries, pieces of her spread about the world.

Molly's lips turned up more in a grimace than a smile. What malicious God had arranged such a turn, twisted a pain so private into something so public. Surely, He knew she'd give up thirty years of paints and brushes, even Ben's gentle touch, for that day, that bike ride, to be obliterated from the slate of time.

Blinking hard, she pulled her socks out of her shoes, shook them loose and eased one, then the other, over her swollen toes. Her quiet place wasn't working its magic, washing away thought so all she heard was the gentle tilt of the water's sonorous voice. She thrust her left foot, then her right, inside her leather shoes, then laced them tightly so her mind would turn to the easy ache, the pain of feet still treading the earth.

Sixty-five. How had she gotten so far? Why did she feel so raw after so long, the past rushing back in the scrawl of a dying man's hand?

She pulled the crumpled letter from her pocket and flattened it against her knee, reading it again the way a child picks at a scab, unable to let it heal. But she couldn't ignore it. She had loved that hand—it had written the major moments of her life. She had come to him with all the innocence of youth, then lost him, her first love, the father of her child. She remembered him the morning Katie was born, his dark hand on her brow, massaging her temples the way she liked, his voice low and encouraging—"That's right, hold it, hold it. Fine, now breathe out." The nurses had tried to take over when the baby's head crowned, but he wouldn't let them. He talked her through the birth, kissed her the moment Katie took her first screaming breath, then counted her tiny fingers and toes twice, just to reassure.

How could that man, the loving one, have left her? Had she changed so much after Katie's birth? Of course, she'd been tired at the end of a day, and not much interested in being touched, but what new mother wasn't overwhelmed? And there was such a thing as commitment. She had believed in commitment.

Thirty years, and she could still feel the anger and bitterness as vividly now as she had then. If they'd been together, a family, Katie wouldn't have been ignored. She wouldn't have ridden out into the streets alone, as heedless of danger as he had been.

"Please come" danced off the page till she closed her eyes against their command. "Why?" she said out loud. "Why should I?" Her words fell in the silent wood, softly as a tuft of seed. Only the stream spoke in its ancient voice, "Peace," it seemed to say.

The word pressed against the barriers she'd built inside, pressed and pressed until she felt them breaking, an almost physical sensation, like ice cracking under the weight of a foot.

She folded her hands over her eyes and did what she hadn't been able to do in thirty years. She wept.

Ben was waiting for her when she emerged from the woods but she didn't see him. The sudden light did something strange to her eyes. Instead of the lawn leading up to a porch and neatly painted front door, she saw the house as it had been when she bought it, two rooms, roof gaping like a mouth open to the sky, support beams listing precariously toward the stream, windows jagged and broken. She saw the hill beyond covered with rocks, not tilled into even rows of lettuce and carrots and sweet peas and squash. She saw the chimney cracked in a jagged line, its tower of field stones caved into its center. Then she blinked and it came into focus. Chaos became order, boards and rocks became home, empty land grew fertile. She saw the life her two hands had wrought.

Ben leaned against the front door, his laughter-creased eyes solemn, his white, uncombed hair falling in a shock across his forehead. No amused grin arched through his grey beard nor did he chuck her under the chin in his playful way as she came up to the door. He had read the letter over her shoulder that morning, watched her eyes grow haunted again, seen her flee into the woods like a hunted deer.

He followed her inside, lit the fire, then perched on the edge of the couch and turned his questioning eyes her way. She sank back into the cushions as if she could dissolve in the fabric and feathers. She didn't want to talk. It would be even more real if she talked, but his eyes told her she had to. He wouldn't push. She knew he wouldn't push. He never had. But there was a gap between them. It had always been there but never so openly as now. He needed a bridge into that other time, that other place.

Her words came haltingly at first. She got sequence confused, went from her divorce back to her marriage, from Katie at the morgue to Katie at the park. It had been so long since she'd spoken the name, it stuck on her tongue like cotton. She had to spit it out. Ben lifted her feet into his lap and stroked them. She didn't feel his hand. She felt Will's, Katie's, the hands of the past beckoning her into forgotten places, lost times—Katie giggling as Molly tickled her on the bed, Will laughing as they ran on the beach, Katie whistling through her new front teeth, Will tossing a ball to her in the back yard. Katie's sleeping head buried in a feathery white pillow. Time hadn't erased the pictures. It had just sealed them in amber, set them on shelves in her mind to be looked at but not touched, never touched as she had touched them once.

She spread her hands over her knees, dug her fingers in deep. They were spotted by the sun, creased with earth, gnarled by time, fingers that couldn't grasp a paint brush some mornings, hands the child wouldn't recognize. They weren't the young ones that had brushed tears from a downy cheek, tied ribbons in Sunday school ponytails, patted powder on a plump, pink bottom. Still, they were the hands that had held the child, the hands that had rebuilt a life, the same hands that had curled into a fist when Will had reached out at the funeral.

The fire crackled and hissed. A log tumbled off the grate into the ashes below. Soon the hearth would be cold, as cold as the back she'd turned to him, as cold as a tomb. It was the nature of fire. The deepest passion would spend itself, even hate.

"You should go to him," Ben said.

She watched the last flames falter, then fade, her hands relaxing, sliding from her knees. Ben drew her close, his warmth a blanket against the gathering dark.

"Will you?" he asked.

She nodded, her brow brushing against the soft bristles of his beard. Even feelings needed a rite of passage, a final resting place. She would hold the outstretched hand, acknowledge what two had lost, not one. It was time to let go.

Chou Meng-tieh

THE WALKER THROUGH WALLS

Burning yet cold,
Your footsteps are wind.
All walls, even those set in bronze,
Prick up their ears
And, as if charmed by the devil,
All crowd towards you.

Every corner of darkness is filled with your eyes.
Your eyes are a net
Netting directions—directions that face you,
Are back of you.

Orion shines night after night on your window.
Your window is sometimes wide open,
Other times shut tight.
Sometimes the window is darker when open than shut.
Ghost light in your eyes, pale yellow dust mist
In your eyes . . . .

Orion says only he has your key.
Orion tells you to open a window,
He will gently close it for you again . . . .

—Translated from the Chinese by Julia C. Lin and
Tan A. Lin

Chou Meng-tieh

YOU ARE MY MIRROR

You are my mirror.
Quiet, I walk in your heart.
Without a foot falling, without a trace
Like a solitary cloud coming out late
From one edge of the sky to another.

Whose painted sky is this? Round and radiant,
Cool and blue. Like your heart. Yes,
There must be something hiding
At your back.
Even if I lit up a thousand eyes with
A thousand hands and stretched out those hands
From those eyes, I still couldn't touch
Your mystery.

Forever, I've felt someone on high
Coldly scrutinizing me, watching my days and nights,
My strengths and weaknesses, coming and going.

No one gets away.
The Koran is in your hand.
The sword, too, in your hand.
Why not scatter a handful of light
To net all the shadows?

Friday, whose Friday are you?
Who is your Friday?
From the eleventh snow storm I wake,
No more South, North, East, or West. With night
At my back, I turn my eyes darkly inward,
And look inside.

—*Translated from the Chinese by Julia C. Lin and*
Tan A. Lin

80   *Jan van der Hayden*

Czeslaw Milosz

AND YET THE BOOKS

And yet the books will be there on the shelves, separate
    beings,
That appeared once, still wet,
As shining chestnuts under a tree in autumn,
And, touched, coddled, began to live
In spite of fires on the horizon, castles blown up,
Tribes on the march, planets in motion.
"We are" they said, even as their pages
Were being torn out, or a buzzing flame
Licked away their letters. So much more durable
Than we are, whose frail warmth
Cools down with memory, disperses, perishes.
I imagine the earth when I am no more:
Nothing happens, no loss, it's still a strange pageant,
Women's dresses, dewy lilacs, a song in the valley.
Yet the books will be there on the shelves, well born,
Begotten by people, but also by radiance, heights.

Czeslaw Milosz

OLD WOMEN

Arthritically bent, in black, spindle-legged,
They move, leaning on canes, to the altar where the
    Pantocrator
In a dawn of gilded rays lifts his two fingers.
The mighty, radiant face of the All-Potent
In whom everything was created, whatever is on the
    earth and in Heaven.
To whom are submitted the atom and the scale of
    galaxies,
Rises over the heads of his servants, covered with their
    shawls
While into their shriveled mouths they receive His flesh.

A mirror, mascara, powder and cones of carmine
Lured every one of them and they used to dress up
As themselves, adding a brighter glow to their eyes,
A rounder arch to their brows, a denser red to their
    lips.
They opened themselves, amorous, in the riverside
    woods,

Carried inside the magnificence of the beloved,
Our mothers whom we have never repaid,
Busy, as we were, with sailing, crossing continents.
And guilty, seeking their forgiveness.

He who has been suffering for ages, rescues
Ephemeral moths, tired-winged butterflies in the cold,
Genetrixes with the closed scars of their wombs,
And carries them up to His human Theotokos,
So that the ridicule and pain change into majesty
And thus it is fulfilled, late, without charms and colors,
Our imperfect, earthly love.

Artur Lundkvist

EFTER LÄSNING AV FÄRÖISKA DIKTER

Så litet i handen och så stort i hjärtat, detta smärtsamt
   älskade land,
   svarta öar i nordatlantisk dimma likt smolk i ögat, men
gröna, gröna på nära håll, ett gräsets yttersta hem i världen,
   öar vars tyngd är omätlig, med klippor vars rötter når
   ända ner i jordens innersta,
   under en himmel med ett överflöd av stjärnor, en
   gnistrande ocean i rymden.
   Bränningen spottar och fräser som vildkatter, farliga
också när de leker, och klippryggarna rullar sig som valar,
   fåglarna lever som munkar i klippväggarnas nischer,
klädda i sina kåpor och kapuschonger,
   sommarskymningen mellan trähusen är violett som syrener
   och doftar av nyslaget hö,
   svalorna virkar det sneda ljuset och vägarna ringlar
bort som säckvävsremsor i gröngräset,
   brännvinskruset stå på den raglande kistan som bärs
av sex män, vars skrovliga psalmer övergå i folkvisor.
   Den bleka solen blåses ut i höstdiset och drivveden hopas,
skurad av havet tills fibrerna framträder som i gamla
   trägolv,

Artur Lundkvist

AFTER READING POEMS
FROM THE FAEROE ISLANDS

This agonizingly beloved land with so small a hand
and so big a heart,
　　black islands in North Atlantic fog, like specks
in the eye, but so green at close range; this
most distant haven of grass on Earth,
　　islands of immeasurable weight, the roots of their
rocks reaching deep into the core of the planet,
　　under a sky abounding with stars, a fiery ocean
in space.
　　The breakers spit and hiss, wildcats, dangerous
also at play; the backs of the wet rocks rolling
like whales,
　　the birds live like monks in their high niches
of stone, dressed in hooded cloaks,
　　the summer dusk between the wooden houses is
violet as lilacs and smells of new-mown hay,
　　the swallows knit the slanted light and the roads
wind through the green grass as seams in burlap,
　　　the jug with hard liquor sways on top of the reeling
　　　　casket
carried by six men, their coarse-voiced psalms transmute
into folk song.
　　The pale sun is extinguished in the mist of fall
and the driftwood gathers, polished by the sea until
fibres are laid bare as in old wooden floors,

suckandet från vindfyllda orglar övergår i larmet från
den stora vinterorkestern,
    och ju längre någon kommit ut i världen ju starkare
    ingen är lycklig och ingen riktigt olycklig i detta navel-
strängarnas tyranni,
    med denna ständigt värkande ömhet hos en blå tand i
havet.

the murmur of wind-filled organs is heightened
to the roar of the vast winter orchestra,
   and the farther someone has travelled out into the
world the stronger he feels the tugging from the
islands' chains of year rings,
   nobody is truly happy nor unhappy in this tyranny
of umbilical cords,
   with this ever tender ache from a blue tooth
in the ocean

—Translated from the Swedish by Lennart Bruce

Stein Mehren

From THE KILESUND WOODS

Somewhere between language and substance
between the image and the unknown
between the sign and the unrecognizable

I call the things
and the things eat out from the words
eat up their names, and become

—Translated from the Norwegian by Robert Hedin

Stein Mehren

AS DAYS COME

There are days
when the sun comes from everywhere
days that slide through the doors
before we are awake
there are birds
that fasten days to the sky
with long, irresistible stitches

There are suburbs
where paths run together
in surging streams of footsteps
there are cities where your hair floods
like sun through the streets
where faces swirl
through us like leaves in the wind

There are days
when the grass billows through me
in long violent shudders
days when the sun rises
in my own body, days
when I simply come to you, as
days come

—Translated from the Norwegian by Robert Hedin

90   *Heister*

Ruben Vela

LIFE OF CHURA, THE GRAVE DIGGER

Before birth Chura was destined to serve the God of Darkness because his mother, ripe with youth, sought license for the prostitution of her body.

From the time he was small Chura showed a pious humility in the face of the horrible duties that his profession obligated him. He buried the bodies of those who had died, staying with them for entire days at a time to ensure they never returned to the world of the living. And so in this way he established with the buried, curious and very strange relations, and they distinguishing him as their favorite guardian, warned him constantly against the sufferings, misgivings and disillusionments that life usually offered.

Wanting to reconcile all this wise advice with the most advanced ideas of his time, Chura married a young virgin of great beauty, dead at the peak of those attributes, and with whom he regularly performed the obligations that marriage imposed, yet never succeeded at having children—it was assumed—for the reason of the ex-virgin's narrow hips or from the uncalculated frigidity that the dead wife was acknowledged to have had in the presence of amorous affections by her young husband.

Informed about what they considered to be an infamous profanity, the Priests ordered Chura's execution, a decision that had to be suspended because of fierce protests on the part of those who received his daily condolences. The case was reversed based on the verdict of the Oracle from the Island of the Sun whose Word ordered everyone present to meet again to hear sentence after a hundred years, starting from that date.

—*Translated from the Spanish by Zoe Anglesey*

Ruben Vela

LIFE OF HUASCAR XUMA, MATHEMATICIAN

Huascar Xuma lamented his humble condition as slave until he was sixteen years old, when the Great Priest, struck by his carriage and intelligence, provided him a liberal education, whereupon Huascar Xuma perfected the arts of rhetoric and mathematics.

During his youth, he held a very important rank in the Empire, although there are those who claimed he owed his high position to their good graces.

A jealous woman wanted to poison him at a banquet, but the deities came to his rescue—they induced unmitigated vomiting. From then on, because of this, one side of his body was left paralyzed.

One day he withdrew to a cave to emerge pale and scrawny, convincing everyone he had returned from the depths of hell in whose infernal school he had learned so much, that from that day on, he reduced all things to a unifying number, as to a universal element and the origin of all things.

He opposed the Priests of Fire who negated the infallibility of the God-Number. Taking an earthen jar, puncturing it full of little holes, Huascar Xuma plugged the holes with beeswax.

The jar full of water, he painted an image on it of the God-Number symbolized by a sphere and he challenged the Priests of Fire in the name of the God-Number.

Huascar Xuma placed the jar on the sacred altar. Instantly the beeswax melted from the heat of the flames, popped out of the holes, the water poured forth putting out the sacred flames and the image of the God-Number painted on the jar glowed victorious in the shimmer of the dying embers. In this manner, he bestowed upon himself victory over the Priests of Fire.

Huascar Xuma taught the existence of one-hundred eighty-three different worlds situated inside an equilateral triangle contained within a sphere. He understood the properties of atoms and its unifying principle multiplied by infinite parts that mutually sustain, forming the matter of which all things are composed.

The violence and rapidity of a mysterious illness took him to the grave, at the time when he intended to define the natural probability of the Number that governs the particular relation existing between God and humans.

—Translated from the Spanish by Zoe Anglesey

Naomi Shihab Nye

EVEN AT WAR

Loose in his lap, the hands.
And always a necktie,
as some worlds are made complete
by single things.
Graveled voice,
a bucket raised on old ropes.
You know how a man can get up,
get dressed, and think
the world is waiting for him?
At night, darkness knits
a giant cap to hold the dreams in.
A wardrobe of neckties with slanted stripes.
Outside, oranges are sleeping, eggplants,
fields of wild sage. The same air
which nourishes them carries headlines
that will cross the ocean by tomorrow.
Bar the door.

Sang Koo

어느 回想

아시아드 육상 三冠王
임춘애 소녀의
TV에 비친 얼굴을 보니
그 표정이 매우 낯익다.

기억을 더듬고 더듬은 끝에
20대 초반 일본 도꾜 유학시절
하숙방 벽에 붙여 놓았던
모딜리아니의 女人像을 떠올렸다.

나는 그때 그 哀憐한 모습이
어찌나 좋고 그립던지
저런 여인네에게 장가를 들겠다고
친구들에게까지 떠벌렸다.

마침내 그런 여성은 만나지 못하고
도리어 푸짐한 느낌의 아내와 맺어져
이미 마흔 두 해를 넘긴 이제사
바로 그런 소녀가 나타나긴 했는데…

Sang Koo

A MEMORY

Triple gold medalist woman runner
1986 Asian Olympic Games—
when her face appeared on TV,
I had an instant sense of recognition.

Recall took me back—age 20,
Tokyo, where I was a student—
on the wall of my boarding house,
a Mondrian painting of a woman.

I was so deeply attracted to her
as the expression of my ideal,
I told everyone she was the woman
I wanted to marry.

However, I never did meet her.
Instead I married someone quite different
and now, 42 years later, again
the face that first attracted me.

하기는 괴테는 **70**에 **18**세 소녀와
熱愛를 했다던가?
지난해까지도 생존한 헨리 밀러도
70세에 求愛電報를 쳤다던가?

허지만 나는
글쎄올시다./

거울을 집어보니
오늘따라 흰 머리 흰 수염이
더 세어 보인다.

And yet, Goethe fell madly in love
with an 18 year old—or so I'm told—
and Henry Miller at 70 proposed
by telegram to a young girl.

But I—
it's doubtful.

Especially today,
looking in the mirror,
an old greybeard.

*—Translated from the Korean
by Byong Mok Kim and Elizabeth Bartlett*

Henrikas Nagys

FRAU PANNWITZ: *VATER UNSER*

Achtung, Achtung . . . dreba dienovidžio dangus
išraižytas tūkstančiais baltų linijų.
Unter den Linden—jokio žmogaus. Tik spengia
priešlėktuvinių patrankų salvės ir dreba žalvariniai
žirgai, nuo tolimų duslių dunksėjimų, viršum Berlyno
pergalės vartų arkos . . . Frau Pannwitz savo namo langus
užkamšė skudurais. Mes bėgam begaliniais laiptais
į dvokiantį ir tamsų rūsį . . . *Vater unser* . . .
Frau Pannwitz—pusaklė, sulinkusi, tarytum neštų
žuvusio vyro ir sūnų lavonus, nuolat šnabžda
ir šnabžda tą pačią maldą: *Vater
unser, der Du bist im Himmel* . . .
O dangų seniai mums atėmė sudrėkę rūsio skliautai
ir baugiai mirkčiojančios, ant linguojančių vielų,
lemputės. Skaičiuojame minutes, sekundes, — didelio
ir merdėjančio miesto pulsą . . .
Frau Pannwitz degančiam Berlyne
šnabžda už mus visus:
*Vater
unser* . . .

Henrikas Nagys

FROM A WAR DIARY: FRAU PANNWITZ

Achtung, achtung . . . The midday sky shakes,
carved with thousands of white lines.
Unter den Linden—not a soul. Only volleys
of anti-aircraft cannons ring out and brass steeds
tremble from the distant muffled sputtering
above Berlin's arch of triumph . . . Frau Pannwitz
has stopped up her windows with rags.
We run down endless stairs into the dark and dank cellar...
Vater Unser . . . Frau Pannwitz—half-blind, bent,
as if she were carrying the bodies of her husband and sons,
constantly whispers and whispers
that same prayer: *Vater*
Unser, der Du bist im Himmel . . .
Though the heavens have long been replaced
by damp cellar vaults and the sputter
of lamps on swinging wires. We count
the minutes, the seconds—the pulse of this great
and dying city . . .
Frau Pannwitz whispers in burning Berlin
on behalf of us all:
Vater
Unser . . .

                    —*Translated from the Lithuanian by Jonas Zdanys*

Henrikas Nagys

1.

Nebuvo pavasario:
po žiemos atėjo
žiema.
Kaip pasakoje,
kaip sapne.
Keista:
ledai kai užklojo
dangų, veidą ir ežerą—
nepastebėjau:
nebuvo vasaros,
nei rudens:
po žiemos atėjo
žiema.

2.

Apkabinkime rankomis saulę—
teneateina žiema.
Teneateina naktis.
Teneateina gruodu,
palaidojusi visą gentį
smėlio kalne.

Henrikas Nagys

THERE WAS NO SPRING

1.

There was no spring.
After winter came
winter.
As if in a story
or dream.
It was remarkable:
though ice covered
the sky, my face, and the lake,
I didn't notice:
there was no summer,
no fall.
After winter came
winter.

2.

Let us embrace the sun—
may winter not come.
May night not come.
May it not come in clumps of frozen earth
having buried generations
in mountains of sand.

Teneateina Arktikos sąsiaurio
amžinuoju ledu.
Teneužgriūva, kartu su Sibiro vėju,
tamsioji tyla.

Apkabinkime rankomis saulę,
apkabinkim saulėtekį,
tegul būna ir būna ir būna
diena.

May it not come
in the eternal ice of Arctic straits.
May dark silence not come
with the Siberian winds.

Let us embrace the sun—
embrace the sunrise.
May day be and be
and be.

—*Translated from the Lithuanian by Jonas Zdanys*

106 *Henri Raymond de Toulouse-Lautrec*

Helen Barolini

LA GIARDINIERA

The telephone rang too early for a Sunday morning. Donna Scortese reached for it at her bedside, feeling by the torpor in which she groped that it was not time for her mother's weekly call. So undeviating was it, at nine each Sunday morning, that she prized it as the only firm punctuation in her run-on, dangling life.

"Is Leon there?" The voice was brisk, wide-awake, preemptory. Donna recognized Joyce, the woman friend of Leon, who lived in Donna's home. 'Leon the Lodger' she quipped among her friends, making it seem light and playful that she had a boarder in the large, empty house where she would otherwise be alone.

Donna reached in the darkened room towards her watch. Seven thirty . . . not so early. "No," she breathed into the receiver. "Leon's gone camping. Back after Labor Day." She followed Leon's instructions of what to say if anyone called for him while he went upstate with his son.

"Do you know what time he left?"

Recollecting the muffled sounds that had become part of her sleeping state somewhat earlier—the steps on the stairs, in the kitchen, and the closing of the front door—all of which Donna was always conscious of, whether it came late at night after she had gone to bed, or early in the morning before she got up, she made a guess. "About six." She was abrupt, annoyed.

"Six in the evening?"

"No." She emphasized each word, "This morning."

"Thank you." The phone was hung up quickly.

Why wasn't Joyce informed of Leon's trip with the kid? Was something wrong between them? Now Donna was fully awake and there was no use reattempting sleep. This thing between Leon and Joyce, this constant checking between partners that dragged her into their doings . . . the uncommunicativeness that made one partner a drifter on the fringes of the other's life—what was it all about? It seemed incredible to Donna, and mean, that he hadn't said anything to Joyce. Was he dropping her as he had Paula?

In the year Leon had been in her home, Donna had learned to distinguish the various females who called him: the wife he was separated from and his teen-age daughter called rarely and very concisely—no conversation, just name and number messages. Paula, his first woman friend, had called often; she had a soft, apologetic voice and seemed to care a lot for Leon. Paula and Donna began to ask each other how they were and to chat a bit. Donna told her she was a widow, that her three children had grown up and left. "That's what they do," Paula chuckled. Donna always gave Leon the messages. At first he called Paula back, then he didn't. Paula would find excuses. "Donna," she'd say, "did you tell Leon I called? You did? Well, he must be busy—I haven't heard. Well, it wasn't that important. I'll probably see him around anyway." Then her calls got less frequent until there were no more. Even before that, Joyce's began. Joyce did not chat. Donna did not like her tone and felt Leon was making a mistake. But it was predictable. Leon couldn't handle Paula's caring so much. It was what happened between Donna and Murray Buddenberg, except that it was Bud who cared too much and wanted too much, and Donna who, like Leon, wanted less.

Murray Buddenberg was never quite gone from Donna's house; he persisted in her memory and feelings just as he persisted in sending her cards attesting to his love. Only the evening before they had dinner together like two people who had just met at a singles group and were on circumspect behavior, testing. None of the pain of their betrayed expectations came between them, nor any of the laughter of their good times either. They were judicious, hesitant.

Donna got up to make coffee and decide her day. From the kitchen she looked out through sliding glass doors into the distance of river and mountains, the view that lifted her heart each morning. It was gorgeous late August and a day of absolute clarity with long, deep shadows contrasting with tree-filtered patterns of light, a huge sky full of billowing clouds, and a tang of coolness in the air. On the counter near the coffeemaker, Donna's eye was caught by the lettuce seed packet which had lain there all spring, all summer, near the discount coupons for Brim, cheese, garbage bags, toothpaste. She was able neither to toss it away, nor to decide to use it. It was just there, like her life, waiting for a decision.

She picked up the packet which was, actually, a novelty greeting card. "Lettuce Never Part" it said over a drawing of a pale green head of lettuce. Inside it was signed, "All my love, Your Bud." The sealed verso contained seeds of head lettuce with instructions for early spring planting. The packet lay there since late in March, months after Donna told Bud not to call or bother her anymore. She resented his calling himself her Bud. But she liked the lettuce message and was touched by Bud's continuing thought of her as a gardener. It had been their plan to live together in her home (his was gone, sold for his divorce settlement), and gardening was just one of the things she would teach him.

They had come together, both wanting to make up for past losses, and had simply ignored the signs of their unsuitability. "I want it to always stay like this, never change," he said at first, uprooting himself from his past life and moving into her home. She, impatient of his growing absorption of her time, her attention, her activities, her very thoughts, felt smothered by his zeal and constant profferment of love. Just as the children, leaving, had done, she cried out, "I need my space!" while he, bewildered and hurt, accused her, "You have time for everyone but me! I want us to be together all the time and share everything. I love you!"

Love! Why should a grown man need so much love! she asked herself until she knew the answer. He was still the son who had been king of his mother's universe from his birth until ten years later when a sister was born, not to supplant him, but to make all the more apparent his reigning dominion. And now he expected to be Donna's whole center. And that, for her, widowed for years and used to her own ways, was inconceivable. They stayed together, with good times and bad, for a year. Then Bud moved to a condominium and Donna, unwilling to sell the house, yet hard put to meet expenses and lonely with no one there, decided to rent a bedroom with bath and use of the kitchen.

Leon was what the real estate people called one of the new homeless: people in the process of separation or divorce who needed temporary housing. A couple would split and suddenly two shelters were needed instead of one. It was their largest growing market, the agents said.

Donna knew who Leon was. She had once spoken to him with a complaint in the supermarket where he was manager. He was hard to forget—so tall, with such black, bushy hair and bristling moustache, and with dark eyes that fixed upon her with disconcerting intensity while she spoke. She felt uneasy at first, estranged in her own home and tubless (he got the bathroom with the bathtub and shower since it adjoined his room and she took the other with shower alone), but she found him considerate, polite, unobtrusive, and hardly ever there. He spent most of his time at work, and then with Paula or Joyce and seemed to come back to the house only when his laundry needed doing.

When they did meet in the kitchen occasionally, at early morning or in the evening, it was always with a shock that Donna saw this big black-haired man using her utensils and putting his convenience foods away in the cupboard she had emptied for him. Once, during a snowstorm she had invited him to share the minestrone she had made. For Christmas he gave her a fruit basket. He did little repairs around the house and always paid the rent punctually and asked if she needed anything from the store. No matter how remote their contact, just the fact of Leon's car coming and going in the drive made Donna feel better.

She settled into a routine; she had her part-time job, she had time to do what she wanted, she had some friends. She missed the idea of a companion in her life as she had imagined Bud would be, but she didn't miss his attempt to control her. Con-artist! salesman! pressure-cooker! she hurled at him in their last bitter moments.

She began to figure: she was fifty-two and there was no better or worse time, there was only what she was given now.

Just a few weeks earlier she had driven to the Berkshires with a woman friend, also a widow and very militantly eager to remarry. Driving through Williamstown, Donna thought of having been there with Bud: they had bicycled through town and found raspberries at a roadstand which they bought, a pint each, and ate then and there, gluttonous, childlike, greedy. The nostalgia surprised Donna. For two days she fought off a desire to send Bud a postcard. She rationalized that she had never responded to his Lettuce Never Part card, and that she should. But why? She struggled indecisively until, on the third day of that Berkshires trip she bought a card showing the Clark museum, addressed it to Murray Buddenberg and wrote: "Remembering raspberries, Monets, and good biking. Donna." She would never, in his style, sign it, "Love, Your Donna." She felt there was something crude, pushy even, about the possessive form used that way.

He called her after getting her postcard as she knew he would. When they had dinner, she was touched at how glad he was to see her and she told him she missed him, too. "If you only knew how much I love you and still want to be with you," he said. But love alone doesn't make it possible, she told him, still doubting.

The shock was that in the time they had known each other, she had formed an attachment (no, a need) that she could not dismiss. It was simply there; Bud was still part of her life for better or for worse. Without having performed a wedding ceremony (which he wanted, she didn't), they were, in some mysterious way, wedded. And marriage, she was startled to learn, was indissoluble. Though she had been taught this in her Catholic schooling, she had never believed it. Now she knew that beyond dogma, it was true in a human way. What is joined really cannot be put asunder; even with the redoing of minds and allegiance and feelings that separation demands, something is bonded and sticks. Forever.

Now, on this August Sunday morning, too early to get the Times, too late for sleep, alone in the house, she fingered the package of seeds and considered. August 29th. Was it too late? It could be the late crop—lettuce liked cool weather and the days were getting cooler. "Lettuce Never Part," the packet implored. She knew she wasn't considering the lettuce alone and she scorned herself for indulging a metaphor as obvious as soap opera. And yet what was she? or Leon? or Paula, Bud, Joyce—any of them?—what, if not soap?

Bud had taught her a new fact of life: constancy counts. She thought she had loathed his ill-bred persistency, his salesman's pitch; now she was moved by the simplicity of his adherence. Where else was constancy? she asked herself. In the memory of a husband a dozen years dead? In work which was a pastime, not a career? In her scattered children who were impatient of telephone calls and too busy to write or to spend any time with her? They thought it was good for her to have a boarder: "to keep you company" was the euphemism by which they denied the problem of her life.

Donna went out dressed in an old shirt of Bud's and loose drawstring pants, clogs. She went to the patch of ground on the rise beyond the carport which she and Bud, in their first enthusiasm had cleared and reclaimed. There they planted the vegetables that had been such a revelation to him. "Thirty-two years I was married in Great Neck and could have had a garden!" he exclaimed. He was excited at the prospect of going out to pick a fresh tomato and said he owed it all to her, he had never known a person like her. "I was always told don't get my hands dirty. How could I know good things like tomatoes came out of the dirt?'' he said in his self-mocking and rueful way.

She laughed when he talked about his background. Other times she grew morose, knowing they were not suited to each other. We rub each other the wrong way, she said; we're mismatched; we come from two different worlds.

Now the neglected garden sprawled before her, a severe reproach. Languidly, back in May, acting on some atavistic instinct, she had put in tomato and basil, because what was summer without them? She even imagined that perhaps one of the girls would come by and she could joyfully heap her with the garden bounty. But long silence made her negligent. She forgot to water the plants; she didn't weed. When she thought of the plants, it was only to admonish them: Make it on your own, just as I have to.

Looking at the result, Donna was shocked and sorry. The basil, usually flourishing and fragrant, was stunted and lost among the weeds. The tomato plants, left unstaked, were straggling along the ground with some undeveloped green fruit among the yellowing leaves. Where had the time gone? What had she done rather than tend her garden?

To Bud she used to brag of coming from tough-minded, sturdy peasant stuff, a pose she liked to affect to contrast all the more (she thought) with her grand style and intellectual achievements. In fact, she did love the physicalness of hard, outdoor work and felt she owed that to her Calabrian forebears who had worked fields of veritable stone and thistle and made them bloom. Now her life was like the abandoned fields of the old country—arid, uncared for, walked away from.

She stood there considering: it was no longer just a matter of putting in lettuce. It was a larger issue: it was staying alive. She went to work, breaking up the parched ground with a hoe, pulling out the rank weeds, uncovering grubs and stones. ''Lettuce never part'' rang in her ears. And it made sense. Let us in some way stay together; let us keep the connection. In what way she could not yet tell. I let Bud walk away, she told herself as she spaded the ground; I wanted him to grow on his own. But nothing works that way, not plants and not people. And she saw, as she worked, the sight of herself and nine-year-old Lollie, years before, going up the hill to plant the flaming red weigela.

Donna felt the sun getting high and strong as she filled a wheelbarrow with uprooted weeds. She found still unopened bales of peat moss and fertilizer in the carport and wheeled them up to the garden site. Hoeing, spading, sifting and raking the earth, she then forked in peat moss and fertilizer to enrich the soil. She wasn't doing just a furrow for the lettuce seeds, she was reclaiming the whole plot. She took down the poles and netting to which the previous year's dried out pea foliage still clung, cleaned them off, and re-set the poles to stake the tomatoes from which she pinched dried stems and leaves. They looked miserable and leggy, but perhaps now that they were lifted from the ground they would revive. She loosened the earth around them, yanked out the resistant crab grass, and threw fertilizer around the plants. Finally, she planted the lettuce seeds.

She stood back to look at her work. It was beginning to look like something. She felt satisfied. Then she scowled, "Christ, Almighty!" The forsythia! The damn overgrown bushes with their long, reaching suckers would soon take over the vegetable garden if they weren't cut back. Donna went back for the pruning shears and started in on them. Just like Bud, she thought as she hacked vigorously at the overgrowth. He would take her over completely; he wanted to make her "his wife," his possession. I want to take care of you, he cried, I love you and will take care of you as no one else ever has! I want you to be mine.

And she did not want to be his wife, she had been a wife already. No, she told him. There's no reason! What's the sense? She wanted them to be friends, partners. She liked this new time for women to be separate human beings in their own right and not just clinging vines on a foundation of male works and days; she liked the feeling of non-dependent companionship between men and women. But Bud was frightened and disoriented. I can provide for my family, he said defensively. I'm a human being, I have my rights, too!

As Donna cut back the forsythia, more shoots were exposed to be cut. The ground was thick with the cuttings and she tossed them into an old mulch pile under the lilacs. We need a fence here, she thought, a tall fence to keep back the forsythia. Maybe Bud would come over and help her put up a fence; they'd pick apples from the trees and she'd make him fresh applesauce. The trouble was, Bud was exuberant, like the forsythia. And like the forsythia, he had to be kept back, otherwise he'd take over everything. What he didn't understand was that cutting back was good, it kept the vigor in the main stem rather than dispersing it in side-shoots.

Having finally trimmed back the bushes and cleared the cuttings from the plot, she then arranged the garden hose to jet a fine spray over it.

Donna straightened up, wiped sweat from her forehead, and looked down the slope of the back lawn to the three apple trees which stood in a row. She sat down to rest, positioning her back against the trunk of the huge pine tree where outdoor Christmas lights were still entwined in the branches, and rested her arms on her raised knees. She stared thoughtfully at the apple trees; they were three different varieties, all green, and she had never learned their names. One for each of you, she used to say to the children. I'm not the sour one! Laura, the boldest, used to exclaim. Now it was a long time since they had been there at picking time, and never, anymore, all at once. The smell of the fall kitchen when the girls were young had been pungent and pleasing with the smell of cooking apples and all of them had helped in the gathering, peeling, preparing.

Donna thought of the chestnut trees of her own girlhood: how she delighted in the fall, walking home from school, to fill her pockets full of those smooth, glossy horse chestnuts that showed through the spikey green burrs. Then the blight had come and taken the trees.

Next it was the elms which sickened and died. They had

lined the street where she had her first home as a married woman, overhanging the roadway and sidewalks, shading the Victorian houses and making a veritable tunnel of cool under which she strolled her babes on summer days.

Now it was said that the dogwoods were going. Those beautiful spring trees of the New York suburbs, new and precious to Donna's upstate eyes when they moved to Westchester. She waited for them each spring and each spring they were again layered stars standing out, white and pink, from the woods, pricks of lacey light in the green.

One could weep at the losses, Donna thought. Where were the children? Gone as surely as a husband, as marriage, as the chestnuts and elms, and as the dogwoods soon would be.

The apple trees remained like sentinels in her memory, touchstones, reminding her of their joyous planting when they first moved to that beautiful place. One for each child. And Laura's wedding pictures taken in front of them. The fall after Bud moved in with her, the trees stopped bearing. Terrified, she called in a tree man who pruned them drastically, trimming and shaping the old trees into pieces of gaunt, minimal sculpture: the totem of her life pared down from too-huge expectations. There they stood, Giacomettis, spare and unpromising, all lines, during all that difficult year she tried to live with Bud and began to doubt, as he did, that they could. The trees kept their severity, promising nothing, through the summer. One day she looked out and they were laden with fruit.

Would the children ever be so miraculously recovered and fruitful to her hopes? She had tended them and helped them grow strong; now they accused her of "forcing," they said they had been trampled, bludgeoned, smothered.

Again Donna thought of Lollie and the flaming red weigela plant. She flushed, feeling an onrush of heat. Visiting Lollie, who had married in California, Donna had marveled at her daughter's wonderful garden and, because Lollie was so serene and communicative in that garden, in an impulse of confidentiality with her, Donna had said, "I am not sure that Bud and I can stay together. We're unsuited to each other."

Furious, Lollie had turned on her. "He's as wrong, as much a misjudgment on your part as when we planted that flaming red weigela at home. You can't force things just because you want them that way! You couldn't force that weigela to grow where it wasn't suited just because you wanted it there, and you can't force Bud to be what he isn't!"

Lollie stood there, her eyes fixed in accusation, while Donna, startled, tried to think what she meant. And there came to her, the memory of a winter day when she and little Lollie chose and ordered from a catalogue illustration a beautiful, but indistinct, flowering plant called flaming red weigela. They had been enthralled both by the gorgeous color of the picture and the exotic name. When, in the spring, the plant arrived, she had gathered Lollie into her enthusiasm and they had gone out to plant the bare stalk. "What is a weigela," Lollie asked. "I don't know, we'll see," Donna had answered gaily, full of expectation. "Then how do you know where to plant it," asked the wise child. "It doesn't matter," said the feckless mother, "we'll put it where it will look nice."

And disregarding instructions that said the bush liked full sun, Donna chose a spot along the shady path up to the hill-top that overlooked their house. Wouldn't it be fine, she said, to have a bush of flaming red flowers to point their way up the hill! Donna put it where it pleased her and trusted to its survival. No, *imposed* its survival. The weigela never took.

How humiliating it was, then, in Lollie's garden to have her mistakes so furiously thrown back at her, saved for so long. She saw suddenly that Lollie had been disappointed in her belief of some marvelous plant, as grand and triumphant sounding as a Vivaldi Gloria and she blamed her mother for not letting the marvel appear; and perhaps for all other marvels expected in vain. The irony was that later Donna discovered that a weigela was nothing marvelous at all, only the very ordinary bush of her childhood neighborhood yards. She never told Lollie, it didn't seem important; and maybe that was the mistake. But was it so grievous?

And why did they accuse her of trampling over them? As if anyone could trample Laura! she thought, thinking of the hard shell of self-centeredness with which her eldest child had always isolated herself. Was that what planting was? always to be in the hand of the unforeseeable?

But no, she told herself. There are always barren spaces and barren times when one just has to hold on and wait. It isn't always a flowering and blooming. She had wanted the children to be sturdy in their own growth, not anticipating them, compact in their strength, turning against her, the gardener.

That detestable metaphor! She thought of the scorn all three would heap on her for such tacky thoughts. "You're so naive," they said. "So literal."

And she agreed: all that nurturing and tending! She began to hate the idea of planting and cultivating, the idea of herself as some silly optimist, making aesthetic choices. Was she some goddam humanist thinking that what she touched with good intentions was bound to blossom? The hell it would! Weeds prevailed, weather turned, plantings failed. Ask any farmer! The secrets of seed and people were mysteries. Donna felt slack, her energy gone. She was no gardener of others; not even herself.

Hating it, she couldn't drop the metaphor. It clung to her thoughts, holding like the poison ivy on the wall at the bottom of the yard, and just as banal and pernicious.

Tears came to her eyes. Goddam you Murray Buddenberg, she cried, why don't *you* plant the goddam lettuce; why is it always *me*?

But women were always the gardeners, like those women during Italy's *risorgimento* who were known as *le giardiniere*, and were the female affiliates of the secret male societies pledged to help liberate nineteenth century Italy from foreign rule. *Alla giardiniera* now came to mind—in the garden manner—her mother's summertime stew of fresh vegetables; and she remembered the neat backyard rows of her Italian grandmother's garden in its upstate soil. They planted. They harvested. Why must she end up questioning and thinking and circling around things endlessly, trying to understand?

She felt possessed of the figure of speech that had forced her into the day to plant the lettuce seeds. But it was too late! Did she think that, filled with goodwill and warmth towards Bud because they had met for dinner the night before, she could go out and plant their relationship anew? And that, late in the season, it would take because she willed it so? The experience of years sat on her shoulders, aching now from the toiling. She put her head on her knees and closed her eyes.

And yet, she told herself, to balance the going and dying and blighting, there is still some persistent life-force which doesn't question, wants no answers, simply is. Why not let the mystery alone?

She raised her head to the trees. Such a good crop of apples this year. She got to her feet and went back to the plot to adjust the hose. She was satisfied with her work. She wasn't just soap; there was still that strain in her of tough Calabrian peasant resistance; she would survive, as they had. Though times were different, it was, in the end, all the same.

In fact, it was not too late. There was still time for a fall crop of peas, spinach, kale, cabbage, as well as lettuce. She would grow kale and invite Bud for a Portuguese soup of kale and linguica like one they had had at the Cape. She could do it herself. She could be a *giardiniera* in her own cause. There were a lot of things still to do. First she would call Bud and tell him she had planted the lettuce.

Was that another mistake of judgment, like the flaming red weigela?

No, thought Donna. I am not forcing, he is choosing.

And if I am choosing too, then it will take.

Donna looked down towards the apple trees. They had been restored and were fruitful. I'll say a prayer to San Rocco, the saint of the impossible, she told herself. I'll call Bud and tell him. She smiled as she thought of what his response would be. "From your mouth to the ears of God!" he'd say.

120   *Elliot Erwitt*

Linda Pastan

balancing act: for N.

like Chinese acrobats
we climb on

each other's
shoulders

four generations
balanced

so briefly
in time

me kneeling
on my mother's frail

shoulders
my son's ankles

hard against
my neck

his child
held in one hand high

above his head
four

of us looking out
in four

directions
hooked together

by nerve
and DNA

hurry
the lights

are going
down

Elizabeth Bartlett

SPELL BEAUTY

Before I heard the word or could read the word, I knew it existed. It was a feeling, something I felt about special things. A look. A touch. A warm cheek. A beam of light. A canary singing. My mother's smell. Each special thing gave me a special feeling.

Beauty. When I learned the word, I realized it applied both to special things and to special feelings. Beauty. They had it. My feelings had it. It was an exciting discovery. There was an outside beauty and an inside beauty. Was there any way I could connect them?

Some did it with painting. Some with music, with dance. Perhaps I could do it with words? If I took a sheet of paper, a clean white sheet of paper, and on it connected the outside and inside beauty—I thought of a shimmering page of words. Oh, if my feelings could become shimmering pages!

But first I would have to learn to write. Spelling. Grammar. Punctuation. Phrases. Vocabulary. So that my words could duplicate the world of sight, sound, touch, smell, taste . . . Until I forgot the feelings inside me, in trying to find the words for the things outside. The more words I wrote, the farther I got from their inner source. Until beauty itself became a word. Spell beauty.

It took me a long time, but I finally realized that beauty is a mutual gift, exchanged between self and the world. When special things give rise to special feelings, the connections we call art enhance the relationship. Art does not replace life; words can not substitute for it. Beauty has its own existence.

Ai Qing

DREAMS

Waking hours
Are crammed with fantasy
Then dreams
Drop in to visit while you sleep

Perhaps an early childhood sweetheart
Or an old buddy arriving from far away

Grief writhes on an inner-spring mattress
Ecstatic rendezvous occur on a straw pile

While poverty-stricken you offer gifts
Once you're affluent you get robbed

Either it's a false alarm
Or the inkling that more is amiss

—Translated from the Chinese by Edward Morin
and Dennis Ding

CANTO LLANO

XXIII

Materia, madre, mar, María,
nombres que vienen del origen
llenando el sabor y el sentido
de un mismo jugo en sus raíces.

Materia que es la madre pura,
tendida a parir lo que existe,
místico ensueño de inocencia
recogiendo las formas vírgenes.

Mar hecho del agua del caos
y del esplendor de los límites,
regazo amargo de María
para El que nos hizo partícipes
Lávenos bramando la mar
como una madre al hijo triste,
y en el seno de la materia
María matinal nos güie.

Cintio Vitier

From PLAIN SONG

XXIII

Matter, mother, maré, Maria,
names which come from the core,
filled with the taste and with the sense
of water coursing through
the same fiber and root.

Matter is the pure mother,
stretching to give birth to all which exists,
mystical in its dream of innocence
gathering all perfect forms.

Maré, sea, made of watery chaos
and the splendor of limits,
the bitter lap of Maria
that He shares with us.

Wash us, sea-mother,
as a mother would her sad child,
and so in the heart of matter,
O Maria of morning, guide us.

—Translated from the Spanish by Maria Bennett

128   *Peter Stackpole*

FOG

On an unspeakably cold and foggy night one November in San Francisco, something terrible happens to a woman named Antonia Love. She is a painter, middle-aged, recently success-ful, who has invited some people to her house for dinner (one of whom she has not even met, as yet). But in the course of tearing greens into the salad bowl and simultaneously shooing off one of her cats—the old favorite, who would like to knead on one of her new brown velvet shoes—Antonia, who is fairly tall, loses her balance and falls, skidding on a fragment of watercress and avoiding the cat but landing, *bang,* on the floor, which is Mexican tiled, blue and white. Hard. Antonia thinks she heard the crack of a bone.

Just lying there for a moment, shocked, Antonia imagines herself a sprawled, stuffed china-headed doll, her limbs all askew, awry. How incredibly stupid, how dumb, she scolds herself; if I didn't want people to dinner I could just have not asked them. And then: Well, useless to blame myself, there are accidents. The point is, what to do now?

As she tries to move, it is apparent that her left arm indeed is broken; it won't work, and in the effort of trying to move it Antonia experiences an instant of pain so acute that she reels, almost faints, and only does not by the most excruciat-ing effort of will.

The problem of what to do, then, seems almost out of her hands. Since she can't for the moment get up, she also can't call her doctor, nor 911. Nor, certainly, can she go on with making dinner.

Fortunately her coming guests are old close friends (except for the very young man she doesn't know, although he seems to think he has met her somewhere). And, further luck, she is sure that she unlocked the front door, its bell being hard to hear, back here in the kitchen. And so, her friends will arrive and they will come on in, calling out to her, and she to them. They will find her ludicrously positioned, they will help— although possibly she is really quite all right, and will manage to get up by herself, any minute now.

A new flash of pain as she tries to move convinces Antonia that her arm is really broken, and again she castigates herself for clumsiness, for evident ill-will toward her friends, determined self-defeat. For steady progress toward no progress at all—oh, for everything!

In addition to which she has probably scared her cat quite badly. He is nowhere around, although she calls out to him, "Baron! Baron?"

No cat, then, and no live-in lover either, since Reeve is at the moment off on one of his restless trips, somewhere; Reeve who in an off-and-on way lives there with Antonia, the arrangement being that both are 'free.' And just as well he is gone, thinks Antonia; he so hates debility, hates bodily things going wrong. (But in that case why has he chosen to live, more or less, with an 'older woman,' whose body must inevitably decline?) Antonia wonders if Reeve is alone on this trip (she knows that he sometimes is not), but she finds that she lacks just now the stamina for jealous speculation.

Her arm really hurts badly, though; she wishes someone would come, and she wonders who will be the first—who will come in to find her in this worse-than-undignified position? Will it be her old friend from school days, attractive Lisa, who is bringing the strange young man? Or will it be Bynum and Phyllis, who are also old friends—or, Bynum is. He is a sculptor, and Phyllis, his latest wife, a very young lawyer. Antonia believes they are not getting along very well.

Or (at this new notion Antonia smiles rather ruefully to herself) it could always be tall, thin, sandy Reeve himself, who is given to changing his mind, to turning around and away from trips, and people. Reeve, a painter too, is more apt to come home early from trips on which he is accompanied than from those he takes alone; but even that is not a formulation on which anyone, especially Antonia, should count.

Antonia is aware that her friends wonder why she 'puts up' with Reeve, his absences, his occasional flings with young art students—and she considers her private view of him: an exceptional man, of extreme (if occasional) sensitivity, kindness—a painter of the most extraordinary talent. (On the other hand, sometimes she too wonders.)

Antonia knows too that her friends refer to Reeve as Antonia's cowboy—

Reeve is from Wyoming.

She tries next to lie down, believing that some rest might help, or ease the pain which now seems to have become a constant. Never mind how appalling the spectacle of herself would be, her oversized body sprawled across the floor. However she can't get down, can't reach the floor; the broken arm impedes any such changes of position. Antonia finds that the most she can achieve is leaning back against table legs, fortunately a heavy, substantial table.

Perry Loomis, the unmet guest, is a journalist, just getting started, or trying to in New York. He could surely sell an article about such a distinguished, increasingly famous woman, especially since Antonia never gives interviews. Now, having cleverly engineered this meeting, and being driven in from Marin County by Antonia's old friend, Lisa, Perry is overexcited, unable not to babble. "It said in *Time* that a lot of speculators are really grabbing up her stuff. Even at thirty or forty thousand per. She must hate all that, but still."

"It's hard to tell how she does feel about it," Lisa rather crisply responds. "Or anything else, for that matter. I think success has been quite confusing to Antonia."

The bay is heavily, thickly fogged, slowing, impeding their progress from Mill Valley into town, to Antonia's small house on Telegraph Hill. Not everyone slows, however; an occasional small, smart sportscar will zoom from nowhere past Lisa's more practical Ford wagon. Scary, but she does not even think of asking this young man to drive. They met through friends at a recent gallery (not the opening) at which Antonia's work was being shown. Perry described himself as a 'tremendous Antonia Love fan' and seemed in his enthusiasm both innocent and appealing. Which led Lisa fatally to say, "Oh really, I've known her almost all my life." Which was not even quite true, but which, repeated to Antonia, led up to this dinner invitation. "Well, why don't you bring him along when you come next Thursday? I'm almost sure Reeve won't be here, and poor Bynum must be tired of being the token man."

"And she's so beautiful," rattles Perry. "That Thomas Victor picture, fabulous. Was she always such a beauty?"

"Well, no," says Lisa, too quickly. "In fact I don't quite see—but you know how old friends are. As a young woman she was just so—big. You know, and all that hair."

"But I met her," Perry reminds her firmly. "At that thing in New York. She had on the most marvelous dress, she was ravishing, really."

"Oh yes, her green dress. It is good-looking. I think she paid the earth for it. That's one of the points about darling Antonia, really. Her adorable inconsistencies. A dress like that but never a sign of a maid or even a cleaning person in her house." And just why is she sounding so bitchy? Lisa wonders.

"Maybe she thinks they'd get in her way?" Perry's imagination has a practical turn. As a schoolboy, which was not all that long ago, he too meant to be an artist, and was full of vague, romantic plans. However, during college years, in the late seventies, he came to see that journalism might better serve his needs, a judgment seemingly correct. However, his enthusiasm for 'artists,' in this instance Antonia, is a vestige of that earlier phase.

"Well, she's in any case a marvelous cook," Lisa promises, warmly. And then, somewhat less charitably, "Her cooking is surely one of those things that keeps young Reeve around."

"But isn't he a painter too?" Saying this, with an embarrassed twinge Perry realizes that he has imagined Reeve, described in Antonia Love articles as her 'young painter companion' as a sort of slightly older version of himself. He had looked forward to seeing just what of himself he would find in Antonia's Reeve.

"Of course he's a painter, that's nine-tenths of the problem right there. Reeve's from Wyoming, we call him Antonia's cowboy. But they should never—Oh, look. *Damn.* There must be an accident on the bridge. Damn, we'll never get there."

Before them on the downward, now entirely fog-shrouded approach to the Golden Gate Bridge, what now seems heavy traffic is halted, absolutely. Red brake lights flicker, as thick cold moisture condenses and drips in rivulets down windshields, windows, as somewhere out in the depthless, dangerous bay the foghorns croak, and mourn.

"Oh dear," says Perry Loomis, feelingly. Although this attractive, rather interesting 'older woman' was kind enough to bring him to his object, the desired Antonia, he thinks he really doesn't like her very much. (Are she and Antonia Love the same age? he wonders. This one looks younger, he thinks.)

"Indeed," says Lisa. On the whole an honest woman, she now admits to herself that she agreed to bring this Perry along not entirely out of kindness; there was also (she confesses to herself) some element of fantasy involved, specifically a romantic fantasy of herself with a younger lover (Lisa has been twice divorced, most recently, two years back, from an especially mean-spirited lawyer). And then, Oh God, she thinks. Do I have to spend my life trying to be Antonia?

Reeve, who did indeed start out for Oregon, and alone, has now made a wide detour via the Richmond-San Rafael Bridge and is headed for Berkeley. Where, as Antonia might have guessed, had she the energy, there is a girl, Sharon, in whom Reeve is 'interested.' At this moment, heading along the foggy freeway toward the Berkeley exits, he longs to talk to Sharon, talking being so far about all they have done.

It's very difficult, living with Antonia, he would like to tell Sharon. Here she is so successful, everything people work for, and she doesn't believe it. In her mind she's still starving and probably lonely. I mean, it's very hard to live with someone whom nothing can convince that she's all right. Nothing can convince her that people love her, including me.

Sharon is one of the most beautiful young women that Reeve has ever seen; he rather suspects that she was hired in the Art Department, where she works, on that basis—she was formerly a model. A darkly creamy blonde, with dreamy, thick-lashed blue-green eyes, Sharon holds her perfect body forward like a prize; she moves like a small queen—and she would not understand a single word of all that Reeve would like to say. To Sharon it would all be the ancient complaints about a wife.

In fact the only person who could make the slightest sense of his ravings is Antonia herself. Reeve, a somewhat sardonic, self-mocking young man comes to this conclusion with a twisting, interior smile. And, on an impulse, passing Sharon's exit, which is University, and heading toward the fog-ladened Bay Bridge, he speeds up the car.

"Phyllis and Bynum, Lisa. Perry. I'll be back soon. Sorry. Stew and risotto in the oven. Salad and wine in refrig. Please take and eat. Love Antonia."

This note, taped to Antonia's door, was found by Phyllis and Bynum, one of whose first remarks to each other then was, "Who on earth does she mean by Perry?"

"Oh, some new young man of Lisa's, wouldn't you say?"

"But what could have happened to Antonia?"

"One of her meetings, wouldn't you imagine. One of her

good works." This last from Bynum, the oldest friend of Antonia's, who has very little patience with her, generally.

That exchange takes place on the long stairs leading up to the small, shabby-comfortable living room in which they soon sit, with glasses of wine, engaged in speculations concerning their hostess.

"Something could be wrong?" Phyllis ventures. A small, blond, rather pretty woman, she is much in awe of Antonia, whom she perceives as exceptionally *strong,* in ways that she, Phyllis, believes herself not to be.

"I doubt it." Big gnarled Bynum frowns.

This room's great feature, to some its only virtue, is the extraordinary view afforded of the city, even now, despite the thick fog. City lights still are faintly visible, everywhere, though somewhat muffled, dim, and the looming shapes of buildings can just be made out, against the lighter sky.

Phyllis, who is extremely tired (a gruelling day in court; but is she also tired of Bynum, as she sometimes thinks?), now lounges across a large, lumpy overstuffed chair, and she sips at the welcome cool wine. (The very size of Antonia's chair diminishes her to almost nothing, Phyllis feels.) She says, "Obviously, the view is why Antonia stays here?"

"Contrariness, I'd say," pontificates Bynum, himself most contrary by nature. "I doubt if she even notices the view any more."

A familiar annoyance tightens Phyllis's throat as she mildly says, "Oh, I'll bet she does." She is thinking: if Bynum and I split up I'll be lucky to get a place this nice, he doesn't have to keep putting it down. This could cost, oh, close to a thousand.

"Besides, the rent's still so low," continues Bynum, as though Phyllis had not spoken, perhaps as though he had read her mind.

A pause ensues.

"God, I'm so hungry," says Phyllis. "Do you think we should really go ahead with dinner?"

"Baby, I sure do." Bynum too is tired, a long sad day of not-being-able-to-work. And he too is hungry. "Antonia could be forever, and Lisa and her young man lost somewhere out in the fog."

The immediate prospect of food, however, serves to appease their hunger. They smile pleasantly at each other, like strangers, or those just met. Phyllis even thinks what a handsome man Bynum is; he looks wonderful for his age. "Was Antonia good-looking back when you first knew her?" she asks him.

"Well, she was odd." Bynum seems to ruminate. "She varied so much. Looking terrific one day, and really bad the next. But she was always, uh, attractive. Men after her. But the thing is, she doesn't know it."

"Oh, not even now?" Phyllis, disliking her own small-scale, her blond pallor, admires Antonia's larger, darker style. Antonia is so emphatic, is what Phyllis thinks.

"Especially not now." Bynum's smile and his tone are indulgent.

"Do you remember that really strange thing she said, when she told a reporter, 'I'm not Antonia Love'?" asks Phyllis. She has wanted to mention this before to Bynum, but they have, seemingly, no time for conversation.

"I think she meant that she could only view herself as created," Bynum explains, authoritatively.

Phyllis is not sure whether he is speaking as a fellow-artist or simply as an old friend. She asks, "Do you mean by the media?" She is aware of enjoying this conversation, perhaps because it is one, a conversation.

"Oh no, so much more sinister," Bynum assures her. "By herself. She thinks she's someone she's painted." He chuckles a little too loudly.

And loses the momentary sympathy of his young wife. Declining to comment, though, and remembering how hungry she is, Phyllis gets up to her feet. "Well, I don't care how lost Lisa and what's-his-name are. I'm heating up dinner."

She goes out into the kitchen, as Bynum calls after her, ''I'll be there in a minute.''

But several minutes pass, during which Bynum does not follow Phyllis. Instead he stares out the window, out into the dark, the enveloping, thickening fog. Into dimmed yellow lights.

He is fairly sure that Phyllis will leave him soon; he knows the signs—the ill-concealed small gestures of impatience, the long speculative looks, the tendencies to argument. How terribly alike they all seem, these girls that he marries. Or is it possible that he sees none of them very sharply, by herself—that he can't differentiate? One of them made this very accusation, referring to what she called his 'myopia.' In any case he will probably not miss Phyllis any more than he missed the others, and in a year or so he will find and marry a new young woman who is very much like Phyllis and the rest. He knows that he must be married.

A strong light wind has come up, rattling the window panes. Standing there, still looking out, Bynum has a brand new thought, or rather a series of thoughts. He thinks, Why do they always have to be so goddam young? Just who am I kidding? I'm not a young man. A woman of my own age or nearly might at last be a perfect companion for me. A woman artist, even, and he thinks, Well, why not Antonia? This place is a dump but she's so successful now, we could travel a lot. And I've always liked her really, despite our fights. This Reeve person must surely be on the way out. She won't put up with him much longer—so callow.

''Bynum, come on, it's all ready,'' Phyllis then calls out, as at that same instant the doorbell rings.

It is of course Lisa and the new young man, Perry, who looks, Bynum observes, far too smugly pleased with himself.

Introductions are made, warm greetings exchanged: ''But you look marvelous! Have you been here long? Yes, I'm sure we met at the gallery. How very like Antonia not to be here. But whatever could have happened?''

"Actually it is not at all like Antonia not to be here," Bynum announces. He is experiencing a desire to establish himself as the one of them who knows her best.

Lisa: "Well, actually you're right. She's almost compulsive about serving food on time."

Phyllis: "She's made a marvelous dinner. Smell! Come on in, I was just about to serve. I thought I might as well do what she said."

Over dinner, which indeed is excellent—a succulent veal stew, with a risotto—Bynum scrutinizes Lisa, and what looks to be her new friend. Lisa is looking considerably less happy than the young man is, this Perry, in Bynum's view. Could they possibly have made it in the car, on the way over here, and now Lisa is feeling regrets? Even to Bynum's somewhat primitive imagination this seems unlikely.

What Lisa actually—and acutely—regrets is simply having talked as much as she did to Perry, as on the way over they remained locked in the fog-bound traffic. She not only talked, she exaggerated, over-emphasized Antonia's occasional depression, even her worries over Reeve.

And, even while going on and on in that way, Lisa was visited by an odd perception, which was that she was really talking about herself: she, Lisa, suffers more than occasional depressions. It is her work, not Antonia's (well, hardly Antonia's) that seems to be going nowhere. And Lisa, with no Reeve nor anyone interesting in her life, at the moment, is worried that this very attractive young man will not like her (she has always liked small, dark, trimly-built men, like Perry). Which is really why she said so much about Antonia—gossip as gift, which is something she knows about, having done it far too often.

The truth is—or, one truth is that she is deeply, permanently fond of Antonia. And another truth is that her jealous competitiveness keeps cropping up, like some ugly, uncontrolled weed. She has to face up to it, do something about it, somehow. Maybe a therapist?

"What a superb cook Antonia is," she now says (this is true, but is she atoning?). "Her food is always such a treat."

"The truth is that Antonia does everything quite well," Bynum intones. "Remember that fully little spate of jewelry design she went into? Therapy, she called it, and she gave it up pretty quickly, but she did some lovely stuff."

"Oh Bynum," Lisa is unable not to cry out. "How can you even mention that junk? She was so depressed when she did it, and it did not work as therapy. You know perfectly well that she looked dreadful with all those dangles. She's too big."

Perry laughs as she says this, but in a pleasant, rather sympathetic way, so that Lisa thinks that maybe, after all, he understood? understood about love as well as envy?

Below them on the street now are the straining, dissonant, banging sounds of cars: people trying to park, trying to find their houses, to get home to rest. It is hard to separate one sound from another, to distinguish, identify. Thus, steps that must be Antonia's, with whomever she is with, are practically upon them before anyone has time to say, "Oh, that must be Antonia."

It is, though: Antonia, her arm in its bright white muslin sling thrust before her, in a bright new shiny plaster cast. Tall Antonia, looking triumphant, if very pale. And taller Reeve, somewhat disheveled, longish sandy hair all awry, but also in his own way triumphant, smiling. His arm is around Antonia's shoulder, in protective possession.

First exclamations are in reaction to the cast: "Antonia, how terrible! However did you? How lucky that Reeve—How awful, does it still hurt? Your *left* arm, how lucky!"

Reeve pulls out a chair for Antonia, and in an already practiced gesture with her good, lucky right arm she places the cast in her lap. In a somewhat embarrassed way (she has never been fond of center stage) she looks around at her friends. "I'm glad you went on with dinner," is the first thing she says. "Now you can feed us. God, I'm really starving."

"I came home and there she was on the floor—" Reeve begins, apparently about to start a speech.

"The damn cat!" Antonia cries out. "I tripped over Baron. I was making the salad."

Reeve scowls. "It was very scary," he tells everyone present. "Suppose I hadn't come home just then? I could have been travelling somewhere, although—"

This time he is interrupted by Bynum, who reasonably if unnecessarily states, "In that case we would have been the ones to find Antonia. Phyllis and I."

"I do wish someone would just hand me a plate of that stew," Antonia puts in.

"Oh of course, you must be starved," her friends all chorus. "Poor thing!"

It is Lisa who places the full, steaming plate before Antonia, Lisa asking, "You can eat okay? You want me to butter some bread?"

"Dear Lisa. Well actually I do, I guess. God, I hope I don't get to like this helplessness."

"Here," Lisa passes a thick slice of New York rye, all buttered. "Oh, and this is Perry," she says. "He's been wanting to meet you. You know, we drove down from Marin together."

Antonia and Perry acknowledge each other with smiles and small murmurs, difficult for Antonia, since she is now eating, ravenously.

"Real bastards in the emergency ward," Reeve is telling everyone; he obviously relishes his part in this rescue. "They let you wait forever," he says.

"Among bleeding people on gurneys," Antonia shudders. "You could die there, and I'm sure some people do, if they're poor enough."

"*Does* it hurt?" asks Lisa.

"Not really. Really not at all. I just feel so clumsy. Clumsier than usual, I mean."

She and Lisa smile at each other: old friends, familiar irony.

Now everyone has taken up forks again and begun to eat, along with Antonia. Wine is poured around, glasses refilled with red, or cold white, from pitchers.

Reeve alone seems not to be eating much, or drinking—for whatever reasons of his own: sheer excitement, possibly, anyone who thinks about it could conclude. He seems nervy, geared up by his—their recent experience.

The atmosphere is generally united, convivial, though. People tell their own accident stories, as they will when anyone has had an accident (as hospital visitors like to tell the patient about their own operations). Bynum as a boy broke his right arm not once but twice, both times falling out of trees. Lisa broke her leg on some ice. "You remember, Antonia, that awful winter I lived in New York. Everything terrible happened." Perry almost broke his back, "but just a fractured coccyx, as things turned out," falling off a horse, in New Mexico (this story does not go over very well, somehow; a lack of response can be felt around the room). Phyllis broke her arm skiing in Idaho.

Reeve refrains from such reminiscences—although he is such a tall, very vigorous young man; back in Wyoming, he must have broken something, sometime. He has the air of a man who is waiting for the main event, and who in the meantime chooses to distance himself.

In any case, the conversation rambles on, in a pleasant way, and no one is quite prepared to hear Antonia's end-of-meal pronouncement. Leaning back and looking around she says, "It's odd that it's taken me so long to see how much I hate it here."

This is surely something that she has never said before. However Antonia has a known predilection for the most extreme, the most emotional statement of any given feeling, and so at first no one pays much serious attention.

Lisa only says, "Well, the city's not at its best in all this fog. And then your poor arm."

And Bynum? "You can't mean this apartment. I've always

loved it here." (At which Phyllis gives him a speculative, not-quite-friendly look.)

Looking at them all—at least she has everyone's attention—Antonia says, "Well, I do mean this apartment. It's so small, and so inconvenient having a studio five blocks away. Not to mention paying for both. Oh, I know I can afford it, but I hate to." She looks over at Reeve, and a smile that everyone can read as significant passes between the two of them.

One of Antonia's cats, the guilty old tabby, Baron, has settled on her lap, and she leans to scratch the bridge of his nose, very gently.

And so it is Reeve who announces, "I've talked Antonia into coming back to Wyoming with me. At least to recuperate." He smiles widely (can he be blushing?), in evident pleasure at this continuation of his rescuer role.

"I'm so excited!" Antonia then bursts out. "The Grand Tetons, imagine! I've always wanted to go there, and somehow I never dared. But Reeve has this whole house, and a barn that's already a studio."

"It's actually in Wilson, which is just south of Jackson," Reeve explains. "Much less touristic. It's my folks' old place."

If Antonia expected enthusiasm from her friends about this project, though, she is disappointed.

Bynum of them all looks most dejected, his big face sags with displeasure, with thwarted hopes. Phyllis also is displeased, visibly so (but quite possibly it is Bynum of whom she disapproves?).

Lisa cries out, "But Antonia, what'll I do without you? I'll miss you so, I'm not used to your being away. It'll be like New York—"

To which Antonia smilingly, instantly responds, "You must come visit. Do come, we could start some sort of colony. And Bynum, you can use this place while I'm gone if you want to."

Perry of course is thinking of his article, of which he now can envision the ending: Antonia Love off to the wilds of Wyoming, putting fog-bound, dangerous San Francisco behind her. He likes the sound of it, although he is not quite sure that

Jackson or even Wilson (wherever the hell that is) would qual-
ify as 'wilds.' But there must be a way to find out.

In any case, he now sees that he has been quite right in his
estimate of Antonia: she is beautiful. At this moment, radiantly
pale, in the barely candlelit, dim room, her face is stylized,
almost abstract, with her broad, heavy forehead and heavy
dark brows, her wide-spaced large black eyes and her wide,
dark-painted mouth. It will be easy to describe her: Stylized,
abstract.

She is of course not at all his type (he actually much prefers
her friend Lisa, whom he has decided that he does like, very
much; he plans to see her again)—nor does Perry see himself
in Reeve, at all. He senses, however, some exceptional connection between the two of them, some heightened rapport,
as though, already in Wyoming, they breathed the same
heady, pure, exhilarating air.

Antonia is talking about Wyoming now, her imagined refuge.
"Mountains, clouds, water. Wildflowers," she is saying, while
near her side Reeve smiles, quite privately.

And Perry believes that he has struck on the first sentence
of his article: "Antonia Love these days is a very happy
woman."

Jayanta Mahapatra

THE HILL

Over the faraway hill nothing moves.
Is its own darkness swallowing it?
The empty hooves of clouds pass over it
but bring no rain.

From the road, the crude slap
of a whip against bullocks' flanks
carries in the morning wind.
Otherwise all else is quiet.

Even the palms hide their high heads
in the bare sky, like all resolves.
For somewhere either children have died
or have not died.

With hundred-year faces
the orphans of Bhopal
stare at the lost hill
of an inchoate world.

Jayanta Mahapatra

IN THE DARKNESS OF NIGHT

In the darkness of night someone
touches your hand.
The world is not easy for you.
You will always have to think, to know.
Hidden eyes slice the fruit. Can you hear?
Ah, these masters of surprise,
of *gherao,* and of the steep plot.
The drums of knowledge roll on.
Shouts break from night's throat.
Day after day. What
do you wish to find in the sky?
The far-off stars, the golden line
on the hand where you were touched?
Darkness. Deal with it gently.
It saves. It
kills.

gherao: encirclement

Jayanta Mahapatra

THE NAKED LIGHT

No reason for human nature
to think kindly of the hour.
Time catches us in the act
of straightening ourselves, as if to say
that what has happened should never have happened.
Did the magician who had hidden
among the branches of years
lose his powers suddenly that night
and make his way to the jungle's edge?
Or was the thought of too important darkness
relieved by a search for tragedy,
by the piously bowed head of pain?
A flower turns the afternoon sun black
and Jerusalem's glory merely reveals
the weakness of dawn.
These feelings I experience today
have no plans for the future.
My mother's voice trembles quietly
in the backyard among uneven grasses.
And when all reason for trusting the stars
has gone, I find my own place here,
the naked light unable to draw me into it.

Sarah Kirsch

IN SUMMER

Sparsely settled, this land.
In spite of mammoth fields and machines,
The villages drowse
In boxwood gardens; the cats
Rarely get struck by a stone.

In August stars fall.
In September the hunt begins.
The graylags still fly, the stork makes his way
Through unpolluted meadows. Oh, the clouds,
They fly like mountains over the treetops.

If you don't get a paper here,
The world is as it should be.
In plum-jam kettles
Your face mirrors itself handsomely
And the fields gleam red as fire.

—Translated from the German by Jean Pearson

Ángel González

¿SABES QUE UN PAPEL PUEDE . . . ?

¿Sabes que un papel puede cortar como una navaja?

Simple papel en blanco,
una carta no escrita

me hace hoy sangrar.

Ángel González

DO YOU KNOW THAT PAPER CAN . . . ?

Do you know that paper can cut like a razor?

Just white paper,
an unwritten letter

makes me bleed today.

*—Translated from the Spanish by Steven Ford Brown
and Pedro Gutierrez Revuelta*

Ángel González

EL CONFORMISTA

Cuando era joven quería vivir en una ciudad grande.
Cuando perdí la juventud quería vivir en una ciudad
    pequeña.
Ahora quiero vivir.

Ángel González

THE CONFORMIST

When I was young I wanted to live in a big city.
When I lost my youth I wanted to live in a small town.
Now I want to live.

—Translated from the Spanish by Steven Ford Brown
and Pedro Gutierrez Revuelta

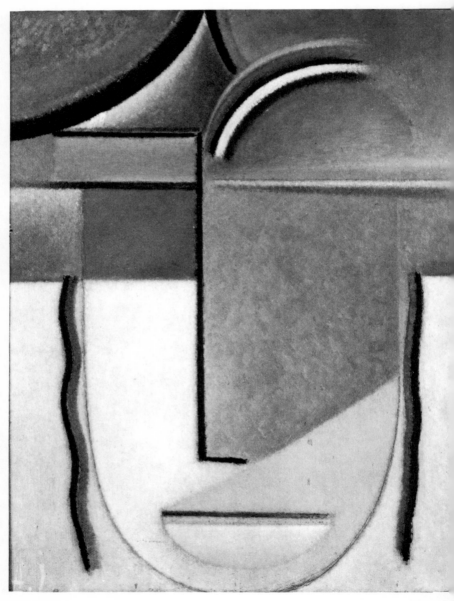

152   *Alexei Jawlensky*

Joyce Carol Oates

COUNTY DETENTION

Outside the detention center guards from the county sheriff's office wore brown uniforms and holsters with pistols strapped securely around their waists, inside the center guards wore blue uniforms and carried no weapons. No, no one carried weapons, not even the officers assigned to the segregated floor where the most dangerous inmates were kept in isolation cells. Asked why, the Sergeant (middle-aged, stocky, genial, wearing a badge that identified him as Instructor of Firearms, Harburton County Department of Corrections) said with a smile that since the center was a maximum-security facility, once the alarm went off "you couldn't get out in a tank." Every gate, every door, every window—all were bolted electronically. The place went tight as a drum. No one had escaped yet though a few had tried.

Also, he added, with a smile that might have been teasing, "If guards carry guns there is always the possibility that the inmates will take the guns away from them, right?"

There were three visitors to the center, two men and one young woman from the State Department of Public Advocacy. "You'll have to be frisked before we go into the facility," the Sergeant said. "It's only a formality. But it's always observed." A matron had to be summoned downstairs from the women's unit on the seventh floor to frisk the young woman. The matron was black, heavy-set, unsmiling but not unfriendly, never looked Nicole in the face, never acknowledged her as a person, but frisked her with quick, light, practiced pats—deft touches at her sides as she obediently raised her arms, again at her thighs—so quick, so perfunctory, the frisking wasn't even embarrassing, must have been common as a handshake. The male lawyers were frisked by a prison guard in an equally mechanical way. Even the Sergeant was frisked. When they asked him why he smiled and said, as if he'd been asked this question innumerable times by visitors, "Why not?"—then, seeing their puzzled expressions, he said, "A county officer might smuggle in contraband, right? Just like some lawyers have been known to do, right?" And he smiled again, patient, not evidently mocking.

He led them along corridors, in and out of elevators, up a brief flight of steps in a windowless stairwell that smelled mysteriously of fried potatoes and yeast. He was telling them about the inmates in the facility, the kinds of people they would be seeing but would not be talking with. "First thing to keep in mind: don't feel sorry for the men in here. Or the women either. Keep in mind that nobody holds a gun up to anybody's head, makes 'em commit a crime. Now we got all kinds here in detention. I mean all kinds. Petty theft, drugs, armed robbery, murder, manslaughter, rape. In protective custody right now, you won't be seeing him, there's this guy, white guy, you may have read about, raped and killed a little girl in the park?—nine-year-old girl, her parents weren't only a hundred yards away? White guy, twenty-eight years old, going to business school nights. Also there's arson, drunk and disorderly, wife beating, child beating, child molesters. Sex offenders go to the state facility at Swedesboro but there're some here waiting trial. Here's where they wait trial if they can't make bail. Basically we got four kinds of inmate: arrested and can't make bail, on trial right now (the sheriff's men take 'em back and forth to the courthouse, shackled), convicted and waiting sentence, overflow from another facility (like the women up on seventh, half of 'em are serving sentences here 'cause there's

no room for them at the women's correctional at Pittsfield).
State's running out of money. Up on fifth which you'll be seeing, they're using the gymnasium for inmates, mattresses on the
floor, also some of the isolation cells, the padded cells, are in
use, I mean for the inmate to sleep in at night, during the day
he's released to the cell block. Any questions?''

The Sergeant signalled with a magisterial sweep of his hand
and a heavy plate glass gate opened automatically, noiselessly.
Nicole noticed cameras, tiny camera eyes, mounted above
doorways, in corners, spaced at regular intervals along the ceiling. Every square foot—every square inch—of the facility was
monitored by television guard. It was all under surveillance,
under strict control. Except for the kitchen unit where the entry
was by way of a guard: here the Sergeant called out *''Key up!''*
in a loud voice. Before the t.v. system everyone had to wait
a lot, he said. Spent half the time waiting to be let in a gate,
let out a gate. ''Guard'd be carrying twenty keys,'' he said,
''there was always the danger of a prisoner overpowering him.
Now if the alarm goes off like I say it'd take a tank to get out
and outside the walls the sheriff's men would be waiting for
'em.''

Had he ever been involved in an attempted break-out?
Nicole asked. Had inmates ever taken anyone hostage in his
experience?

''Not in my experience, ma'am,'' he said politely.

A young black guard appeared with the key and unlocked
the gate to let them in. They entered uncertainly, staring. The
kitchen was enormous, a half-dozen inmates, in green prison
uniform, were working close by. Fluorescent lighting, odors of
fresh-baked bread, fried potatoes, disinfectant, a slightly sickening warmth as of intestinal gas. . . . The kitchen unit was the
favored place for inmates to work, the Sergeant said. New
appliances, new linoleum floor, big freezing units, microwave
ovens over there on the wall. Remodeled a year or two ago.
This is the place where food is prepared for five other facilities in the county, the Sergeant said. ''First it's cooked in here,
right. Then they freeze it. Then it's shipped out by van. Then

at the other place it's slid in the ovens, the microwave ovens, and unfroze and cooked. 'Course the food tastes like," he added, lowering his voice, "like you know what. But the inmates like it O.K." The visitors laughed nervously. Nicole saw a moustached black man not far away, unpacking a box of cans, moving like clockwork in his prison uniform, a tall white perfectly starched cook's hat set on his head. Close by was another, younger black man scrubbing a large tarnished pot, his hair covered by a net. On the other side of a long wooden counter a stocky black woman, middle-aged, her hair also covered by a tight black net, was hauling a tray of buns out of an enormous oven. The gleam of perspiration on very dark skin, like tiny jewels. Quick sliding of the eyes away, not-seeing, not-acknowledging. The white visitors and the white Sergeant with his loud affable voice might well have not been there, the kitchen work proceeded as if unobserved. Of course, Nicole thought uneasily, they were play-acting; not for the white visitors but for one another. Oddly, they seemed quite at ease in their green costumes and head gear amidst giant tins of Crisco, Hunt's Tomato Sauce, Campbell's Beef Soup. They might have been alone, absorbed in their work, muscular arms bulging as a box of tin cans was heaved onto a counter, lips stretched in a smile of wariness, or was it a grimace of resentment, or was it nothing but a tic, a twitch, signifying nothing.

"Sure smells good," the Sergeant said, indicating the tray of hot buns; and the black woman had no choice but to smile, embarrassed.

"As to where the inmates feed," the Sergeant said, leading them out into a corridor, "—in their cell blocks usually, unless a man is sick or in isolation, a man or a woman, I mean. They feed three times a day as you'd expect, twenty minutes allotted for the main meal. It's no problem getting 'em to eat," he added. "Some of 'em big boys can clear a filled plate in two minutes."

One of the lawyers asked if the food was nutritionally balanced?—he assumed so.

"Oh sure," said the Sergeant. "Like I said it's no problem getting 'em to eat."

This was her first visit to any of the state's prison facilities and Nicole was wearing her dark blue woollen suit, tailored, not too severe, fitted rather loosely to her body. She was tall, rangy, small-breasted, with somewhat muscular legs, long narrow feet. With the suit she wore a white silk blouse with a mannish collar and cuffs; a lawyer's costume. She was nervous, kept glancing up toward the ceiling (but why? it was only a ceiling, and rather low), feeling an odd premature fatigue. The Sergeant kept a brisk pace, spoke loudly, easily, patiently. Nicole could not determine whether he resented his visitors this morning—they were laywers after all despite their low-paying present jobs with the state—or whether he rather liked being in a position of authority, leading them forward along mysterious passageways, stopping them at bolted doors, answering at length their questions. She had had to check her purse outside the facility and didn't seem to know what to do with her hands.

In the windowless laundry room three black men—two of them big-boned, hulking—were slowly folding sheets, towels, uniforms. They wore the facility's green uniforms but their shirts were unbuttoned to the waist; their stomachs pushed outward against their beltless trousers. As the Sergeant spoke of the laundry "operation" the men gave no indication of listening or of being aware of the visitors. Slowly, with no rhythmic pace or beat, as if each action were somehow new and even improvised, the men folded towels, sheets, uniforms, hauled more laundry out of the enormous driers, showed faces trickling with sweat. Nicole was uneasy at the Sergeant's loud voice. It was far too loud for the airless room, the low concrete ceiling.

Odd, Nicole thought, but evidently customary, for the tour of the detention center to begin with the kitchen and the laundry room. You saw immediately, in a way too casually, the inmates at work, set off from the guards primarily by their prison uniforms: green for the inmates, blue for the officers. The atmosphere was subdued, routine, dull rather than oppressive. In the laundry room the heat from the opened driers wafted outward, the visitors too were uncomfortable. Nicole's smart wool suit was too warm. She wished they might leave. For the inmates *were* listening, watching out of the corner of their eyes. . . .

She wiped her face carefully with a tissue. And in the corridor outside more inmates, slow-moving, expressionless, pushing laundry carts heaped with soiled laundry. *It will never end,* Nicole thought.

The Sergeant spoke of the newly re-instituted death penalty in the state, a subject of great concern to the public advocate's office.

"Now you're naturally going to encounter a more dangerous inmate sometimes," he said confidentially. "For instance he's waiting trial, right? and figures he's going to be found guilty. Or say he's already been found guilty by the first jury and he's in there waiting for the second trial—fifty-fifty chance he'll get the death penalty. Time's running out, right?"

The lawyers asked if the Sergeant thought the re-institution of the death penalty was a good idea, or a mistake, but the Sergeant was not to be drawn into a debate. He shrugged his shoulders. Sentiment swings back and forth, he said.

"Some criminals themselves," he added, "I don't mean murderers but guys with lesser raps, they believe in the death penalty themselves 'cause they know the general situation. They know how things are."

Outside on the roof was a volleyball court, the Sergeant said, for use in good weather. Inmates were allowed two recreation periods per day under normal circumstances. Now that the gymnasium was in use there was a problem, he said. "There's a lot of nervous energy the inmates got to work off. Specially after visiting hours, right? The ages in here're seventeen to twenty-five—that's your problem right there—also the anger they got to contend with."

The infirmary, and women's detention, and a middle-aged matron with her hair in a grandmotherly bun led a handcuffed young black woman past, on her way to the courthouse, the Sergeant said. A half-dozen women were led down the hall by another matron, an ill-coordinated procession. On their way to the medical unit for examination: the doctor's in this morning. Nicole saw that they were all black—various shades of black—except for one almost-pretty blond, thin, faded, with a grayish grainy skin, slack lips, eyes hollowed and evasive, very much aware and resentful of the white visitors. Nicole, embarrassed, looked away. ". . . Drugs, prostitution, bad checks," the Sergeant was saying, "once in a while you get some surprises like armed robbery, murder, but mainly it's petty crime, street crime. The detention center is actually the street only it's behind walls. Right? That's why," he went on in a slightly lowered voice, "the race distribution is what it is. Seventy percent black throughout the state system, big percentage of Hispanics, only ten percent white, maybe less. Here you'll find more blacks, not too many Hispanics. They can't make bail, that's the main thing. The same distribution with the women. Lots of 'em are in and out of here like clockwork. Arrested, can't make bail, or maybe the pimp doesn't come through for a day or two, then she's back on the street and gets arrested a few weeks later. Faces get to be familiar, the judges get to know them." Another straggling line of women in green dresses, ten, eleven, twelve, all black, one with a plump swollen face and enormous breasts, the youngest looked like a child, startlingly young, eyes downcast, shamed, mouth bruised, hair in fastidious corn rows, the merest flicker of a glance at the white visitors, a very dark white-rimmed gaze, *Don't you stare at* me, *howcome you standin there starin at* me.

The Sergeant was speaking with unusual force of the "common fallacy" that drug addicts suffered in prison. "Sure they set up a ruckus, scream that they're dying, going crazy, all that," he said, "but it isn't true. Never was. Except for the hardcore addicts that *are* dying, by which I mean heroin, a really heavy user of heroin, and they're shipped to the hospital right away. A hardcore addict is finished, there's no coming back for 'em, but the rest of 'em, some of these women for instance, they make do when they understand we're serious, they get cleaned up fast. Off drugs and off meth and that's that. As soon as they're admitted to the facility. And they don't die either."

In the elevator he said: "The worst thing for the women is being deprived of their children. That's what hits them hardest. The men—it's different for the men. A man might try to hang himself but not for that."

Nicole was thinking, Why am I here? but she knew why she was here, she did nothing without a purpose.

They were not to be taken through the segregated unit. But the Sergeant answered their questions about it, spoke at length, special security, padded cells, emergency training. Men who went berserk in their cell blocks, attacked their attorneys (sure it happened once in a while even with private attorneys), threatened other inmates, guards. A man has a lot of anger in him, the Sergeant said. A normal man.

Through a plate glass door they looked into an empty corridor. At its far end two guards stood talking. The cells along the corridor were special cells, canvas padding on the walls, no he didn't know exactly how many of the cells were in use at the moment. The man who'd raped the little girl was in another section, in protective custody. They'd put him in there for his own good. "There aren't many middle class inmates in the facility," the Sergeant said. "Not many white men or women. People with money can make bail, right? A few years ago, though, there was this guy in the rackets, Mafioso, million-dollar bail the judge set, the guy was given protective custody at his own request and that's the last white man in this particular unit in my memory, I mean of that class. Gives you an idea how rare it is, right?"

Through the guard station window they were looking into the gymnasium. It was disconcerting to see a number of mattresses spread out on the floor, rumpled sheets, pillows, one black man lying on his stomach on a mattress, arm stretched along the floor. High overhead the fluorescent lights burned. The lights are never turned off, the Sergeant said. Dimmed a little. But never turned off. For obvious reasons.

Nicole's head had begun to ache, it might have been the fluorescent lighting, the Sergeant's brisk affable voice. She had not been prepared for the sudden intimacy of the inmates' quarters here—the solitary man lying in what was after all his bed, another sitting with his back to the wall behind the basketball net, others idly pacing about, very like caged animals. Exactly like caged animals. Yet more oddly a long table had been set up in the center of the gymnasium where several attorneys were conferring with their clients; no one appeared to take notice of them. The fluorescent lights gave the space the eerie intense quality of a stage setting but nothing was happening or would happen. The man had been lying on his mattress, Nicole supposed, a long time.

"A temporary unit," the Sergeant said. "But it's been in use about six weeks."

The Sergeant spoke of the problem, the chronic problem, of inmates who extorted other inmates, hit them for cash or favors, ganged up on them in the showers. They knew when a man was weak, he said. They knew in five minutes. "Not much you can do if they really want to hurt somebody, it's in the showers they do it, beatings, rapes, the inmates never inform on one another, or almost never, they got to be hurt pretty bad before they'll do that, or terrified. Sometimes you see it, a guy's just broken. Can't take it. A white guy if he's in with too many young blacks, even an older black guy without connections, they know in five minutes who's a mark and they never let up. They're hard. They got a lot of anger to contend with."

One of the lawyers asked a question and the Sergeant said: "Yes, rape is a problem, always is, a place like this, wouldn't be normal, would it, if it wasn't?—these're healthy young guys, like I said seventeen to twenty-five years of age. Lots of nervous energy to work off. Also, like I said, they're angry.''

Nicole had a flash of memory—her own unmade bed, that morning, an empty bed, a twilit room—she lived alone, by choice (she would have said after a moment's hesitation)—she was thirty-one years old and too ambitious to get on with her professional life, too impatient for the slower, repetitious, self-circling rhythms of domesticity to live with another person; even had there been another person.

She would make her way among angry people—men, women—blacks—"indigents"—but she was not herself angry; she had refined herself of all anger, and of nearly all emotion; polished and honed and ground down fine as a precious stone. She had finished high in her class in law school, she had been praised and encouraged, at least to her face, by certain of her professors. Throughout her life she had been praised and encouraged, elementary school, high school, college, made to think nervously well of herself and to expect a good deal for herself, more perhaps than the world would grant her: for many are praised, many are encouraged, but few are finally chosen. She had ambitions for law, for herself "in Law." She would do research, she would teach, she would do good, do actual *good*, if only she was allowed.

That rumpled bed, sheets damp after a night of disturbing but immediately forgotten dreams—a nest of sorts, a refuge. There she plotted. "Aspired." She had had to demean herself and to an extent exhaust herself in order to get a job she would have thought might be hers so much more readily, for was she *not* quick, bright, zealous, even brilliant, as her professors claimed?—her only liability being that she wasn't all these things and a man as well.

But angry?—no. She wasn't angry, she knew anger to be a purposeless emotion. Better dogged stubborn persistent self-promotion. Polished, ground down fine as a precious stone.

Now the Sergeant was showing them one of the facility's numerous thirty-man cell blocks. This was the heart of the detention center, the cell block for male inmates, replacing, as they probably knew, the old-fashioned jail or prison system, tiers of cells in corridors and large open "yards"—the kind familiar from prison movies, maybe?—hundreds of convicts loosed to a common space, milling and surging about aimlessly, like cattle. But the thirty-man cell block was different.

These cells were arranged in double tiers in a three-sided rectangle around a fairly spacious area, a common room of sorts, where a number of tables were set. The fourth wall of the rectangle was given over to the guards' station so that the inmates were always in view. The effect, Nicole thought uneasily, was very much like that of an interior cage at a zoo—the men contained like penned-in animals—pacing about, or standing idly, or sitting at tables where they read newspapers, or played cards, or simply sat staring off into space. Seeing them so intimately, at such close quarters, she felt a stab of shame, or fear. If they should look toward the guard station window! If they should happen to see her! There were so many men, such a force, it seemed, of men, a different atmosphere entirely from the makeshift quarters in the gymnasium. This was the real prison, these were the real prisoners.

All the inmates were black and most of them were fairly young except for a single white man of about thirty-five—very thin, sallow, with a drooping blond pony tail, pacing nervously about, his mouth twitching as if he were arguing with himself. The Sergeant was citing statistics. Explaining the meal-time procedures. Speaking of the theory of the thirty-man cell block. Speaking of the distribution of inmates—the administrators at the center tried to keep gangs broken up, ages varied—"It's primarily the street in here, like I said"—they sometimes put, for instance, an English-speaking Hispanic in with Hispanics who didn't know English so that he could help them out—they usually put white men in together so that they wouldn't be isolated and victimized. But if things got really hot for a man, say a young white man, a certain type, no connections and not able to protect himself, they'd take him out and put him in protective custody for his own good. "There's a lot to contend with," he said. "After all you got career criminals in the facility, guys with prior convictions going back to when they were kids, you got perverts, murderers, the lot. Then some young guy is brought in on a drug bust, he can't hope to protect himself. It can get pretty rough sometimes, in the showers especially. We just can't control all that goes on, in a place like that."

A few of the inmates had noticed Nicole. Their eyes started up, whitely alert, word must have flown about, now two or three of the more daring—big, husky, dark-gleaming youths— eased away from their companions and strolled, idly, casually, slantwise, in the direction of the guard station. Nicole went rigid in a paroxysm of alarm and embarrassment. How could this be happening, here of all places!—how could they dare! They were staring at her, heads held high, faces tight, taut, staring, intense and staring, their movements stealthy and innocent at once: and Nicole edged away from the window as discreetly as she could, tried to shield herself by standing behind the Sergeant, tried not to look down into the cell block. She hadn't known how uncertain, how weak she had been feeling for the past half-hour or more, she hadn't realized how drained she was, the fluorescent lighting, the hum of the ventilators, the tiny camera eyes, the indefinable odor of the prison—the "facility"—how close she felt to tears. Except of course there was no reason for tears. And no reason for panic. She was safe behind a thick plate glass window in the company of several officers and her own colleagues from the public advocate's department.

It crossed her mind that none of the officers was armed. That the plate glass window was after all only glass.

The Sergeant, talking, a forefinger raised, seemed to be addressing her; he turned, half-sat on the counter, inadvertently exposing her to the inmates' stares. *A woman! a woman!* word flew through the cell block and one by one the men turned to look, even the older black men sitting dispiritedly, even a few men lounging in their cells at the rear, craning their necks, alert, curious, wondering. The young blacks, the bold ones, arrogant, cocky, now drifted back and forth in front of the guard station, heads turning on muscular necks, shoulders raised, a flash of teeth, lewd mocking grins, they were conferring together in angry laughing asides, they were assessing the woman, the white woman, peering at her over their shoulders. Nicole felt sick; helpless; unable to detach herself from the guard station without seeming very odd, unable to bear the inmates' brash sexual attention. How dare they, down in the cell block, pass judgment on *her*—a white woman, a lawyer, an employee of the public advocate's office whose professional commitment was to them or to people like them! She could not hear their blunt crude words but she felt the impact of the words as surely as if she were within earshot.

Yet the Sergeant continued to speak in his calm, affable, unhurried voice, as if nothing were wrong. One of the lawyers asked a question; the Sergeant replied; then went on to explain, to give the history of. . . . Why did he notice nothing, Nicole thought, faint with apprehension. Why did he not shield her. Why did he not lead his visitors quickly away.

(What most disturbed her about the incident, afterward, was her sudden forced awareness of herself as a *woman* in a context in which *woman* had no role, did not apply. She was a professional person in the company of other professionals; not a *woman*. It stunned her to be forced into the awareness of *woman*, which is to say herself—*her* self—and to be forced too to realize that if she were in actual danger she would have to be protected by men. Yet more ignobly, helplessly, she saw herself as the black men probably saw her—a tall dark-haired woman past the first bloom of youth, the skin tight about her eyes and forehead, lips nervously pursed, coloring rather sallow. All her life she had cultivated a smile meant to be sudden and dazzling, knowing her features only ordinarily attractive she had cultivated a certain vivacity, an employment of her eyes, she was quick, sharp, witty, keen, but only if she were allowed the space to be so. Her posed photographs were sometimes gratifyingly pretty, her candid photographs were plain and humiliating. In the black men's crude assessing eyes she was disappointing. In their fevered little world she was not even young.)

Again she tried to position herself behind the Sergeant, again he shifted, accidentally—or was it deliberately?—and exposed her. By this time a dozen or more of the inmates were milling about directly below the guard station, some of them with their backs to the window, legs and feet springy as if they were about to kick loose in an improvised dance. White woman, white bitch, who's *she!* White bitch come to visit! They were rowdy, they were children, afire with cunning, delight, what would they not do if they could grab hold of her! Man, what would they not do!

Nicole was not going to be intimidated though her head ached and she felt short of breath. She asked the Sergeant a thoughtful question or two; she wanted the inmates to know that they had no power over her, not even to harrass. Yet as the Sergeant answered she was incapable of following his words. *Why don't you help me!* she wanted to cry.

Now it seemed to her clear that the Sergeant and the other men, even her lawyer colleagues, were well aware of the situation. They sensed the inmates' excitement, they were allowing the inmates their sexual aggression. (The men were even gesticulating among themselves now, Nicole thought. Though she didn't dare look directly at them. Though she didn't dare turn her flushed bright gaze away from the Sergeant.) Lewd, mocking, contemptuous—scornful of her as a woman, as a sexual object worthy of their interest—excited by her presence in the cell block yet angrily disappointed by her appearance, by *her*—such shame! such primitive anxiety!—she knew beforehand how she would lie sleepless and humiliated in her bed, reliving these long excruciating minutes, seeing, in her bed, the faces of the inmates more clearly, deciphering the meanings of their foul gestures, their mouthed words, seeing too her own stricken diminished self, hiding behind the middle-aged man in the officer's uniform. Nicole, in her smart tailored suit, her white blouse with the prominent collar and cuffs, Nicole as a professional woman at the start of an ambitious career. She would experience again the faint terrifying sensation in her chest, the shortness of breath, the pain behind the eyes. What would they not do to her, the pack of them, if they could get their hands on her!

The Sergeant asked if they had noticed that cell directly across the way?—where a man was lying on a cot, legs and torso partly visible. That was the "suicide watch" cell where inmates were put whom the guards watched twenty-four hours a day. Maybe they had already tried to kill themselves, maybe they'd only threatened it, or were acting strangely. So they were assigned to that particular cell in any of the cell blocks.

"Sometimes one of 'em will surprise us," the Sergeant admitted. "One nobody suspected of being suicidal, I mean. You can't always predict." He paused. One of the lawyers asked a question. "Hanging's the most common method, of course, since they don't have access to firearms," he said. "But they're not successful more than one time out of, say, ten."

The rest of the tour passed for Nicole in a haze of anxiety and pain. It was absurd, she had no reason to be frightened, she was perfectly safe and the experience in the cell block was already behind, soon she could analyze it, objectify it, fit it into her life—her life as a professional woman in a man's profession—soon it would be mere personal history: like the humiliations she'd suffered over the years, long buried, freshly resurrected, a scornful remark made by a boy in high school, mocking laughter from a carload of boys as she stood waiting to cross a street, her first lover's inexplicable loss of affection for her, simple interest in her, simple tact: the petty demeaning nuggets that constituted the underside of her life. *But this is not me!* Nicole wanted to protest. *I am so much more!*

She walked like a somnambulist, head wracked in pain, eyes burning as if she'd been staring into the sun. Corridors, elevators, stairwells. They were shown another cell block identical to the first—here the inmates were all black—but the

Sergeant had no reason to linger. Next, the officers' dining room. She glanced up apprehensively at the low ceiling, the unadorned concrete walls, the narrow barred windows. Would they like some coffee? No? Nicole wiped her face carefully with a tissue, hiding her eyes for a brief merciful moment. She could not bear it any longer. She could not bear it.

That indefinable odor, diffuse in some places, concentrated in others, as of intestinal gas; something stifling, warm, over-warm, stale, sweet, sickening; mysteriously familiar.

She was having a panic attack, she could not control what was happening.

But what was panic?

The sudden mad conviction that she was in danger. The conviction that she was trapped. That something was unnatural, wrong, terrifying. That it would kill her, pressed down so low.

But nothing was wrong, she knew that very well.

She wasn't mad, she wasn't even an emotional woman, observe how calmly she listened to the Sergeant, the intelligent questions she asked of him even after the others had fallen silent.

The Sergeant, that amazing indefatigable man!—having been talking now for an hour and fifty-five minutes nearly without pause yet still affable, earnest, no longer even obliquely mocking, quite clearly proud of his position, enjoying his authority over the young attorneys from the public advocate's office. They were not altogether certain who they were or what they hoped to become—what they *could* become, given the perimeters of their work—but he knew who he was and took pleasure in it. Telling them now about the inmates' canteen privileges. About medical and psychiatric services. About other detention centers in the state.

They were stepping out of an elevator on the first floor and there, waiting to enter, there, so suddenly, like a nightmare flash in a movie, were three young black men in prison uniform in the custody of a single guard: not handcuffed: their arms loose at their sides: slope-shouldered, sullen, hooded eyes and fat lips swollen with blood. And for an instant Nicole could not move. Stood paralyzed in the elevator; staring. Yet the others behaved as if there was nothing wrong, as if they were not in immediate physical danger (the guard was un-armed, they would have to pass within a few inches of the prisoners), so Nicole, dazed by this new assault, her eyes misted over with pain, forced herself to follow them, to step out of the elevator in a manner that might be judged normal, and of course nothing happened, the young black men showed not the slightest flicker of interest in the white visitors or in the sallow-skinned white woman, no danger, no risk, no reason for terror.

No one had noticed, Nicole thought, she'd covered herself perfectly.

"Tired?" asked the Sergeant, teasing.

For of course they were all, the three of them, exhausted.

But to conclude the tour the Sergeant took them down to the control center on the ground floor, where several officers sat sipping coffee, smoking cigarettes, staring at a vertiginous array of small television screens. "It's revolutionized the pri-son system," the Sergeant said proudly. "Electronic surveil-lance. Twenty-four hours a day." Nicole looked at the television screens and saw quivering images that turned into corridors, stretches of empty space. Occasionally a human figure appeared as if the tiny tremulous dots on the screen had coalesced and come to life. "But it's damn wearing on the nerves," the Sergeant said. "Watching the screens like that, so close, you know, so attentive. After a few hours you're shot. Like your head has been emptied out." He paused. He looked at them, at Nicole, she thought, in particular. "Any questions?" he said.

Outside in the street she looked up, blinking at the sky. And then she remembered what she had been missing.

Courtesy of National Museum of Modern Art

170   *Yun Hyo-jung*

Nam Cho Kim

TO ME

I.

If you want to go, do so,
go, even if you have to step
over a thousand sharp blades
to a summit
covered by snow
ten thousand years . . .

There you and I can fight
about life,
about death.

It is there we can share
eternal values,
human truths—
not by dying
but by loving
and living,
by truly living.

If we want to go, let's start—
even if the sunlight
is filled with gunpowder,
let's go.

II.

Your authority is over
like the student taking a test
who can not go back and take it again.

You have used up
your one opportunity
of being judged—
you could not make
even one man happy
and now
must take the consequence.

From now on,
living with regret—
self-condemned
and resigned to punishment.
So,
don't raise your palms,
begging the world
for another chance.

—Translated from the Korean by Byong Mok Kim
and Elizabeth Bartlett

Nina Cassian

WHAT IS KEEPING THE CLOUDS?

Why are the clouds so late in coming?
What is that shaft of sunlight doing here,
those ragged bits of azure sequins dotted around,
not to mention that stubborn hope
                    that keeps chirping?
I require the ultimate grey, obdurate
and protective, that forbids any adventure.
I want the naked color, the unembellished epithet,
the elimination of the difference
                    between dawn and sunset,
between you and me, you
the dead one, me, the one left alive.

—*Translated from the Rumanian by Naomi Lazard*

Koichi Iijima

SPOON

A scorched and rusty spoon
makes the sunshine all the more
dazzling,
turns it into something
I can scarcely see.
Trees are rustling.
This spoon
is what a man once ate his food with.
What was his face like?
What was he doing?
Since we are all human,
we can
easily infer
that.
Probably he was dazzled by the sunshine
and loved the rustling sounds of trees.
I can understand all this clearly.
But the person who killed him at Auschwitz—
what was he like?
We don't know.
We cannot imagine that so easily.

Handrubbed,
withdrawn from a big handkerchief,
a mere spoon
conveys limitless words.
We thought we had come far from that year,
but one spoon takes us back infinitely.
January
sunlight
spreads serenely,
trees still rustle, won't stop shaking.

—Translated from the Japanese by George Uba
and Shoko Okazaki

Αξιον εστι ὁ πικρὸς καὶ ὁ μόνος
ὁ ἀπὸ πρὶν χαμένος ἐσὺ νά 'σαι
   Ποιητὴς ποὺ δουλεύει τὸ μαχαίρι
στὸ ἀνεξίτηλο τρίτο του χέρι:

   Οτι αυτος ὁ Θάνατος καὶ αὐτὸς ἡ Ζωή
Αὐτὸς τὸ Ἀπρόβλεπτο καὶ αὐτὸς οἱ Θεσμοί

   Αὐτὸς ἡ εὐθεῖα τοῦ φυτοῦ ἡ τὸ σῶμα τέμνοντας
Αὐτὸς ἡ ἑστία τοῦ φακοῦ ἡ τὸ πνεῦμα καίγοντας

   Αὐτὸς ἡ δίψα ἡ μετὰ τὴν χρήνη
Αὐτὸς ὁ πόλεμος ὁ μετὰ τὴν εἰρήνη

   Αὐτὸς ὁ θεωρὸς τῶν κυμάτων ὁ Ἴων
Αὐτὸς ὁ Πυγμαλίων πυρὸς καὶ τεράτων

   Αὐτὸς ἡ θρυαλλίδα ποὺ ἀπὸ τὰ χείλη ἀνάδει
Αὐτὸς ἡ ἀόρατη σήραγγα ποὺ ὑπερκερᾶ τὸν Ἅδη

   Αὐτὸς ὁ Ληστὴς τῆς ἡδονῆς ποὺ δὲ σταυρώνεται
Αὐτὸς ὁ Ὄφις ποὺ μὲ τὸ Στάχυ ἑνώνεται

   Αὐτὸς τὸ σκότος καὶ αὐτὸς ἡ ὄμορφη ἀφροσύνη
Αὐτὸς τῶν ὄμβρων τοῦ φωτὸς ἡ ἐαροσύνη

Odysseus Elytis

From THE GLORIA

Most worthy bitter and lonely one,
lost from the start,
Poet who works the knife
with his indelible third hand:

For this is Death and that is Life,
this the Unexpected and that the Established

This the line of the plant bisecting the body,
That the lens' focus burning the spirit

This the thirst following the fountain,
That the war following peace

This the Ionian watcher of the waves,
That the Pygmalian of fire and monsters

This the ignited wick from the lips
That the invisible tunnel bypassing Hades

This the uncrucified bandit of pleasure
That the Serpent united with Virgo

This the darkness and that the beautiful frenzy,
A springtime in a downpour of light

—Translated from the Greek by Edward Morin
and Lefteris Pavlides

Edith Bruck

NOI

Per noi sopravvissuti
è un miracolo ogni giorno
se amiamo, noi amiano duro
come se la persona amata
potesse scomparire da un momento all'altro
e noi pure.

Per noi sopravvissuti
il cielo o è molto bello
o è molto brutto, le mezze misure
le sfumature
sono proibite.

Con noi sopravvissuti
bisogna andare cauti
perché un semplice aguardo storto
quello quotidiano
va ad aggiungersi ad altri tremendi
e ogni sofferenza
fa parte di una UNICA
che pulsa col nostro sangue.

Edith Bruck

US

For us survivors
every day is a miracle;
if we love, we love hard
as if the loved one
could disappear from one moment to the next,
and we too.

For us survivors
either the sky is very beautiful
or very ugly; half measures
subtleties
are prohibited.

With us survivors
you have to go carefully
because a simple crooked glance—
a daily one—
adds itself to other tremendous ones
and every pain
forms part of the unique one
that pulses with our blood.

Noi son siamo gente normale
noi siamo sopravvissuti
per gli altri
al posto di altri.
La vita che viviamo per ricordare
e ricordiamo per vivere
non è solo nostra.
Lasciateci . . .
Noi non siamo soli.

We aren't normal people:
we have survived
for the others
in place of others.
The life we live in order to remember
and remember in order to live
is not only ours.
Let us be.
We are not alone.

—Translated from the Italian by Ruth Feldman

182   *Robert Doisneau*

Thomas E. Kennedy

GASPARINI'S ORGAN

For GW, the true Fantastico

1. The Birth of Gasparini

My name is Vincente Gasparini. I was born in sin, died in scorn. I gave to life my blood, my labor, my art. I do not rest.

My father was Arturo Gasparini, watchmaker, fitter of jewels, springs, miniscule gems and catches into intricate mechanisms to measure the rhythmic tick of that tedious gravity which melts the faces of beautiful women.

The day of my birth, I walked with *mon père* upon the side-walks of an unknown city—Vienna? Paris? Utrecht? Where? When? I do not know. I know only the warm, soft palm of my father, holding my own small hand as we stepped along the clangoring street. Fruit vendors screamed like fighters, fishwives shouted in black skirts, their red fingers fumbling amongst iced wares. Steel-rimmed wooden cartwheels rumbled over cobble stones. Scabrous cats slunk amongst sacks of grain to crack the necks of rodents. Alewives fed the furies of men in taverns who sought with spirit to escape their minds. Shouts, laughter, anger, mourning. Whores in brothels snored, happier in sleep than ever when awake, and amidst this clamor, a one-eyed man with pock-marked face stood holding a box in hands whose dirt had become the grain of their flesh, nails broken and grimed. His mouth smiled, his single-eye saw beauties beyond that street, a pale eye it was, the color of boiled blue

cotton, while the box in those hands gave forth the most delicate, exquisite melody my ears ever had sung. I was perhaps
six. Or eight. I don't know. It hardly matters. I stopped. My
father stopped. This ringing quiet melody overpowered all
other sounds of that afternoon, all misery, all appetite, *all*
paused in the gentle, delicate shelter of that sound.

I, Gasparini, was born.

2. Gasparini Learns his Skill

The box was at once so simple and so intricate. The hand
of my father purchased it for me, reached into his leather *pung*
and removed more tinkling coins than that one-eyed pock-
marked face could master with a sneer. I, Gasparini, saw the
light fade from the boiled cotton of that eye as he pocketed
the silver and copper pieces, as my father fondly slung the
singing box over his shoulder. I, Gasparini, saw this one-eyed
man vanish into the misery of that street to the alehouse, the
whore, to fill his belly, spill his seed, to buy a rope perhaps,
to rent an attic with a stout beam.

I, Gasparini, had sinned the sin for which man is not responsible but for which he nonetheless must pay.

I, Gasparini, *knew*. Yet I did not know. I *saw*. But had first
to experience before this vision, this knowledge became the
reality to which man is sent. We all must see, must yearn, must
labor, yearn, and die. Life is insufficient, yet in its very insufficiency, in the yearning for completeness, in the wound of that
yearning, we live, and it must comfort us. It must produce the
cosmic smile as fingernails rake pleasure from the itching flesh,
as the box reels out music to fill the singing ears, as silver pur-
chases the box that small boys take home and dismantle, seeking the secrets of its music.

It was of fine cherry wood, fitted together with pegs and the
sheerest, finest glue, wood that shimmered at the touch of
sound, that moved in the thrall of music. Wood. Wood trans-
mits, but has no talents. It has features, but of itself is dense
and still. The wood of the grand piano conveys the majesties

of fingers to the ears that fill the concert hall, but fingers are fingers, keys keys, strings and hammers nothing but another insensate layer before dead wood conveys the art of these elements to the hungry ear.

Yes.

Within the cherry wood of that box which had stilled, for an instant, the misery of that city street was a brass comb, a bronze cylinder fitted to a crank. Nothing more. Nothing.

When I saw these simplicities, the hairs at my neck stirred, my eyes opened. I sucked a draught of air into my nose. I understood at once that the tits on the cylinder were synchronized to the teeth on the comb, that the turning of the crank brought these two elements into contact, that the pluck of tit on tooth rang out a note, that the spinning of teeth and tits constituted time as it related not to the ticking of minutes but to the ringing of melodies.

Asthma struck me at that moment. I sucked in air. It wheezed in my throat, scarcely filled my lungs. My throat might have been the split reed of a woodwind. I recognized the appearance of misfortune, I recognized the first of my misfortunes, I realized that whatever price the universe exacted of my entrée to these secrets would simply be paid. Choice? Yes, perhaps there was choice of a sort. The sort of choice a lonely man might have gazing into the eyes of a smiling woman. And if the woman is a whore? Whores and Whores. Prices and prices. Some fees are subtle. Some whores offer a love truer than the love of mother or wife. Some whores stand with God.

I, Gasparini, destroyed that box of music. I was nine. Or twelve. I don't know. I sat in my chamber. The four walls of the box laid apart in the red light of sunset through the window, a cylinder in one hand, an intricate comb in the other. I felt the mean evil of knowledge on my face as surely as if I had been gazing upon the nakedness of a woman—that was the way we used to gaze upon a woman's nakedness back then in those innocent years.

3. The Death of Gasparini's Father

Perhaps you ask where my mother was, *who* she was, *what* she was? You who speak from this late century ask who or where or what was Gasparini's mother? Ask, yes. Ask. Ask your own self. Ask.

My father on his death bed called for me, Vincente, to say farewell. He was old. He said to me, "You have learned my trade, your fingers are clever, you know the way to correct the instrument which measures time so that it is devoid of all false-ness, clear of the hungering ego which besmirches all human effort."

Did he truly say this? Did he truly take my twenty-year-old hand in his old gray one? Did he smile upon his son? No. In truth, he spat bloody phlegm onto his bedclothes, clung to me as to life. His eyes rolled with fear, and I helpless to comfort him. He said, croaked rather, "You . . . You . . ."

And died.

You, what? A curse? A blessing? A request?

He was burned in a pine box. I watched his smoke rise from the high yellow brick chimney of the crematory on a bright winter day and wondered at my eagerness to get on with what I wanted to do, had been waiting to do, aware without thought that only his death would free me to my task, unwilling to look into the heart of what his death had done to me, unwilling to feel the pain of losing the warmth his hand gave to mine, the gaze of his pale blue eye upon me, the approval of his nodding head as he saw my fingers clever at their interests in the mechanical objects of his factory, never guessing that his son was planning the usurpation of his entire industry.

I had inherited the business of Arturo Gasparini. Three shops and a showroom. Twelve employees. A stockroom of golden and silver models. Precious metals sculpted by skilled fingers, fitted with tiny gems of diamond and ruby.

I, Gasparini, cared for by my mother, sought out by the mothers of the city's maidens. I, Gasparini. Who among them could know that I had already long before bartered for my fate, given my future, exchanged it for the sound that rang from the friction of a brass tooth against the bronze tit?

This was Gasparini's passion: Brass on bronze.

4. Gasparini Takes a Wife

There were years in which my vision fogged. I tired of the work room, the gearwheel, screwdriver, the watchmaker's pincers, the music box maker's pliers and saws and clippers and hammers and glue.

I constructed boxes for lonely gypsies who travelled with monkeys that tipped small hats for coins and flung their excrement at the children of their benefactors. I constructed boxes that sang of Jesus the Saviour, that played minute masterworks, that tinkled great melodies on small teeth.

These wonders brought me a modicum of economic reward. I acquired a house on Staworoski Boulevard, had an option on a second such house. Yet somehow I knew that never would I have three such abodes. Two houses on Staworoski Boulevard. This was the fate of Vincente Gasparini. Small music, small rewards.

And what of my passions, my dreams? I desired greatness. I desired immortality. I desired the power of music. I desired women. I had always desired women. My desires for women were such that they made me wonder. A woman's lips, what were they after all? A woman's thighs? A woman's fingers, feet, teeth, tongue . . . Lovely creature. God could only be a woman, man an attendant angel. And how happy the universe if Woman is God. For then *God* desires, and we all are saved by virtue of our very flesh. No woman hates her child, not for long. Woman is earth and creator. And women *do* love, that is why they are slaves, that is why if God is woman we are in luck, for then God is a slave of love. She may rage incontinently against us, but still will want us, for women and, thus, God, never cease to desire.

These were the thoughts of Gasparini as he tired of his cogwheels and cylinders and brass tits and little melodies vibrating through cherry wood. These, in any event, were his feelings at that time when the unfamiliar name of passion wove garments of flame which drove him from his work.

Gasparini married. Took a woman of black hair and plump thigh who admired his skills to bring forth music by raking a tortoise-shell comb across his thumbnail, striking wineglasses with spoons, whistling through the knuckles of his thumbs into the joined cup of his palms.

She had shining brown eyes and provocative lips, teeth that were strong and challenging and breasts that had never known humility.

I, Gasparini, never loved her. I only burned for her mysteries, for the secret music of her thighs, her breasts, her buttocks that were foreign to shame, her lips and teeth which teased and tempted, glinted secret wishes, hidden fancies.

We wed, this woman and I, Vincente Gasparini, and both were riven with disappointment. The season of our passion was comprehensive but short.

I constructed synchronized boxes which kept our love in symphonic structures, Wagnerian undress, Bachian ecstasy, Beethovian passions, Vivaldian joys and completions.

There was a time, a brief, fleeting time, that my lady's body was sufficient answer to all the insufficiencies of existence, her pink tongue between glinting teeth a succulent mystery more important than all the weight of cosmic ignorance, her shining eyes the master, the mistress of all weariness. The teeth of her smile shone and caused the blood to race toward the center of my body. She offered her knuckles for my lips and I knelt with joy, certain that I was chosen for a celestial visitation.

And Gasparini was visited. By new lives. Gregorius and Mathilda. Children of passion. I, Gasparini, could relate to you details of procreation which could form the basis of legend. I, Gasparini, maker of music boxes.

5. Gasparini's Children
These two little ones taught me love. To gaze into their small

faces was to feel in one's own blood, in one's own eyes, in the movement and senses of one's own body the sacredness of life. If I shouted, and they trembled, I wept. If I smiled, and they smiled back, my heart lifted with joy.

On Sundays, we walked together in the city, one on either side of me, their small hands in mine, and I knew that if such love, such a sense of life's connection could exist amongst all men, amongst all creatures, life's beauty would be unbearable. Yet it was that beauty we sought, for life's lack of beauty was what led us to our deaths. I took them walking down the same streets through which my father had led me those many years before, my hand in his that afternoon on which the pock-marked face of the one-eyed man smiled, the life surrounding him transformed, my life transformed, with these small elegant notes and rhythms. And I said to my children every time we passed the spot at which I had inspired my father to aid me in committing my sin against that man, "In this place, many years ago, *my* father took me walking, and my fate was decided. You, my children, shall decide your own fates."

I laid a palm on either side of their faces, their light shining eyes gazed up at me with such utter trust, that cursed me for a fool. My eyes filled. I knelt in my morning suit on the muddy street and embraced them.

They fueled my work. Their smiles, the music of their laughter was lighter, more fluid than any musical instrument, certainly more so than any box. To see them in summer on the shore running naked on the beach, their small feet slapping the hard, wet sand as the breakers formed round their ankles, as they ran, laughed, dove into the waves and came up again, in furious happiness with their bodies, filled me, somehow, with a pain of sadness I scarcely could bear.

I, Gasparini, maker of music boxes, realized that I had not fulfilled the contract drawn up for me that day so many years before when I caused the death of that one-eyed man.

The creation of life, procreation, is for us all. That which I yearn to create, which I had bartered my future for, was the completion of insufficiency, even if only an instant's completion, the production of a beauty strong enough to withstand the heart's sadness.

6. Gasparini Loses a Finger

Why? You may ask.

What is this life? What asketh man to have. Now with his love, his children, now in the grave.

What requireth a man of his days? Wife, offspring, food, drink, shelter.

Yes. What? Nothing, other than to fulfill the destiny of his birth. That toward which he must labor in great agitation and hope and pain to find, if he is a good and just man, his undoing.

Yes.

I began again to seek the music I had heard on that city street that day years before, my small moist hand in the warm strong softness of my father's hand which, with silver and copper, had purchased the box whose illusions had so charmed me.

Yes, illusions. Illusions. There was no music in those boxes. There was only the friction of tit on comb. There was no human breath, no pluck of fingertips, no press of warm lips, no flick of intricately boned and blood-fed wrist. No. There was only brass on bronze. Mechanics. This could as well be the ticking of a clock as of music.

I stopped building these boxes, stopped selling them, stopped producing the materials with which they were constructed, stopped oiling my tools, stopped.

I, Gasparini, stopped.

I brooded.

We had a certain quantity of monies out amongst the lenders, a certain reputation, a certain respect.

But I drank genever and beer and wine in public places, stood small and fat in the center of public squares and shouted insults at people I did not know, took upon myself to demonstrate against the bourgoisie: I entered the shop of a cravat salesman. He approached me in his *petit bourgeois* finery, his son, apprenticed, at his heels, his posture equally bowed as his father's. Only my reputation kept me from being thrown out.

"Monsieur Cravat," I asked, "can you be led by the nose?"

His shoulders lifted, his chin lifted, his nose lifted with it. He said, "By the nose? Not I, Sir."

Between the knuckles of my bent first and second fingers I entrapped the bulbous veined potato of a nose and proceeded to lead him round his shop from cravat rack to cravat rack. He cried out in pain. I was incensed. He whimpered. I laughed with fury. His nose began to run onto my knuckles. I whipped my hand away in fright. Wiped it on my pants. Seized him by his own red cravat with its diamond stick pin. My aim was to lift him up, this little man, to lift him up to my own height until his face turned blue and he sputtered and gasped and begged for mercy, and when I did not give him mercy, until he seized it for himself, until he wreaked revenge upon me. But to my chagrin the cravat was not an ordinary one. It was a false cravat attached round his neck by a new substance called elastic. When I seized it and tried to lift him by it, only the cravat lifted. The elastic stretched. My frustration almost made me weep, but a sudden furious inspiration led me instead to drag the cravat down to his feet and let it go so that it leaped from my hand and smacked him on the chin. He staggered backwards, blushing. His eyes did not meet mine. He began to chuckle. A nervous, sick giggle. At that moment my eyes met the eyes of his son. The boy was perhaps twelve years old. His eyes were the color of pale amber, filmed over with salt and moisture. I saw at once what I had done. I raced from the shop. Paused in the doorway. Dug into my pocket and drew forth the bills that were wadded there after my visit to the wine room. I turned back to the cravat salesman, extending the crumple of bills toward him. It was more money than he would earn in a year, two years. He gazed upon it, his eyes full of desire, lifted his face to mine.

I said, "I beg your forgiveness. I beg you."

He approached me, palm open.

In a voice slight as the sound of a tiny, unoiled hinge, his son opened his mouth and spoke a single word: "Father."

The cravat salesman drew back his hand, opened his palm, swung, roundhouse, smacked the bills from my grasp. I turned and fled. He followed me throwing bills at me, crumpling them in his hands so that they bounced off me like small, weightless pellets. I ran back into the wine house. Dug into my pockets, but they were empty, found myself back on the street on my hands and knees gathering those small crumpled pellets of money. The cravat salesman watched me through the window of his shop, his eyes torn between dignity and regret.

Soon the name of Gasparini was without value, without interest other than for a laugh, or for those who sought the opium of their own superiority.

I, Gasparini, was a public fool. Even as I sought the music of the celestial spheres, even as I toyed with every manner of metal or wood for tunes that would thrill my god-abandoned heart, I continued to seek the bottom of my well, to insult my fellow creatures, to humiliate my fellowman in the eyes of his offspring.

One night I drank so much that even the most jaded hangers-on turned from me. I was so drunk that I do not even know what I did or might have done, for the entire night was a blur, but I must have achieved the end I had sought for so long: my total, public humiliation. I woke next day in a pool of waters, alone, confused, in great physical and psychic pain, but clinging to an idea. The idea was of a system of belts and wheels which could create wind that might be driven by a funnel through a rubber gasket into the mouth of a French horn.

Where this inspiration had come from I could not know. It came to my besotted mind. It came of my degradation, of the abuse of my body and mind, came not as the reward of virtue, but as the reward of self-destruction. It came to me as light comes to lit candle. The burning of its own essence. It came to me in terrible drunkenness, but stayed with me when I woke.

There followed years of trial and of error. I was determined that no matter what the world may experience, it must know the peace that I myself had known as a boy when I heard the music box in the hands of the one-eyed man, my own small hand warm and safe inside my beloved father's. I worked with tits and combs and bellows and belts, learned that punches in a sheet of paper greatly economized the amount of space required and thus potentialized a machine which could play an entire symphony. What I lacked were the sounds of violins, French horns, drums. Pianos we could duplicate to some extent, and bells and such, but not real instruments.

It was clear to me that this was the next thing I must do.

I, Gasparini, must find a way in which the finest of all music could be played in the greatest of all detail so that music whose likes never have been heard before could resound amongst us all even when the violin, trumpet, or French horn were not present—or rather when no human talent was there to unlock their music.

I, Gasparini, built such a machine, and it cost me nothing less than everything. I labored all the hours of my days. Even as my wife lay dying, I labored, taking only a few moments to bid farewell to that faithful shrew, nagging even as she exhaled her last. My children grew to be strangers, my beloved small children grew to be strange adults who did not know me. My fortune dwindled to nothing. My health failed. I lived on bread and broth boiled from bones salvaged out of trash barrels in the bloody yard behind the butcher shop. My brain, cleared finally of alcohol, labored in new fevers of exploration, vision, delusion.

At night as I slept at my workbench or huddled in a blanket on my pallet on the floor, a one-eyed face visited my dreams and in that eye all the resigned sadness of death and human misery shone, of the wrong death, for always, it informed me, one's death is the wrong one.

In fevered, sweating dreams, I was visited by the cravat salesman, the son of the cravat salesman. The son gazed upon me with burning eyes. "I have no father," he said. "You have taken my father," he said. "My father has died the wrong death."

The boy and the one-eyed man together gazed upon me: "Your death too, Vincente Gasparini," they said to me, "shall be the wrong one. That shall be the gift reserved for your age, to place a crown upon your lifetime's effort."

I labored through a cruel winter whose winds bit like tiny evil mouths at my flesh, whose icy waters soaked into my shoes, rotted my socks, my feet. I lost the tip of one finger to the frost. It aches. Still now when all is taken from me, when I am nothing but the sighing of air in haunted evenings, still now that lost finger joint aches.

The machine upon which I labored was laughed at in the town. Gasparini's folly, they called it and laughed. Foolish men with puny dreams, insipid visions, laughed at me, Gasparini, who was driven by unknown furies to the accomplishment of this fate, this wrong death which the universe craved of me. This punishment which I had sought for myself finally by committing the worst sin of which I was capable.

I, Gasparini, labored to fulfill a destiny of greatness so that the gods could have their reason to strike me down.

I, Gasparini, rose to their sport with the shield of dignity; this, too, they snatched from me as one might snatch an object from an infant, as one might snatch the dignity of a father from his son.

7. Gasparini's Organ

I built it on wheels so that it could be rolled into the street, harnessed to a horse, drawn into the center of the town draped in sheets sewn together to conceal its mysteries until the moment of its presentation. Already burning in the furnace of its boiler were the last sticks of furniture in my workroom, the last hafts of my last tools.

They laughed at me on the main square as I fed these sticks into the mouth of the boiler, as the steam built to its moment of greatness. They laughed, the grubby merchants laughed. They said, "Ah! See! Gasparini pees in his pants to get warm!"

I was calm. I unharnessed the horse and led her away, returned to shoo the arrogant children of arrogant fools who clustered with taunts round my *Folly*, lifting the skirts of its draping.

I, Gasparini, grasped the edges of the sheets and slowly drew them from the humps and contours of my machine.

A stillness began to settle on the crowd as the sheet dragged back, as the gleaming wood of a grand piano was revealed, a row of brass—trumpets, French horns—a cluster of violins in the corral of a circular bow, each neck grasped by ten delicate metal fingers, as a dozen sticks of varied weight hovered over snares and bass and kettle drums.

I, Gasparini, gazed slowly across the faces of the crowd, uncertain now of something they had so easily embraced, uncertain now that Gasparini was indeed a fool. And their frightened eyes seemed to say, if Gasparini is *not*, after all, a fool, what then does that make us?

A single lever awaited my touch. The steam was released into the bellows, the conveyor belt moved into gear, the ten-yard long punch paper began to feed from its pile of rectangles into the brain of Gasparini's organ.

Gasket lips leaned forward to the brass mouth of a French horn and blew the opening notes of *Morning, Noon and Night in Vienna*. I knew my people. They needed not *great* music; they needed a music whose art entered them, not music which called forth their own art of human greatness.

The single brass voice was answered almost at once by the majestic synchronicity of the entire orchestra offering an introductory fanfare. The square was filled with the music of an entire orchestra, of a symphony. Violins bowed forward in their harness to be sawed, plucked by metal fingers, circular bow. Cellos roared quietly. Horns called out—trumpets, woodwinds, the French horns—were what gave the majesty. This was the greatest, the *only* moment of my life. I was filled with beneficence. For the first time in how many years I was able to admit to myself that I might have failed in my quest. Only now in success could I allow that doubt the air. I trembled at the risks I had taken, the prices paid all without guarantee. My entire life might have ended in my workroom with a failed instrument, my aged worthless body in the corner huddled under a moth-eaten blanket, frozen.

Tears filled my eyes as an elegant oboe line traced intentions into the air of the still square where the townspeople hung upon it only to be dashed within the violent response of the entire orchestra in concert, building toward the conclusion, the last violent explosions of harmony stuttering to resolution behind a viola's wandering, an oboe's plaintive search for admission, where all ended in a silent resonance of clash and harmony.

For a moment, silence. Then the square erupted in applause, cheers echoed upward amidst the encircling stone walls, palms beat themselves raw against one another. Coppers and silvers, too, were flung by the handfuls into the air to dance and jingle at my feet.

"Gasparini: Long life! Gasparini: Long life!" they shouted.

A stout, vested man threaded through the crowd toward me.

His suit was flannel, three piece. He smoked a cigar contemplatively, nodding many times before he spoke.

"Gasparini," he said. "You are a great man."

I bowed in humble acknowledgment.

"But you are nowhere."

8. Gasparini's Greatness

This vested person with the thick lips and cigar also had eyes which could envision. He turned them upon my organ; the gaze focused not upon its gleaming surfaces, but on the magnificent horizons of its possibilities.

"Gasparini," he said. "My name is Rupert Pozzezioni. I, too, like yourself, have vision, but not your genius to transport those visions into this dimension of the senses." He slapped his chest with all his fingers, felt his face, his lips, his eyes, sucked on his cigar and inhaled the smoke, paused, raised one finger.

"But," he said. "I have something you no longer have. A factory. My factory is flourishing. You traded your skills as a fabricant for art. I do not have art. But I have the factory. Currently it manufactures steamship supplies. One entire department of that factory is at this very moment idle, awaiting a good idea." He touched his nose. "My vision, coupled with your genius, can make of you a man of international fame, of world-recognized greatness." He gestured with his palms to the heavens. "The Great Gasparini. London, Rome, Paris, Vienna, Moscow, Prague, Berlin, Utrecht, Philadelphia: The Great Gasparini. Gasparini's organ. They will flock to hear it and see it, to be transformed by it. They will marvel. Who, they will ask, is this genius who has made this thing. *Auteur! Auteur!* they will shout, and I shall say to them, he is called Vincente Gasparini, and they will shout and clap for you as they did today, this handful of insignificant bumpkins. They will shout your name, Gasparini. You: Gasparini."

Rupert Pozzezioni gazed into my eyes and nodded slowly. "Gasparini, I want you to hear me now. I want you to listen. I am a practical man. I will convey you to the greatness. And I do not and will not lie to you. You, Gasparini, your *creation,* Gasparini's creation will be known and hailed in each of these cities I have named for you. I say this to you."

Rupert Pozzezioni did not lie. Not very much at least.

The factory department was created, tooled, commissioned, calibrated. Pozzezioni himself did nothing. He walked about in a three piece suit smoking his cigar, available for consultations and decisions. He had a team of engineers to prepare the conveyer belts and assembly line and mechanated operations necessary for mass production.

To me, he said, "Gasparini, I trust you. I am surely a fool, but I will take a chance to let the heart prove its love. I will not ask you to sign any papers. Think what you could do to me, Gasparini, ey!"

To his engineers, he said, "Improvise. Simplify. Use your fancies if you have them. Had Gasparini been bounded in his fancy by that which already exists, this great organ would not exist today. Now you men in building the machine that will duplicate this feat a hundred times, must look again beyond that which already is to discover the art of the possible. Cost-benefit. Think: cost-benefit. Eat: cost-benefit. Sleep: cost-benefit. The future of this very world, this expanding, hungering world depends on: cost-benefit. The most for the least to the most."

To me, he said, "Gasparini, the French horns got to go."

"Never," I said. "Never. The French horns must stay. Without the French horns we lack passion!"

"Gasparini," he said. "The French horns are a twentieth part of the entire production and demand a tenth part of the economic outlay. Furthermore, Gasparini, the French horns cause an irregularity of contour which makes packaging for the hold of a modern steamship vastly more difficult and, Gasparini, that which is vastly more difficult is vastly more expensive."

"Without the French horns," I said. "My dream and vision is defiled."

"*With* the French horns," he said, "your dream and your vision begin and end here, leaving you once again, old maestro: nowhere."

My lips trembled. I swallowed. I saw him see these signs. His voice lowered, became tender.

"Gasparini," he said. "You are such a dreamer."

"And you, sir," said I, "are such a *merde.*"

He shrugged. He smiled. He placed a fresh cigar between his fleshy red lips. He winked.

9. The Death of Gasparini

Still, I saw the day when my instrument in a rank of one hundred flanked the docks in huge wooden crates, hoisted into the holds of a dozen ships. It was an instrument which resembled mine, though it had only half the strings, half the brass, no tuba, no French horns, and only an upright piano. It was programmed to play a medley of Strauss waltzes and Sousa marches. Across the front plate of the piano, etched in porcelain the color of boiled blue cotton, were the words "The Pozzezioni–Gasparini Music Maker." The machine was activated by inserting a five pfenning coin into a brass slot.

On the dock, Rupert Pozzezioni, standing before the gangway of the flagship of the commercial fleet, removed his *pung* and scooped out a handful of coppers and silver pieces which he pressed into my palm.

"Gasparini," he said. "I want you to stay in your romantic workshop. Do not change a thing. When they learn of your greatness in the great cities of the world, when they come to bring you fame, I want them to see." He pulled down his lower eyelid with the tip of his finger. "I want them to see what it cost you. I want them to see that for the genius, for the true artist, cost is nothing, benefit all. I want them to see the great Gasparini in the truth of his greatness." Now he was mounting the gangplank. I watched him from the dock, holding my cardboard suitcase, mouth open, charmed, yet uncertain. He smiled, bit the end from his cigar, spit it into the sea, winked and ordered the withdrawal of the gangplank.

"Wait!" I shouted, the spell shattering like thin glass. "Thief! Liar! Take me with you!"

The ship's horn hooted, the ship slid forward in the waters. White smoke bellowed from the stacks into the grey winter sky. Pozzezioni stood at the railing of the stern and called through a bullhorn. "I never lied to you, Gasparini. All that I promised you has come to be. You are a nice man, Vincente. The world also needs your sort. Bye-bye!"

That night, seated on the concrete floor in a corner of my freezing workroom, my tattered wool blanket around my shoulders, a bottle of plum brandy between my thighs, I drank myself dull, and froze to death. The process was gradual, death followed life as the nail follows the finger. The procession was logical: first the chill, then the stupor, then the letting go.

10. Gasparini's Afterlife

In the end, of course, all, all is vanity. All is gone. The merchant, Pozzezioni, dead now for many years, a great man in his own right, dead and forgotten, his riches squandered by his children and grandchildren, the fruits of his efforts, second-rate mass produced music machines, forgotten. Three of the original hundred still survive in old cafés in unvisited sectors of fading capitals. All that was mine, too, is gone; my wife, never again met, not even in the afterlife. I suspect she has no afterlife, though I hope she has and that it includes music. The same for my poor children, who nonetheless I am pleased to say found happiness in their lives and even buried their neglectful father and once or twice a year visited his grave, upon which they planted flowers and a stone with my name and dates and the words: "Inventor of the Gasparini Organ." Could I speak to them, I would say, "Please change that to 'creator'," but a stone is a stone, better than no stone at all, and believe me, it was a comfort as I lay there in that cold wooden box, to hear the gentle thump of their knees as they knelt on my grave, hands clasped before them, faces lowered, eyes shut, turning their thoughts to the earth where I lay rotting. Now, they too are gone, childless, and my family line has ceased, my grave is untended, my body long since turned to dust. Only I still pace the earth, unseen but breathing.

My organ sits as a curiosity in the National Museum in Utrecht, rarely played, though sometimes on special occasions, once a year or two, the curator, a black-haired big-nosed man of great charm and love of mechanical music makers holds a special exhibition, and I always come to hear it play itself, and this is the reward of my infinity. This is the treasure that I laid up in heaven for myself. For every time I hear the organ play, I am again on that street with my small hand in the large, warm hand of my father, seeing the marvelous blue eye of that pock-faced man holding the music box which transcended all except for love.

As long as the organ plays, that reality of love survives, and all of existence for those few moments transcends all threats to it. It is enough, I think, to run a world on.

Gevorg Emin

CLIMB

I had been climbing steadily
and paused
when voices from below rejoiced
''Aha, at last, he stops.''

They're wrong, of course, I will go on
because
only the falling rock stays
at rest where it drops.

—*Translated from the Armenian by Diana Der Hovanessian*

Gevorg Emin

GOSSIP

The barking dog does not stop the caravan.

If you should read tomorrow
in some poison pen
Gazette
that you have stolen
a star from heaven
(and there's even
a witness
to your theft)
do not bother to deny it,
nor defend yourself. Lies
thrive on gossip.
And each denial gathers aura
to the lie.

Somehow accept
a small degree
of guilt. For instance,

if you were reported
seen in Paris
on Brigitte Bardot's knee,
say: Oh, how you wish
that it were true.

Or if accused
of robbing Chase Manhattan
laugh, saying you wish
that too could be.

In this world each does
what he needs to do.
Dogs must bark
but the caravan proceeds.

—*Translated from the Armenian by Diana Der Hovanessian*

204   Maitreya

Tu-Jin Park

THE CLIFF

How to manage, to climb that steep, awesome scarp.
Frozen rocks, covered with icicles,
how to get by.
It might as well be a billion feet high.
So blue, it merges with the sky,
how is it possible to climb up there.
Even the stars fail to reach the top,
they fall and flutter like birds,
while the sun itself freezes, drops,
and shatters into morning frost.
So furious the wind and storm,
twilight and rainbow hide helpless below.
A philosophical metaphor.
As we climb, we also are halted,
we also fall and flutter our frozen wings.
Peace and freedom. Revolution and aggression.
Everything fails and falls down,
a bloody mess.
It's either dream, faith and love—or despair.
How, where can we succeed
in climbing this cliff?

The question burns in the chest like fire,
it rumbles in the heart
like a tormented flag
desperate to reach the summit.
How, when to stake that flag
at the top, at last.

—*Translated from the Korean by Byong Mok Kim
and Elizabeth Bartlett*

Alicia Ostriker

WHAT YOU'VE GIVEN ME

What's worse than having no word from you?
                                                    —Rumi

For my birthday, you came over laughing,
Set down a box with a present in it,
And went away laughing.

I know what you've given me
Is inside. But sometimes I'm frightened
I'll spend my entire life

Like this, pulling off tissue
Wrappings, and never
Come to the present.

Ricardo Feierstein

DE LA NOSTALGIA

No quiero, no quiero ya
dejar de lado mi pasado y mis humores
ni la ancha placidez de un lejano río
ni navegar del medio hacia la costa
sin saberme alto, judío, americano.
No quiero, no, plumerear melancolías.

No estoy, no estoy en eso
de andar sacudiendo las nostalgias
como un mechón de pelo sobre la frente
o un perro lanudo después del baño
lanzando lluvias como bumerans.
No estoy, no, queriendo vivir en el pasado.

No digo, no digo hoy
que el hombre es la suma de sus recuerdos
pero ellos cuchichean el rumor futuro
acumulan vida en un tonel abierto
como sangre que late y se percude.
No digo, no, que es excluyente. Sólo aporte.

Ricardo Feierstein

NOSTALGIA

I'm not willing, not yet willing
to set aside my past and my temperament,
nor the wide contentment of a far river
and navigate from the center to the bank,
without acknowledging myself tall, Jewish, American.
I'm not willing, no, to embroider my spells of gloom.

I am not, not in the habit
of shaking out nostalgia as I go along,
like a lock of hair across the brow
or a woolly dog after the bath,
throwing off cloudbursts like boomerangs.
I'm not willing, no, to live in the past.

I'm not saying, I'm not saying now
that man is the sum of his memories,
but they do whisper rumors of the future,
they collect life in an open barrel
like blood pumping and pulsing.
I'm not saying, no, that it's excluding.
                              Only affirming.

—*Translated from the Spanish by J. Kates and Stephen Sadow*

Maxine Kumin

MAGELLAN STREET, 1974

This is the year you fall in
love with the Bengali poet,
and the Armenian bakery stays open
Saturday nights until eleven
across the street from your sunny
apartment with steep foc's'l stairs
up to an attic bedroom.
Three-decker tenements flank you.
Cyclone fences enclose
flamingos on diaper-size lawns.

This is the year, in a kitchen
you brighten with pots of basil
and untidy mint, I see how
your life will open, will burst from
the maze in its walled-in garden
and streak toward the horizon.
Your pastel maps lie open
on the counter as we stand here

not quite up to exchanging
our lists of sorrows, our day books,
our night thoughts, and burn the first batch
of chocolate walnut cookies.

Of course you move on,
my circumnavigator.
Tonight as I cruise past your corner,
a light goes on in the window.
Two shapes sit at a table.

212   Juan Gris

Giorgio Manganelli

THE EMPEROR AT CORNWALL

At dawn, excited by an unusual and absurd configuration of clouds, the Emperor arrived in Cornwall. But the voyage had been so laborious, so tortuous and misguided that he had a very imprecise recollection of the place from which he had departed. He had departed with three squires and a man-servant. The first squire had run off with a gypsy girl, after a dire quarrel with the Emperor, during a night filled with lightning bolts. The second squire had fallen in love with the plague, and under no circumstance would he abandon a certain village devastated by it. The third squire had enrolled in the troops of the emperor who was his successor, and had tried to murder him; the Emperor had been forced to consider him under sentence of death, and pretended to carry out the sentence by cutting his neck with his little finger; then they both laughed, and bade each other farewell. The man-servant remained with the Emperor. They were both silent, melancholy, conscious they were pursuing an object not so much impossible as irrelevant. They had metaphysical ideas that were very imprecise, and whenever they happened upon a temple, a church, a sanctuary, they wouldn't go into it, because, for various reasons, they were certain they would find there only lies, equivocations, disinformation. When they had arrived in

Cornwall, the Emperor was unable to deny his uneasiness: he didn't understand the language, he didn't know what to do, his coins were examined with suspicious care by untrusting peasants. He wanted to write to the Palace, but he couldn't remember the address: an emperor is the only one who can, or indeed must be ignorant of his own address. The man-servant had no problems. Being with the disoriented Emperor was the one way of not being disoriented himself. With the passage of time, Cornwall was opened to the comings and goings of merchants and tourists: and a professor of history at Samarcanda (Ohio) recognized the profile of the Emperor, who by now spent all his days at the pub, attended to by his taciturn man-servant. The news that the Emperor was in Cornwall spread quickly, and although no one knew when he had been emperor or of what part of the world, the thing was flattering to the natives. He got his beer free from then on. The village which played host to him inserted one of his coins on its coat of arms. The man-servant received a generic title of the nobility, and the Emperor, who now speaks the language of the place a little, will, in a few days, marry the beautiful daughter of a warrior fallen on hard times. He has a watch now and eats apple pies. They say that in the up-coming elections he will be the Conservative Party's candidate, and will lose with honor.

—*Translated from the Italian by John Satriano*

Giorgio Manganelli

THE NEIGHBORS

The slightly myopic gentleman, with the speech impediment, who smokes a pipe, lives in the same building in which a taciturn, reserved, slender and, basically, young lady lives. The gentleman and the lady live in dignified solitude, even though the lady's house has the defect of being excessively orderly, and the gentleman's just the opposite. They meet each other practically every day (a quick and casual meeting) with a slight smile and a half-uttered greeting. Each of the two has thought about the significance of the other in a different way. Without reverie, without love, and yet at some length. Each is slightly, but not disagreeably, disturbed by the presence of the other. Neither of the two has ever thought that so casual an acquaintance could become a more definite and amicable relationship. In fact, they have no desire to get to know each other or to speak to each other. Yet the problem, the utterly minor problem, that each of the two poses for the other, never ceases to disturb their lives, in a negligible but constant way. Each of the two, therefore, has tried to understand whatever could have happened, how that abstract association could have begun, and what that uneasiness could mean, that worry that each represents, and knows he represents, in the life of the other. In fact, each knows that the other has in some way been touched, grazed, and each considers this contact to be a bizarre enigma.

The lady has concluded that the slightly myopic gentleman has certain gifts of hallucination. Thinking carefully, in silence, she has been able to recognize in that face, in that walk of his, in the movement of his hands, even in a certain jacket of his, traces of persons departed for some time, persons irrecoverable and dear to her; and she has said to herself, half laughing, half in tears, that that man is a meeting place of aunts and uncles, parents, even girlfriends from her childhood and a man whom she had once admired and lost. The slightly myopic gentleman has tried to change his time-schedule, his trips out, his habits, so as not to run into the taciturn lady anymore, and that with the aim of interpreting her significance. He has suffered intensely, in a way lacking in sense. But it seems to him that he has understood that in some way he is bound to that woman, by a slender yet uncuttable bond, something that connects the most secluded and ignored places of their existences. That bond is not love, but something that sits between shame and predilection. Both of them are aware of it, but neither of them is permitted to know what it is. Each of their casual encounters is an innocuous theft, which demands to be pardoned.

—*Translated from the Italian by John Satriano*

Lei Shu-yan

CREATION

With the scalpel of time
I cut mystic fissures in the brain.

All that has not yet happened
That has already happened
That will happen
Is rippling water within those fissures.

Where no beauty exists
I would create beauty.

I shall create a planet
In preparation for a crash with earth.

—*Translated from the Chinese by Edward Morin
and Dennis Ding*

Bronisław Maj

Czy mam prawo do przeszukiwania
czasu? do czasu utraconego? Więc
od kiedy? —Mój pociąg dudni
na rozjazdach, stoję w oknie
z twarzą w wilgotnym wietrze: widzę
senne miasteczka wyłaniające się raptem i —
i znikające tak szybko jakby nie całkiem
istniały. O ileż dłużej trwają pola,
w słońcu, rojne od ludzi i zwierząt:
sierpień to pora żniw w moim kraju. To
naoczne mijanie pełnych i niezależnych form
życia, czy ja — mam już prawo? Takie
jak każdy, kto właśnie ujrzał rzeczy,
które na pewno już nie będą jego: życie
podległe czterem porom roku, nieposkromionym
porom serca, niedzielom
w małym miasteczku.

Bronisław Maj

IS IT RIGHT

Is it right of me to keep rummaging
through time, forever behind me? And when
can I begin? The train pounds
on its journeys while I stand at the window
with my face to the wet air. I see
sleepy towns rise up in an instant—
and disappear so quickly they were never
there. So how much longer will these fields continue,
bathed in sunlight, swarming with people and animals—
August the time of harvest in my country. This passage
before my eyes of complete and independent forms of life—
when do I have the right to begin? The same right
that anyone has, who has just caught sight of something
he knows he can never own. Life under the sway
of the year's four seasons, the unrestrained
seasons of the heart, Sundays
in a small town.

—Translated from the Polish by Daniel Bourne

Bronisław Maj

Otwieram okno: jest czerwcowy dzień, są
światła błyszczące na rzece,
która nazywa się Wisła, są mosty, wieże
o kopułach zielonych jak drzewa, są drzewa
jak zielone wieże, są niebieskie tramwaje
pełne ludzi, ich głosów, są wszystkie
głosy, jakie mogą być, jest
wszystko, co tylko umie
być, i tylko to jest
prawda: nie spodziewaj się więcej,
nie pytaj, czas już dojrzeć do tego,
aby być jak dziecko na progu
tajemnicy
otwartej.

Bronisław Maj

ON A JUNE DAY

On a June day I open the window. The play
of light on the river, the river
which happens to be named the Vistula. Bridges,
towers whose green domes look like trees, trees
which look like green towers. There are sky blue
tramcars filled with people, their voices.
There are voices, all the voices
which ought to be here, everything which knows
the art of living. There is no other truth
than this. So don't be surprised, don't ask.
It is time to ripen, to be
like a child tottering on the verge
of a secret
openly revealed.

—Translated from the Polish by Daniel Bourne

Bronisław Maj

Nigdy nie napiszę długiego poematu: wszystko,
co tu poznałem, nie pozwala mi
kłamać: trwa pomiędzy
dwoma haustami powietrza, w jednym
spojrzeniu, skurczu serca. I jestem
tylko teraz i to, co jest tu ze mną,
wystarcza zaledwie na kilkanaście
linijek, wiersz tak krótki jak życie
bielinka, błysku światła na fali,
człowieka, katedry. Kilkanaście linijek
i to, co pomiędzy nimi: nieskończony
błysk światła, wieczne życie bielinka,
człowiek przekraczający
śmierć.

Bronisław Maj

I WILL NEVER

I will never write a long poem. Everything
I have ever known tells me
it would be a lie. This world goes on
between two gulps of air; in a single glance,
a quick contraction of the heart. And I
can only be in one place at a time—with that
which is with me now, good for only
ten or fifteen lines, a poem short as the life
of a garden butterfly, the glint of light on a wave,
on a cathedral, or on a human face. Ten or fifteen lines,
and that, which exists between them: the light
which does not end, the garden butterflies
which will be with us forever, the human journey
to death and beyond.

—Translated from the Polish by Daniel Bourne

Courtesy of San Diego Museum of Art

224   *Julien Dupre*

Sándor Weöres

THE PLAIN

A muddy-wheeled cart goes lurching
between the poplar trees' wide rows
just where the narrow track
cuts from the main road.

Crops, naked fields, horizon
and sky surround the single horse
and driver in a wide frame,
hiding them in fixity that never alters.

The distant here seems very near
and what's near seems far away:
all sing together as one—
everywhere furrows, lumps of clay—

horse, driver and small cart
rolling the working hours away
through slow centuries,
and buried by the nights and days.

—Translated from the Hungarian by Jascha Kessler
and Maria Körösy

Sándor Weöres

ZAJ A HOMÁLYBAN

Ez nem a pásztori éj.
Zuhognak a kődarabok,
megvillanik arcod a ködben.
A menet nyomul tovább
s gomolyognak az itt-maradók
Egyszer ha belestem volna,
mi rejlik a fátyla mögött
a rengeteg éjszakának!
De csak a megbánás füstje,
az omlás pora,
mögötte az ismeretlen
máglyái tetőre hágnak
s a láthatatlan kerekek.

Sándor Weöres

NOISE IN DARKNESS

Not the night of shepherds.
Falling rock,
your face flashing in fog.
The procession pushes on,
swirling those who stay here round and round.

If I'd even once peeped in
at what the veil
of this enormous night conceals!
Only the smoke of repentance,
the dust of crumbling,
and beyond, roof-high,
the pyres of the unknown,
and unseen wheels.

—Translated from the Hungarian by Jascha Kessler
and Maria Körösy

Marek Nowakowski

GLOBUS

From the window is a view of a long shed with a corrugated tin roof. In back of the building is a forest. Above the trees is the setting sun. The metal roof catches the lowering sun's rays and glistens silver.

"It's better to look at it while it's still light," says his wife, wanting to lead us outdoors.

He stops her with an annoyed jerk of his hand.

"Not bad this Adam guy," he says as he stubbornly returns to the subject. "I'm no judge. It's sure not my line of work," he chuckles in his hoarse voice. "So he's a fighter for freedom—truth, ideas, whatever they call it. But not bad!"

He rises from the armchair suddenly. He starts to pace the floor from the fireplace to the opposite wall, where he has hung a copy of the painting by Kossak depicting an episode in the January Uprising. He stalks back and forth in his own living room like a predator in a cage. His gait is tense, nervous. His torso juts slightly to the front and his head bends forward as if any moment he is ready to ram somebody's stomach. He walks silently, his steps soaked up by the plush carpet.

"He really gives it to them with these letters." With the back of his hand he jostles his glasses in their thin gold frames. These glasses have always been his smokescreen. He is always taken for a fool, a weakling. "The one from Mokotow Prison where he challenges both the general and the security minister? He sits behind bars and instead of caving in just keeps attacking! And how does he smuggle these letters? They're pretty long. They'd be pretty thick bastards as well. But someone like him'd be apt to sweet-talk more than one jailguard. . . .''

His wife Danka is amazed at his tirade of praise for this unknown prisoner who is neither his relation nor partner. She follows him closely with her eyes.

His walk becomes faster, more and more prisonlike.

He stops. He props his body on the hewn-out sandstone of the fireplace. The years have been relentless. . . . His temples are gray and a bald spot covers the top of his head. But he is still muscled, sinewy. His neck is like a bull's, no spare tire on his belly.

Suddenly he lurches away from the fireplace, leaning down and grabbing my shoulders as if his hands were a pair of pliers.

"Once upon a time I wasn't so bad myself. No one could break me either!"

He sits back in his armchair, his memories wrapped around him like a shroud.

Danka looks at him intently, not wanting to be left out.

"Remember?" he says at last. "It was in 1947. After that party at Wedel's."

She nods her head immediately. Her pale sickly face instantly looks younger. Both of them immerse into that distant time. A party at Wedel's. Praga, the part of Warsaw on the east side of the Vistula. On the other side remained great heaps of rubble. One big cemetery. In this respect the city on the right bank was lucky. People could live here right from the start. He had a place on Brzeska Street, the very heart of Praga, roiling with black market dealings, smuggling and conspiracies, the occupation vitality still alive and kicking. She lived a few streets off. Now they want to raise this Praga from the dead, trying to outdo each other in their recall of details. The crowded tenements: Targowa, Stalowa, Wileńska, Kamienna, Mała, Szwedzka, Grodzieńska. The back courtyards, pits without sunlight, filled with slender white statues of the Madonna, sheds, stables, dovecotes, stores of coal and fodder, and basements packed with contraband goods. Here was a den of railroad thieves—there an underground printing press. Here they distilled bootleg vodka. There they cranked out newspapers. The streets paved with cobblestones, the gutters filled with every color of the rainbow. Wooden peasant huts with shuttered windows survived from the last century. A small yellow building housed a nightclub with the poetic name "The Oasis." The chaos of the Różycki Bazaar. The train stations spit out thousands of farmers daily who came to hawk their produce and buy goods only obtainable in Praga. Taverns of swindlers and receivers of stolen goods, truck drivers and mechanics. Dark smelly interiors where the tin-plated bar sparkled with a sickly glint and a blind harmonica player obsequiously accompanied the drinking bouts. Secret back rooms with plush couches suitable for pleasure or illegal transactions. The swarming hives of the coffeehouses, the whispers and flitting glances. The hansom cab and rickshaw stands. The onion domes of the Orthodox Church. The false Gothic of St. Florian's. The colorful billboards for The Singer Sewing Machine Company, Enrilo Coffee, and Baczewski Spirits. The vast slaughterhouse stinking of blood and carrion on a Vistula canal. Groups of men perpetually standing in doorways. This was Praga. The city on the right side of the Vistula.

The core has survived till this day, but more and more of that Praga has shrunk and fallen apart, been girded or cut in two by the towers of new apartment complexes and skyscrapers. Still with a little bit of imagination that time can still be evoked—the welter of life right after the liberation. In comparison with the cemetery that remained of Warsaw proper, Praga was a town. It was to Praga by way of a pontoon bridge that people from the other side would come on the first horse-trams and rickety trucks freed from the demobilization, a barker calling out to prospective passengers, "Still room for two ladies. Two ladies and off we go." They came to cheer themselves up at the sight of homes and streets intact, to remember how their own side had looked before it had been leveled. Praga burst its seams with freedom and expectancy. Despite the foreign soldiers in their burly coats and hats with red stars, despite the soldiers' language foreign to them even though it was Slavic, despite the unpleasant recollections of the nineteenth-century Russian partitions, hope still existed and people's heads swarmed with colorful mirages of the future. After so many years of the nightmare of the occupation, it could only get better. The war years were just too sinister. They were too much for human endurance. Now throughout the streets and courtyards of Praga, the saloons wallowing in the stench of beer and cabbage, people would reunite after years of separation, fall on each other's shoulders, raise toasts to a better future or swear their undying friendship. Just as often enemy would come across enemy, hatred would flare, they would lock heads and the blood would flow. It was a life both lush and violent. The shell of the war years had broken and the lava poured out.

People exhibited unknown energy and invention. It was an El Dorado for schemes and opportunity, for activities both clean and illegal, for unexpected fortunes and downfalls. People came and went. Some left Poland forever while others returned from years of exile and wandering. Others hung in limbo, checking out the uncertain situation and weighing their chances, trying to read their fortune from the stars, reality mixed with fantasy. And the sky was hardly clear, a heavy cloud blew in from the east. But still there was an ongoing belief in Western civilization and our attachment to it. We fortified ourselves with a hope in America and kept singing, "America, America, the fabled U.S.A.—" even though the cellars of the secret police on Cyril and Methodius and the militia on Sierakowski were filled with new arrests, and nearby in Rembertów a new camp sprang up surrounded by barbed wire where they collected the Home Army partisans caught by the Red Army as it liberated Poland. Women would come up to the wire and try to bargain with the sentries. They carried bundles of food, warm clothes for their sons and husbands.

Every so often their pleading was successful. Pure grain alcohol played an important role.

"Drink," the Red Army soldiers demanded with relish, then led the captives up to the barbed wire. Painful, heart-rending scenes ensued, people's last words and glances. The Home Army prisoners were soon transported by freight train to the depths of Russia.

At night there was pounding on doors. Voices in Polish and Russian. People were yanked out of their sleep, blinded with flashlights, their wrists twisted before they were packed off to headquarters of the old czarist prison on Eleventh of November Street, known colloquially as The Toledo. Already the vanguard of the new system had appeared. Young men in white shirts and red ties stood outside churches and competed with the religious ceremonies, singing communist revolutionary hymns at the top of their lungs while people watched them in glum silence. Other young people garbed themselves in semi-military dress, in knee boots and hound's tooth riding breeches. They would also wear Western combat fatigues. They often had a small gun stuck behind their belts or in their pockets and glared like wolves at the People's militia, at the voluntary reservists and the members of the Youth Defense League, at the armed military patrols that moved through the streets in small groups. Often there would be confrontations of this sort between kids of the same age, from the same street, courtyard and school. Sometimes these encounters would end in violence. Shots would be fired and at dawn the next day somebody's body would be discovered slumped to the pavement like an empty sack. This was a common sight and people were not too surprised. They would only check to see if it was somebody they knew, or, God forbid, a close friend or brother. Then they would quicken their steps, trying to put distance between them and the corpse as soon as possible. The less one knew the better. Even more important was to keep one's mouth shut. All of these were skills which the Germans had taught. They still came in handy.

As a teenager from Brzeska Street, my friend was hardened

in this postwar atmosphere of stress and contradiction. No one knows how he got his nickname Globus. It probably stemmed from the war years, when he had already showed himself to be a sharp kid with a good imagination, the kind that seems to have the whole world working between his ears. But his head had another function. For years he had specialized in fighting with his head, butting like a ram the stomach of his antagonist. This had its effect on his nickname, too.

In such a dog-eat-dog world the young Globus developed. Shrewdness, strength, cruelty and cynicism were part of that world's Ten Commandments. The weak couldn't keep up. They couldn't take the harsh rules of the game. Often they died. But Globus prospered in the jungle streets of Praga. During the occupation he traded in cigarettes. He made deliveries of bootleg liquor in the bazaars. He travelled out into the countryside to fetch slabs of pork, notorious meat extolled in the songs of the time. He was shot at by police and railway guards. He dodged the roundups for concentration camps which the Germans sprung regularly on the market squares in Praga. He circled like a young predator through all the haunts and dives familiar to him as the back of his hand. With unerring instinct he recognized both friend and enemy, privileged characters and informers. Early on his heart and eyes grew accustomed to death. More than once he witnessed a street execution or a cruel Jew-hunt. This kaleidoscope of life and death was his everyday childhood experience. After the liberation his talents blossomed with all the intensity of a young man coming into his own. Before long he had already come to terms with the new reality. He wormed his way into dealings with the United Nations Relief Agency and it was through his hands that highly coveted American items made their way to the Różycki Bazaar. Soon he held sway amongst his contemporaries on his own street. He experienced for the first time the stupefying charms of notoriety. His fame, caused above all by his great strength, proceeded to fan out even further, taking in all of Praga and even reaching to the other side of the Vistula.

In 1947 Globus had reached his zenith.

Today, he recalls everything himself. Danka adds to the story here and there. She, a constant witness to his life, has stored a mass of details about the exploits of her husband. Her memory is luxuriant, saturated with the atmosphere of those earlier years, thick with emotions which have not yet faded. She even remembers Rex, the shaggy mutt from the courtyard on Brzeska. Rex was homeless and early each day he would wait by the gate of the slaughterhouse on Krowa. There he would growl or whine, threatening or groveling for scraps. The guards and butchers knew him. They admired his resourcefulness and lavishly set out bundles of bones and guts for him. He had his own hiding places in the area. Later he would dig out his loot. In his own dog's life he got by. One day he vanished from the courtyard on Brzeska and was never seen again.

"Some nasty person must have clubbed him to death," says Danka.

Globus has a different opinion. "He died in a battle with another dog. He was weaker and didn't make it."

There was hardly a day when Globus wasn't in a fight.

"It just happened that way," he says modestly.

The biggest fight of all occurred that autumn at Wedel's weekly party.

These parties were held every Saturday in Wedel's prefabricated house. They were attended by the young and old, by factory workers in Praga and Grochów, by thieves, merchants from the Różycki bazaar and con artists from the outlying districts of Marki, Ząbki, Zacisze, Kobyłka. Between dances couples locked in each other's arms went outside for fresh air. Nearby was a pond with a stone bottom. Frogs croaked in the water. The fireflies of lit cigarettes glowed and from above the bald pate of the moon looked down on the partygoers indulgently.

"Those were the days," sighs Danka. I imagine her remembering her first kiss with her boyfriend.

Thus it was Saturday night at Wedel's when Globus won his

crown. The fight was inevitable, the last link of a chain of events that could not be turned back. To this time the other fellow had been known as the top dog, the bruiser of bruisers. Thirty years old, he worked as a sandman on the river. His name was Franek or Antek, and he plied this traditional trade of the Vistula that required no mean feat of brawn, dredging up the golden sand from the queen of Polish rivers. At that time there were still plenty of sandmen around, equally raring to fight or to drink. Saturday was pay day, and during summer or on a warm day in fall the Sunday morning sun would discover them lying side by side on the banks of the river. They would rub their eyes, hawk the phlegm from their throats, spit, then raise themselves off the ground and gaze at the breaking day.

The duel between Globus and the Sandman took place in the usual atmosphere. A small crowd on the parquet dance floor. A group of young men flocked around the cash bar. Suddenly the dance floor cleared as if the couples were touched by a magic wand. The bar emptied. The band never skipped a beat. A group of men encircled the space which would serve as the fighting ring. The two combatants sized each other up. The sandman was enormous, athletic, the veteran of many a fight, the conqueror of Sztajer, Majcher and other champions of the fist. In front of him stood Globus, a slender wiry youngster with the nervous movements of a cat. He seemed to be easy prey for his opponent. In addition he was weak-eyed and had worn glasses since childhood. This made him appear defenseless in contrast with the dangerous giant of the Vistula sandmen. But everyone knew about his hands' lightning quickness. When one hand removed his glasses, the other one was already in action. He finished off with a thunderous butt of his head. The blow that Globus delivered was unbelievable. Opponents toppled as if they had been pulled up by the roots. Now, however, there is no use being intoxicated with the fight between him and the Sandman, the blows and feints in a religiously silent room. It is enough to describe the end.

Globus wants it this way too. Fifty-five years old, he has

never gotten involved in details. He abruptly describes the cap-stone of his youthful glory, the defeat of his major rival.

Danka adds a batch of colorful details. She is once again a fifteen-year-old fallen head over heels for the greatest warrior of Praga.

"He cut him down," Danka repeats. "He literally cut him down. The guy toppled like a log."

Without saying a word Globus demonstrates the sudden swerve of his body, the lowering of his head and then the swift uppercut which sent the Sandman reeling.

Thus ended the reign of the former king. Globus took his place on the throne. He was everybody's guest. Fellows from Brzeska Street, his friends Sunia, Waldek, and Mugsy, formed his retinue. They were proud of the coronation of their pal. For him too it was a great day. In spite of being only eighteen he had worked long and hard for the title of top dog. Also, he felt the eyes of his girl upon him, the ginger-haired Danka, her gaze full of love and admiration.

Danka adds more details. The party continued. She danced and danced with her boyfriend. The Sandman was long gone, and with him his gang from the river. Half-carrying the stag-gering, bleeding giant they made their exit from Wedel's early.

Globus continues. The day after was Sunday and as usual he took a walk with his friend Sunia along Targowa Street. Their itinerary always took them from the Orthodox Church to the viaduct and back. They looked at girls, joked and laughed. Today was a fine autumn day. It was especially fine to Globus as he basked in the glory of the night before. They walked to the viaduct a second time. Right in front of a bar called Turtle's it happened. Globus and Sunia recognized them immediately. Three young security agents from Cyril Street coming straight from the other direction. Each was drunk and felt like king of the world. The slightest thing was enough to set them off. In front of the zoo near the Vistula, Globus himself was witness to a nasty quarrel between a group of these secret police and some merchants who had stalls in the bazaar. Some girls tried to talk them into going, but they pulled out their firearms instead. Luckily some Russian officers were drinking nearby. They took the side of the merchants and put a stop to the whole thing.

"Our brother Slavs," laughs Danka.

Often acquaintances joined the militia or the secret police, but these three on Targowa were not familiar. One was in uniform. The others wore street clothes. They looked up to no good. They took up the entire sidewalk and weren't about to give an inch. Sunia stepped out in the street to go around them, but one of them banged into his shoulder. Sunia stumbled and then bumped into the second one.

"What do you think you're doing, you joker," the second one growled and right away punched him twice in the jaw and delivered a hook to his stomach. Sunia dropped to his knees. This was too much for Globus. His hands started his response and his head finished up. The other guy was laid out flat on the pavement.

"There weren't too many that could take a blow like that from Roman's head and still stand up," interjects Danka with satisfaction.

Danka can't tear herself away from each and every beloved detail. Meanwhile Globus proceeds matter-of-factly, recounting these ancient street adventures with photographic detachment. When the first secret police goon had fallen, the second, the one in the army uniform, reached behind his belt. Metal glistened in the palm of his hand. He pointed a revolver. But he wasn't fast enough, and Globus decked him out on the sidewalk as well. Sunia took care of the third. He had just come to and tackled the guy's legs from behind. Then Globus and he took off running. From Zamojskiego to Grochowska. They ran into a doorway and out the back. From there they went through the rear courtyards all the way to the pond with the stone bottom. The secret police raised themselves from the ground and went into action. It was the Day of Judgment on Targowa Street. The guy in uniform started to pull the trigger. He ran up and down the street firing blindly. He landed two slugs in an invalid sitting in a cigarette booth. Dead on the spot. Passersby hid in the doorways. By now all three of them were emptying their guns on anything that moved. They wounded two, one of them severely in the hip. The victim was transported to the Hospital of the Holy Eucharist.

"Roman was attending night school at the time," adds Danka. "The next night during the break they came for him and took him off to Cyril Street. I accompanied him as his fiancée. I had to wait in the guard post near the entrance. They wouldn't let me go any further. 'Madam Citizen must wait here. Your fiancé just has to answer a few questions. Then he'll be right out.' Finally they just kicked me out on the street. It was windy and cold."

Globus was locked up in the Cyril Street basement. He was taken out for interrogations day and night for an entire week. He was charged with attacking an officer, disarming him and then shooting the kiosk-keeper—a disabled war veteran—as well as critically wounding two others. He already felt the rope on his neck. Besides the young police officers the only witness was the superintendent from an apartment building on Targowa. The scoundrel said he saw everything.

They brought Globus and the man face to face. The snoop blurted out, "He's the one. He's the one that did the shooting," without batting an eye.

"If I could get my hands on him I'd wring his neck," said Globus in reply.

During the interrogations they started to beat him. They put him in handcuffs and punched him in the face. They bruised his kidneys and kicked him like a dog.

"I'll remember you guys," wheezed the defenseless Globus. "I swear on the wounds of Christ I'll remember you guys."

"My memory came in handy," says Globus smiling contentedly. "Years later I met one of them in a dark alley. It was perfect."

Danka wrinkles her brow as she tries to take in the image of that settling of accounts.

"Was I there?" she wonders aloud.

From the basement they moved Globus to the main prison

on the Eleventh of November Street. A nineteenth-century song does justice to this old imperial jail. "Do you recall our home in Toledo? Covered with bars and automatic guns, the guards lined up in rows to meet us, and the savage look on the warden's mug."

The first impression was disheartening, the cell dark and dismal. His four cellmates were unshaven, dirty. They looked like cutthroats.

But they weren't. One was a lawyer. One was a baker. Another was an engineer. Globus can't remember the fourth. All were political. He told them his story. "Confess," they offered in unison. "you haven't got a leg to stand on."

"What do you mean?" said Globus dumbfounded. "I didn't do it!"

The lawyer spoke up. "That doesn't matter. Sooner or later you have to confess. You're a young man. Don't waste your health."

"I couldn't sleep," Globus reports. "I lay awake for nights considering their advice. They were experienced, and they had admitted to everything. Guilty, not guilty, that hadn't been important."

"You have to give up," they repeated with frightening resignation.

The lawyer hounded him daily. "You're just hurting yourself, young man. You have to understand. With them you haven't got a hope."

The lawyer had been in the Home Army, spent the entire war in the Resistance. He had received the Fighting Cross, talked eloquently about Piłsudski.

In the end Globus decided to admit to nothing. The lawyer tapped his finger to his forehead. Crazy.

"But they just had no fight left in them," states Globus.

At the end of three months Globus's case took an unexpected turn for the better. Too many people had seen the slaughter on Targowa Street. The entire city on the right side of the river talked about it. There were witnesses. The real perpetrators were arrested.

"The wolf eating its own young," laughs Globus.

"I felt some kind of change even earlier," says Danka. "They let me bring packages. They were real nice."

They altered the charges against Globus. He was sentenced for taking part in a street fight. He received a year. Only one glorious year hung over him. No more than a long vacation.

"What would have happened if I had confessed? What would I have been to myself," he asks rhetorically. "A jellyfish."

He considers courage the greatest virtue. A warder came into their cell and found a needle. Whose needle was it? A special unit was called in to beat the prisoners one by one. They never laid a hand on Globus. He held them at bay until they finally overpowered him and dragged him off to solitary confinement.

"What's the use of dirtying our hands with this one?" said one of the guards. They left him to lie in peace on the concrete floor.

"It wasn't like that," corrects Danka. "Didn't you say something else at the time?"

Globus closes his eyes. "You're right," he says finally. "One of those clowns said something like this: 'You did pretty well, you asshole.' He was bent over and holding his belly. I must have landed a punch on him. . . ."

They continue conjuring up these old times beautifully. All the atmosphere, color, trivia. I get drunk on these tales along with Globus and Danka, the very magic in the walls of the buildings. I become a teenager roaming the streets of 1947 Praga and drinking vodka in the local taverns.

The reality was much more brutal, but in passing it has become shrouded in the nobility of lost youth and adventure.

"Ehh. But all that's neither here nor there," says Globus sheepishly. "I guess this Michnik fellow just got me going."

I know the story of what happened to him later pretty well. He remained faithful to the Praga Ten Commandments. The post-liberation years stretched out for him as a continuation of the occupation. He moved in a jungle full of danger—but also of tempting possibilities. He knew how to stay cool, to lie low until the time came to pounce. Then he would grab his portion of the big feed and disappear into the underbrush. He had his ups and downs, his moments of triumph and defeat. In this manner his life rolled along and still does. Globus has turned out to be a perfect example of that corner of society that manages to function under its own steam in socialism—falling back on nothing but its own inventiveness, reflexes and raw intelligence. Such people take advantage of the cracks in the walls, the fault lines and atmospheric disturbances inherent in this best of all possible systems. There are not many, but they are all lively and resilient as the plague. They take risks, but they also have a cynical flare for what they are doing—and an abiding distrust of the hands which have built the system and the guards who watch over it. They carry on a dangerous and dirty game, and they hold neither ideals nor empty dreams. Such notions as justice, personal integrity, loyalty, truth are obsolete—fit only for plays in the theater, capable of raising a smile of pity if not one of disgust. There is nothing more alien to Globus than these hashed-over abstractions. For him the collective is one big heap of manure. He judges each individual according to his own personal standard of values. For the naive and incompetent he hasn't a shred of sympathy.

"Stool pigeons and fools," Globus quotes an old dirty saying with relish, "play with each other's tools."

What surprises me is his high regard for Adam Michnik, for Michnik's uneven battle with the authorities—fought with the written and spoken word and paid for with years of doing time. I would expect Globus to say Michnik is merely tilting with windmills. Globus himself is no stranger to prison, and he knows well the struggles of plenty of cohorts and friends who have found themselves in hot water. He tells me of the stone silence of one thirty-year-old titan named Żarówa who kept completely silent during the interrogation, thinking that even the uttering of one word to the officers investigating him would be a stain on his honor. There are other examples that could be invoked. But in all of these cases each had fought for his own interests or had tried to save his own skin or reputation.

I muse over it all at the fireplace. Danka throws on a new log. We listen to the joyous crackle of the flames.

Globus returns to the subject of Michnik. It worries him like a bad tooth. "The man's got guts. He sticks his neck out. Even with an axe over his head he's not afraid."

Globus lurches from the chair and starts to stalk once again about the room. The members of the 1863 Uprising gaze out expectantly from Kossak's painting. Globus has always paced in this manner when excited—before a big business deal, a dangerous job, or dividing up the take. Also, I notice he looks ready to do some damage with that head of his. He adjusts his glasses, fingering their frames, his hands restless for action.

"Leave it all be," I say to Globus, trying to calm him down. "What do all those letters of Michnik mean? A drop in the bucket. You know yourself the authorities have at least given us the right to gab."

Globus bridles. "You're nuts. A letter like that is granite. It explodes in your mind and makes your head swim."

Danka pays more attention to her knitting than to the conversation. The needles click in her practiced fingers. There are several bright-colored balls of wool, but I have no idea if she is making a sweater or winter socks.

"What's this Adam guy like?" Globus asks, coming to an abrupt halt.

"Average height, slender, blue eyes, blond hair—"

"That's not what I'm asking," he cuts in. "What makes him tick?"

"Well, he likes women and booze."

"That's more like it," Globus laughs. "So he's made of flesh and blood!"

"But he doesn't like physical fighting. He doesn't even know how. And he's got a terrible head for business.

"Not important. Does everyone have to? What else—"

"Cold-blooded. Never lets his emotions get the best of him.

Yet ready for anything. He can get fired up when the need arises. At least I think so. He's pretty tough-skinned and stubborn. Maybe even a son of a bitch.''

"Roman is the one who's a son of a bitch," Danka intrudes.

She puts down her knitting and looks out the window. It is already dusk.

"Last winter we had a car accident," she says at leisure. "Roman's fault. He was going too fast."

Globus cuts her short. "You're crazy. This truck leaped out from a side road. There was fog everywhere. What could I do? I had to swerve."

They went into a slide and hit a ditch. The car rolled a couple of times, landing on its roof. Danka was badly bruised and shaken, their only son covered with blood. The gas tank could explode any second. Globus extricated himself first. He then started to pull from the automobile what was the most valuable for him. First his son, then a briefcase filled with money, and only after that he fetched Danka—his own wedded wife.

"That's the way he is," says Danka, not without pride.

Globus sticks out three fingers. "The correct order! Our son represents the survival of our family. The money, well, there was a lot of hard currency, and money, well, that's basic. And a woman. . . ." He doesn't finish, looking instead at Danka and smiling.

"This old son of a bitch could always find another one," she finishes for him. "Some young tart."

Diplomatically I change the subject. I praise their magnificent new house. A real palace. Big rooms, wood panelling. In the basement will be a bar and dance floor. Still not finished, but at least everything is under one roof.

Globus waves his hand. Distaste and fatigue wash over his face.

"This place only brings me trouble. It's hard to build any spread, but this one. . . ."

"If we just make it till spring," says Danka heartily. "We'll have finished building. Our rabbits will be giving birth."

For a little while longer we talk about their construction

woes. Workers, supplies. Everything is like pulling teeth.

"Show your friend our farm," proposes Danka.

She gets up first. Globus lights an electric lantern. We go out into the backyard, and they show me around their domain. In a long, roomy frame shed are hundreds of rabbit cages. The occupants wiggle their noses comically. We continue on to the stable, where Danka and Globus keep a horse and several cows.

"A country gentleman's estate," says Globus. "We have to have a horse."

The corner is fenced off. Inside is Globus's favorite, a pugnacious ram in the company of two ewes.

"A plain nuisance," says Danka. "What do we need a ram for?"

"Shut up, stupid," her husband reprimands. "There has to be a ram."

The ram backs up, breaks into a run and lowers its head.

"He's going to charge!" Globus looks pleased.

It's easy to understand Globus's attraction for the ram. They share a certain specialty of attack. We go back to the house. We sit on the armchairs near the fire. It is completely dark outside, silent. The only sound is the wind blowing.

"This Adam," says Globus. "I'd like to have a partner like that."

"What help would he be to you?" I ask.

"I myself don't know," he replies after a long silence. His fingers drum the arm of his chair. A gold bracelet jingles on his wrist. The sounds rise above the sleepy crackling of the logs on the verge of bursting into flame.

—Translated from the Polish by Daniel Bourne

Yevgeny Yevtushenko

THE KNOCK

"Who is it?"
"End-of-Youth. You weren't
expecting me yet?"
"Well, no. I'm in the middle
of a poem, and on the phone,
and making an omelet.
Can you come later on?"

When I finally opened,
there was no one outside.
Was it a joke?
Had I heard right?
Or was it Maturity I missed
who came and sighed
and now has gone?

—*Translated from the Russian by Diana Der Hovanessian*

246   *Paul Cezanne*

Yehuda Amichai

A HOUSE

Paper flowers and real ones together
in the vase. That's how peace slowly enters my heart.

The only person in the room who knew me
fell asleep in a chair, his eyes open
in some other place.

The candlesticks on the dresser are the soul,
candles burning down in them are the body.
The candlesticks will last a little longer, until they too—

Stairs are the hope of the house,
walls are for leaning your forehead against
like Wailing Walls without a cornice or a roof.
For memory only, and for prayer.

Days pass by like people in the street,
each day someone else who won't come back.
The window is the brother of the door
as sleep is death's sister.

—Translated from the Hebrew by Chana Bloch

Yehuda Amichai

THE OPENING OF THE SCHOOL YEAR

Here, in the enormous gym
they stand together, children and their parents,
all of them halfway to the truth,
and in each one, tears
at the same eye-level.

They stand in straight lines between
the ladders of toil,
beneath the torture-ropes
and the rings of sweaty leather
that are there to be gripped
in despair.

The sound of their songs rising to the ceiling
and the light from outside
swirl together into an unknown future
beside the high windows.

The old child-weary principal
speaks in an exhausted voice. And suddenly
in the silence between two sentences

a rifle
falls
to the echoing floor.

Then the children burst out into the schoolyard
and the sound of their shouting fills the world.

In the cries of children there's
always something of
the cries of the firstborn who were slain in
Egypt.

—Translated from the Hebrew by Chana Bloch

Yehuda Amichai

STATISTICS

For every man run amok there are always two
or three who will calm him, pat-him-on-the-back,
for every weeper, more tear-wipers,
for every happy man, plenty of sad ones
who want to warm themselves at his happiness.

And every night at least one man
doesn't find his way home,
or his home has moved somewhere else
and he rushes around in the streets,
superfluous.

Once I was waiting with my little son at the station
as an empty bus went by, and my son said:
"Look, a bus full of empty people."

—*Translated from the Hebrew by Chana Bloch*

Yehuda Amichai

HALF-SIZED VIOLIN

I sat in the playground where I played as a child.
That child went on playing in the sand. Those hands
    went on
making *pat-pat,* then digging and knocking down,
then *pat-pat* again.

Between the trees that little house is still standing
where the high voltage hums and threatens.
On the iron door a skull-and-crossbones: another
old childhood uncle.

When I was nine they gave me
a half-sized violin and half-sized feelings.

Sometimes I'm still overcome by a great
proud joy: I know how to get dressed and undressed
all by myself.

—Translated from the Hebrew by Chana Bloch

Claes Anderson

Varför alla dessa svar
på frågor vi aldrig ställt
Varför alla dessa slutgiltiga lösningar
på problem som aldrig funnits
Varför alla dessa utsmyckningar
på ting utan användning
Varför alla dessa ytor över in-
genting
Varför dessa falska omsorger
om de redan ohjälpligt försummade
Varför denna höstliga kyla
när det är våren vi väntar på

Claes Anderson

WHY ALL THESE ANSWERS

Why all these answers
to questions never posed
Why all these ultimate solutions
to problems that never existed
Why all these adornments
on things of no use
Why all the surfaces on top of nothing
Why all the insincere caring
for those hopelessly neglected
Why this chill of fall
when it is spring
we're waiting for

—*Translated from the Swedish by Lennart Bruce*

Claes Anderson

Över dina hav med vågor som rynkor
Över dina stränder med sand som porer
Över dina vatten med sjöar som ögon
Jag reser frå dig på morgonen
och kommer fram till dig mot kvällen
Platserna jag lämnar och platserna
jag kommer fram till skänker mig
återseendets och nyupptäcktens glädje och vemod
Min resa i dig är sammansatt
och sker samtidigt i olika riktningar
Innan jag somnar kommer jag ihåg dig
med min huds alla orter
Också avskedet är ett återseende
Avståndet hämtar med sig din närhet

Claes Anderson

ACROSS YOUR OCEANS WITH WAVES LIKE WRINKLES

Across your oceans with waves like wrinkles
Across your shores with grains of sand like pores
Across your waters with lakes like eyes
I travel away from you in the morning
and come back toward evening
The places I leave and the places
where I arrive fill me with the joy and anguish
of rediscovery
My journey in you is complex
I travel in different directions at the same time
Before falling asleep I recall you
with all the habitats of my skin
Even the parting is a reunion
The distance brings with it your closeness

—Translated from the Swedish by Lennart Bruce

256   *Sir Frank Brangwyn*

Samuel Hazo

TO ALL MY MARINERS IN ONE

Forget the many who talk
   much, say little, mean
   less and matter least.
                    Forget
we live in times when broadcasts
of Tchaikovsky's Fifth precede
announcements of the death
of tyrants.
           Forget that life
for governments is priced
   war-cheap but kidnap-high.
Our seamanship is not with such.
From port to port we learn
   that "depths last longer
   than heights," that years are
   meant to disappear like wakes,
   that nothing but the sun stands
still.
      We share the sweeter
alphabets of laughter and the slower
languages of pain.
                  Common
as coal, we find in one another's
eyes the quiet diamonds
that are worth the world.

                      Drawn
       by the song of our keel, who
       are we but horizons coming true?
Let others wear their memories
    like jewelry.
             We're of the few
   who work apart so well
   together when we must.
                    We speak
    cathedrals when we speak
    and trust no promise but
    the clean supremacy of tears.
                       What
    more can we expect?
                The sea's
    blue mischief may be waiting
    for its time and place, but still
    we have the stars to guide us.
We have the wind for company.
We have ourselves.
              We have
    a sailor's faith that says
    not even dying can divide us.

Norberto Luis Romero

THE GUEST

I had scarcely opened the door and entered when I noticed that someone had been in the house. Not in vain are the years of solitude and silence in which one accustoms himself to recognizing immediately the order of objects: Set always in the same place, rigorously precise spots in which objects settle as if they had been born there, they only suffer temporary or routine displacement, but always return to their original—almost sacred—place.

Keys, usually, are the only objects which wander, get lost in the house. Keys are the only things which do not possess a place of their own; they are the only nomadic objects in this rigorous order which governs houses. But an ashtray (an object also subject to a certain pilgrimage) was the sign that someone or something had entered the house in my absence. Despite being in its habitual place, it was moved slightly—too near the edge of the table, where I had never left it for fear it might fall off. Instinctively I set it right and checked to see if it were clean as I had left it the night before, as it was this morning before I left for the office. The first thing I did was to remain very still and silent to listen for any sound which might give way the presence of another person. But the noises were the same as always (like the places of the objects)—the footsteps of passersby coming from the street and the light, monotonous purring of the automobiles. Calmer now, I went through the rest of the house seeking some indication to prove that I wasn't alone or that someone had entered while I was out. I found no trace of another presence. Nonetheless uneasiness possessed me that night and I got up several times to prove that nothing valuable was missing. I had already checked the locks and windows, and they had not been forced.

This incident was soon forgotten, although instinctively I developed the habit, when entering the house, of looking at the little table where the ashtry was, to check that it was in its right place. At certain moments I seemed to feel the vague desire for the little incident to be repeated.

One night, returning as usual, I felt again the very sensation of that day. At once I went to check the ashtray, but I found it as always, clean and in the spot where I had left it the night before. I relaxed and even felt a little foolish before that supposed pursuit. And that night I slept fitfully until I awoke in the middle of a nightmare: *I am going to the mirror as every morning, to look at myself to see that my face is a hole, a hollow, or a transparency, and when I try to find it with my hands I discover that my face is another's, is the face of multiple men who, like me, look at themselves in the mirror every morning . . .*

The next morning I vacillated a good bit before confronting my own face reflected in the steamed glass, and I could verify that in the nightmare there had been something of reality since my face in no way differed from the faces of many men who, simultaneously, would be doing the same thing in innumerable places in the world.

Before leaving for work I had to look for my keys because I didn't know where I'd left them. I looked in the hall, on the tray on the table in the entry, then in the bedroom, on the night table and on the chest, until at last I found them in the library, where I had been reading before going to bed and having that nightmare. It was strange—for the first time I had forgotten them in this part of the house which I frequent so much, otherwise the only place where a certain disorder, caused precisely by continuous use, can be noticed—but an apparent disorder, since basically I know by heart where things are, especially books. I know my library completely and, if you will, it is my real intimacy.

The nightmare returned after a time but with one variation: It was no longer the bathroom mirror where I saw myself and innumerable other faces, but a very small mirror which I have in the library. At once I went to look at myself and met only my own face still puffy with sleep. I was about to leave when I had that very feeling which I had had that first day when I found the ashtray out of place. Again I had the impression that I was not alone, again I sensed another presence. A quick glance at the library confirmed it: There was a book off its shelf and I was sure I had not been the one who had taken it down. Years ago I had read it and I no longer consulted it.

That day at the office I was restless; it was hard to concentrate and often I found myself lost in involuntary thought. Not only were the ashtray and the book out of their habitual places, but there was the nightmare of the mirror and the almost absolute certainly that it was not my imagination, that a presence was occupying my house in my absence. And that afternoon I went directly to the library with the assurance that I would find—used—the same volume off the shelf to which I had taken such care to return it. Lying closed on the table beside my reading chair, the volume easily fell open to the first pages as if it had been read recently. I turned the pages one by one, hoping to find some mark or evidence that the supposed reader had made, but I found only my own finely written notations in the margins. 'It tends to open at about page 76,' I thought. 'If it's true that he comes to read it while I'm gone tommorow, I'll find it falls open some pages ahead.'

I made a meticulous check of my few friends and concluded that none had duplicate keys so I discarded the possible idea that someone was playing a joke on me. Robbery as a motive I had also discarded since nothing had ever been missing and locks and windows showed no sign of having been forced. It was nothing more than the book, an old copy of

Malory's *The Death of Arthur,* which lay open at page 76. I was not at all surprised the next day, when I found the same volume, despite its having been on the shelf, fell open easily a hundred pages on. Besides, I felt quite pleased knowing he shared my literary tastes. Soon I no longer needed to find books or any other object in disorder to perceive, the instant I entered the house, that he had been there. And *The Death of Arthur* was succeeded by other examples which also coincided with my tastes. This more aroused my curiosity about that furtive guest and rid me of all uneasiness or fear of him. I wanted to know who that invisible reader was who appropriated my house and books, and I sought a way of communicating with him. On a bit of paper I wrote *I would like to know you personally* and slipped it between the pages of the book he was reading.

That afternoon I think I even left work a few minutes earlier than usual to hurry home, enter the library and pick up the book, expecting to find an answer. My disillusion was great—I found no note, no name card, no indication that would allow me the faintest hope of knowing him. At once I despaired, thinking that, intimidated by my adventurous attitude and by feeling himself exposed, he had abandoned me as if he considered his presence in my house a crime.

And that night I could hardly close my eyes: The nightmare came back, and since then he stopped frequenting the house. I was annoyed, extremely disappointed, and repented my action. I thought I had lost him forever and I sought him desperately. I went through all the rooms from top to bottom and especially the library, seeking something which would prove that he still came, but that he was careful not to leave a sign of his presence. Not finding anything which might verify it, I gave way to sadness. The little daily surprises had ended. There were no longer any books in disarray, no pages marked by use. The nightmare of the mirror and the faces also ended. Everything returned to normalcy, order, and routine.

Once more I grew accustomed—not without a certain difficulty—to the solitude and silence of the house, until one afternoon, because I felt sick, I returned earlier than usual. I no sooner entered than I realized he had come back; immediately I looked at the ashtray, but it was where I'd left it. I dared not go into the library since I was sure he was there, reading I don't know what, interrupted by my sudden arrival, perhaps as nervous as I. I thought I heard a startled breath—not mine—and on a sudden impulse opened the front door again and rushed outside. I was afraid I had frightened my guest, violated his intimacy as he had violated my own, as I had frightened him those first times, and I thought of the symmetrical pair of mirrors: We were living similar situations. Finally I decided to go back, but my heart was beating violently and before entering I cleared my throat as if announcing myself and giving him time, if he was still there, to leave or at least not to be surprised by my arrival. When I went in, I knew instantly that he was still in the house.

Since then he has not stopped coming and reading my books (which are no longer mine); I haven't returned before the usual time so as not to break that luck of the tacit agreement which we've made and which prevents our hours from coinciding and our meeting each other. Now two or three books are in use; to the obvious disorder of the library one more, scarcely visible, was added—perhaps a notation on the margin of a page, a corner dog-eared as a sign of interrupted reading—and those signs of another often were confused with mine, and there were plenty of occasions to fuse readings, for me to continue a book which he had perhaps begun. About that time I began to stay away on Saturdays and Sundays too, expecting him to notice my absence and come to the house on those days too. I would take a walk, wander the streets, go to a movie or sit in a park. I soon realized he had understood my intentions and had begun to come on those days.

We soon grew used to this new lifestyle. It was pleasant to know that, getting home, I would find some new sign of his presence. A chance incident, rain, brought us together forever. As on any Sunday I had gone out walking at the proper time, but I was forced (perhaps I desired it) to go back before the usual hour, breaking that mutual understanding. When I opened the door and went in, I did not give him time to leave. He was there in one of the rooms, probably the library as usual. Immediately I knew he had sought refuge in the bedroom; I could almost hear his contained breathing and the beating of his heart, as agitated as my own. I hadn't the courage to go in there, nor did he come out to face me. My first impulse was to grab an umbrella, intending to justify my presence and go out immediately. It had stopped raining and the sky was clear.

I confess that when I returned I was afraid I would never feel him near me again. The following day I was confused, I wanted to stay and wait for him to ask him to forgive me for having arrived before the right time. But I was afraid and I only dared leave a note, excusing myself, between the pages of the book he was reading. It seemed stupid and I tore it up. At once I wrote another, which I also destroyed as quickly. Finally I left.

I think there were some days of absence, or at least he was very careful not to leave a sign of his presence. They were days during which I thought I would despair, during which solitude encroached upon me again and dreams (those about the mirror) recurred.

Then I decided to go back to my habitual life, trying to stop being concerned about him, trying to accustom myself again to solitude and silence. I lived my life as I used to and stopped going out Saturdays and Sundays so as to find refuge in my reading as I always had. It was then—I don't know how—that he returned. Then I understood that he wanted nothing from me, simply for me not to change my life for his, since he would not change his for mine either.

With time we have grown used to the changes. Gradually we have adapted ourselves to them and they have stopped becoming surprises or anomalies and have become part of a new routine. It is no longer necessary for me to leave the house for him to come here to read as always; better, he is continually here. Nonetheless we both respect, in part, that old pact. If one of us in in a room, the other doesn't enter it. Our space is perfectly delimited—like that of objects; our paths are never the same nor do they coincide. But there are times when I feel him behind me, very near. I can almost perceive his breathing and the heat of his breath. The desire to turn and look at him, to know him and speak to him, is irresistible, but I control myself, with great pain I control myself, thinking that if I do see him, confront his form and face, which so many times I have imagined, he will leave me forever.

—Translated from the Spanish by H. E. Francis

Rolf Jacobsen

KIRKEN I WALL STREET

Innerst i Wall Street fant jeg en gammel kirke
halvt ihjelklemt mellom skyskrapere av glass og marmor.
De hvite pengetårnene pekte høytidsfullt mot himlen,
men den gamle kirken sto der ydmykt med en framstrakt
   hånd
og ringte med sin lille klokke om noen skulle se og høre.

Livstidsfange eller gissel. De lot den i allfall få leve
nede i skyggen der. Kanskje noen ville komme,
så den gjorde litt nytte for seg. For dette vet de jo, de
   mektige
at det lønner seg
med en blomst til de fattige i ny og ne,
og en skilling til en gammel tjener
i de rikes hus.

Rolf Jacobsen

THE CHURCH ON WALL STREET

On Wall Street I found an old church
half squeezed to death between skyscrapers of glass and
marble.
The money towers pointed solemnly toward the sky,
but the old church stood there calmly with an outstretched
hand
and rang its little bell, that someone might hear and see.

Prisoner-for-life or hostage. At least they let it live
down there in the shadow. Maybe some would come.
—So it made itself a little useful. Because this they know,
the mighty,
that it pays, it pays—
with a flower to the poor once in a while
and a dime to an old servant
in the house of the rich.

—Translated from the Norwegian by Olav Grinde

Courtesy of Santa Barbara Museum of Art

268   Anonymous

Cees Nooteboom

HOMER ON ITHACA

The day is serene, the buzzard sways over his prey,
A great box of silence
is being unpacked.

Over the shimmering bowl of the sea
the other island floats.
All the light is from porcelain
a fragile vase around us.

Yesterday it is happening again.
Today the hero is going to war.
Tomorrow he is coming back.

No, here nothing has ever changed.
Under the olive tree the blind man sleeps invisible
and hides in his eye the secret of the poet.

Sing, heavenly Muse!

—Translated from the Dutch by Leonard Nathan

Cees Nooteboom

SPHINX IN THE MUSEUM AT DELPHI

My eyes are vacant,
my face has been disfigured,
my wings undone,
my lion's body wrecked.

Time made me, time ruined me,
the terror of my judgment has faded,
I exist only
as a word on your tongue.

Now I am as blind
as the man who killed me,
now I pose no more riddles
than the one you can see:

the obdurate, broken, taut,
skull of a doll.

—Translated from the Dutch by Leonard Nathan

Yusuf al-Khal

CAIN THE IMMORTAL

When you turn at the road's
last bend,
you eat the distance with your eyes
as if it were an idol raised to heaven.

You can't go back.
You will either fall
or reach the crossroad
unless some oracle appears
like an image on a wall.
Perhaps this oracle is nothing
but the fist of God.
                              No,
you are leafed with worry.
You've been devoured by stares.
You curse the dust
that fathered Adam's rib
and then run off into a cleft
between two shores—
the region of your exile.
Where is your home?
Your pallbearers are carrying
no one in your coffin.

You really cannot die.

—*Translated from the Arabic by Samuel Hazo*

Ivan Davidkov

ПРОЛЕТ

Събуди ме пукот на пъпки черешови,
от ехото на утрото удесеторен.
И весело тракна резето. —
Не беше ли
открехнал вратата ми
пролетният ден?

Излязох.
Южнякът със гърло пресипнало
говореше на дърветата, до земята

приведени,
и детско хвърчило,
из нечий сън излитнало,
се мяташе като перушинка напреде ми.

Раждаше се песен
на пътища неизброими
и ставаше златна от семе
черната оран.

Два хълма
със своите ръце незрими
люлееха сребърното въже
на кръгозора.

Ivan Davidkov

SPRING

The bursting of the cherry buds awoke me,
made tenfold by the echo of the morning.
And cheerfully the front latch clicked.
Was it the spring day
that had tried to open
my door?

I went outside.
The south wind, with a throat gone hoarse,
was talking to the trees bent to the ground,
and a child's kite,
flown out of someone's dream,
danced like a feather ahead of me.

A song was being born
of countless roads
and the black ploughland
turned golden with seed.

Two hills
with invisible hands

—Translated from the Bulgarian by Ewald Osers

Ivan Davidkov

ОЧИТЕ МИ СА ПЪЛНИ С ДАЛНИНИ

Не ме търсете. Аз съм отпътувал
отдавна. И писмата ви едва ли
ще ме намерят. Кремъчни клисури
след мен вървят със своя
                             дрян разцъфнал.
Каменоломни ми даряват мрамор,
на който да поседна. Там, отсреща,
в бараки ламаринени, червени
от дъждовете, чувам как се гони
ек на длета. И камъкът протяга
ръце и устни, за да се порадва—
след милион години—на небето
и на ливадите. Аз слушам мълком
гласа на тайнството—и си отивам
като откъртен камък по наклона.
Какво спечелих аз през тия дни?—
Прах по обувките—една поема
от глина и от облаци, един
                             изпръхнал къшей,
свидетел на безсънните ми нощи,
и лудото възкръсване на мрамора
и на душата ми
                        под острите длета.

Тояжката със пътя разговаря.
Очите ми са пълни с далнини.

Ivan Davidkov

MY EYES ARE FULL OF MISTY DISTANCES

Don't look for me. For I have long
departed. And your letters are not likely
to find me. Rocky gorges
follow me with their flowering dogwood trees.
And quarries provide marble
on which to sit. There, opposite
the corrugated iron sheds, rust-red
from rain, I listen to the
ring of the chisel. As the stone extends
its arms and lips in order to enjoy—
a million years from now—the sky
and the green fields. Silent, I hear
the voice of mystery—and I walk away
like a dislodged stone rolling down the slope.
What have I gained over these past few days?
Dust on my shoes, one single poem
of clay and clouds, one dry piece of bread,
a witness to my sleepless nights
and the mad resurrection of the marble
and of my soul under the chisel's edge.

My staff converses with the road.
My eyes are full of misty distances.

—Translated from the Bulgarian by Ewald Osers

Vahakn Davtian

INTERPRETATION OF DREAMS

If you dream of flying through the air
that, believe me, is the best sign
even if you wake yourself up so that
you do not fall. It's all the same.
The dream stays with you as a smile.

If you dream of picking a flower, fresh with dew,
or of walking toward a woman holding a red,
warm, palpitating heart to put into her palm
and she takes it willingly, you can know
you will not be rejected in love.

If you dream of the sea, that too is a good sign.
Even if you are leaping into it with your love.
Even though, surrounded by storms, you fail
to reach the desired shore. It's all the same.
The dream augurs well and its benefits stay
with you during the waking day.

But if suddenly in a dream you want to shout
and no voice rises in your throat
or you wish to run and your legs do not move
then that dream forbodes nothing good.

Therefore before you sleep plan to fly,
think of air, breathe it in. Imagine flowers
and seas and plunge in.

   —*Translated from the Armenian by Diana Der Hovanessian*

Courtesy of Los Angeles County Museum of Art

278   *Soga Shohaku (Detail)*

Charles Edward Eaton

THE CRANE

You may have the egret if you will let me have the crane—
That symbol of good fortune and long life has been
For longer than I remember wading in my brain.

The little house surrounded by bamboo, the blue lake,
Need just this serious bird calmly stalking there
To tell me what I wanted all these years was no mistake.

In this house I really live in, really own and know,
I want a sometime refuge, drawn, perhaps, by Hokusai,
As if the heart were always beating round a secret cameo.

You have every right to chandelier, fan, plume, egret—
I love them too in many moods except this secret one
Which comes from moving in an aura, tone of the bird's-
          foot violet.

I like the rough-and-tumble, the rub of hardy fellows,
But in the twilight, I can feel the heart gathering,

coalescing,
Its circular relief—the bird is standing in the shallows.

An hour, an evening, before *lex talionis* must assert its
    right—
Is this how we come at all to notions of good fortune, long
    life:
The splash, the long, slow steps in the water, until the
    crane takes flight?

Josephine Jacobsen

THE MULCHING

Mrs. Salter kept the ten thousand dollars in the house for only forty-eight hours. She was not accustomed to such a thing, and in any case the whole project was a rush of stored-up emotion which had to complete itself or perish.

On Friday she had been aware that Miss Peebles, her favorite cashier, had looked at her with strong and innocent curiosity; Mrs. Salter usually raided her savings account only for a trip, which she would outline to Miss Peebles; but it made her tired to think of inventing a plausible lie, and certainly the facts were private. The departure of the $10,00 would definitely incommode her, but neither seriously nor for long.

The virgin-fresh notes were in two crisp packages, each clasped by a broad rubber band; and Mrs. Salter, never the sort of person who looks over her shoulder for robbers, simply slipped them into the top bureau drawer, under her handkerchiefs. It was necessary that they stay there for forty-eight hours, since she couldn't get to Miss Peebles on a Saturday, and it was Sunday lunch that she was to have with Agnes.

Mrs. Salter had a notion that these Sunday lunches—the only invitations to her mother ever issued by Agnes—were a sort of substitute for the boring and constrained hours Agnes saw others spending in church, or entertaining, or handling brothers, sisters, nieces, or other weights.

Receiving was an activity alien to Agnes since childhood. Obviously she felt constrained to a giving of her somber time, of her sparse house. For many earlier years Mrs. Salter, like her husband, had brooded over how difficult—or was it impossible?—it was to give Agnes pleasure. She was born with a taste for deprivation and a sense that each refusal was spiritual coin stored against some never achieved account. Sometimes Mrs. Salter thought humbly that this might be one of those mysterious and psychological reactions to, or from, the sense of easy-going indulgence, to self and to others, that Agnes, when she was first old enough, defined in a quarrel as "hedonism."

Mr. Salter, a genial and light-hearted man, had given up the struggle long before his wife. It had saddened him to discover that he had participated in the production of what he, also in a quarrel, defined as a masochist. But he was a resilient man, and though his wife knew he continued to wish secretly that Agnes would flower suddenly like a desert blossom, and that it had been possible to have other children, he had gone along relatively happily, enjoying his buoyant wife and life as it came, until it suddenly went, when his heart gave a mysterious leap and stopped beating.

Agnes was then twenty-two—a long-jawed, sharp-eyed young woman who made up in determination what she lacked in geniality. She found looking for flaws in her acquaintances a sort of perpetual treasure hunt, in which cryptic clues led her eventually to her goal.

On this fateful Sunday morning, Mrs. Salter sat at her little glass-topped breakfast table, staring out over the small bright oblong of her flower garden, now invisible to her in her cloud of excitement. There are times when the current of a situation, blocked, baulked, dispersed, will gather and pour into a narrow potent channel. Mrs. Salter felt, mainly, two things. First, that this must—surely must—be a last attempt; a bottomless sense of fatigue waited for her on the other side of failure.

The other was that she believed Agnes to have, somewhere,

her own sense of humor, or at least of the ridiculous; mordant, perhaps, checked and curbed, but there.

She went and got the two packets of notes and laid them before her on the table. There was something innocently absurd about the power of the little wads of green paper. The Presidential face—one, actually, that she had never seen before—stared blandly from its circle.

After Agnes' divorce, she had got a job, which she still held, as a copyreader. One of the rare pieces of advice Mrs. Salter had attempted with Agnes after puberty, was that she hesitate to marry Johnny Trencher. Johnny had just broken up, under somewhat violent circumstances, with his extraordinarily pretty and cheerfully unfaithful wife, an energetic girl named Mavis. Their marriage had rocketed up and down, and Mrs. Salter, who had known Johnny as a tempestuous and attractive adolescent, had watched it with mute sympathy and not much hope. When Johnny finally rebelled, the divorce was rapid and filled with considerable vituperation. Three months later Johnny and Agnes were married. Mrs. Salter, finding in Johnny's eye the innocent conviction that the obverse of what was insufferable must be sufferable, had with trembling driven herself to suggest to Agnes that the marriage be delayed, say for a year, until the roiled waters cleared.

Agnes, touchingly entranced to succeed a conscienceless charmer, fell very much in love with Johnny, and, Mrs. Salter feared, remained so to this day.

The marriage lasted eighteen months, at which time Johnny demanded a divorce. Agnes, who had seen this request approaching since the first months of the marriage, instantly agreed, adopting it as her own idea. Six weeks after his final decree, Johnny remarried Mavis, and their previous life resumed its course.

Agnes got a job as copyreader for a glossy magazine which swam smartly just ahead of the current fashion in clothes, sex and culture. She earned barely enough money to rent her small and dreary house, drive her cramped car, and avoid peripheral expenditures.

Thankful that she felt independent and occupied, Mrs. Salter congratulated her on her job. Agnes looked at her, with her small direct black eyes.

"Really?" she said. "Well, it's a magazine written by morons for tarts."

Mrs. Salter, though in a way she could see Agnes' point, winced. She had found it seldom did good to put things so bluntly, the truth needing a magnet, not a bomb.

Mrs. Salter, who was cheerfully though not heavily rich, had tried in an ingenious number of ways tactfully to share with Agnes what she had been given for no merit of her own, by providence and Mr. Salter. An elaborately casual attempt to provide an appealing dress that would have softened Agnes' grim dourness; a suggestion, after a small windfall in the market, that what she would herself most enjoy at the moment was seeing Agnes exchange her querulous and demanding car for something more restful. Agnes returned the dress and rejected the car.

Mrs. Salter, somewhat inexplicably, loved her daughter very much, though there were moments when she reflected that this had to be a biological phenomenon; and she thought of her with a mixture of affection and a sort of weary distress. Recently she had tried not thinking about her at all, but that had turned out to be beyond her meager resources of self-discipline. Even when she travelled, which she frequently did, the thought of Agnes, willfully joyless, doggedly skimming the edge of poverty, increasingly alone, and now pressing thirty, lay like a faint but gnawing malaise in the day's leisure moments.

Then, a few Sundays ago, Agnes had intimated, in an uncharacteristic burst of confidence, that labor for the morons in aid of the tarts had become unsupportable. "I spend my day with imbeciles," she said, pushing the crust of her quiche about her plate. "And then I'm ashamed of the result."

Forewarned not to leap into this opportunity, Mrs. Salter swallowed the last delicate morsel. Agnes, with no one to feed but herself, was an admirable cook.

"Did you consider just letting the whole tiresome thing go?" Mrs. Salter asked vaguely.

Agnes glanced fiercely around at the limp curtains and exhausted slipcovers.

"Let it go?" she echoed. "This past week I had a bill for $288 on the car. The transmission went."

This statement was a pleasure for Agnes, and Mrs. Salter could feel herself getting angry. The anger stole like an injection into her very veins. And though she had instantly changed the subject, it was then that her idea, part baffled love, part ultimate rebellion, came to her.

When she got home she thought about it. She was a person of tenacious affections, but she was also basically realistic, and she thought of how variously, unobtrusively and affectionately she had attempted to share, and how implacably she had been denied the joy of any sort of giving. It had always been this way; but since the debacle with Johnny Trencher it was as though Agnes felt that any offering from her mother's generous stores, material or emotional, was a devious comment on her own disasters, a sort of subterranean "I told you so," disguised in the language of generosity.

Now Mrs. Salter realized suddenly that she had reached the end of tact, of humility, of effort. The idea of one violent, dazzling assault, one attempt to put forward a sort of glittering joke, overcame her. If not this, then let it indeed be nothing.

She would draw out ten thousand dollars in actual green notes. She had herself never laid eyes on such a visible sum, and certainly Agnes had not. By the suddenness and silliness of the fact, by treating it as toy money, something to be handed over like a comic valentine, she had a notion that she might succeed where timidity and small efforts had died.

She could think of no formula of presentation, and must trust to the moment.

On this unflawed morning in early June, and leaving her offering on the breakfast table, exhilarated, she walked over the lawn to look at her flower bed. In matters concerning herself, Mrs. Salter was lazy, and the kaleidoscope of bloom—

begonias, ageratum, alyssum, geraniums, marguerites—
represented annuals, set out in bud. The tuberous begonias,
in their great rumpled glory, radiated rose, yellow, white,
scarlet. The hugest rose-colored one had a ladybug on one
glossy petal. Extravagance was the word which came to mind.

The green packages deep in her straw bag, Mrs. Salter pulled
into Agnes' brief driveway, behind the rusted rear of the brown
Dodge. Agnes was shaking a mop out of the window. She
withdrew, and as Mrs. Salter mounted the porch steps, came
out and touched her lips to her mother's cheek. To Mrs.
Salter's amazement, she saw that Agnes must have been cry-
ing. She could, of course, have a cold. Mrs. Salter had never
known Agnes to cry since she was a small child, and the sight
moved and yet somehow encouraged her.

Agnes kept no furniture on the porch (and indeed, it offered
no privacy), and they went together into the small dark living
room, with its habitual air of defiant meagerness.

Mrs. Salter, keyed up, would have liked a stiff drink, but she
accepted eagerly the small thick glass of sherry, and Agnes said
''Cheers!''

The word, the room, the contents of her straw bag, indeed,
it seemed to Mrs. Salter, a host of years, crested and pressed
against her heart. She could not wait. She could not. She
prayed for love to make her shrewd.

''Cheers!'' she almost shouted, and she put down her glass.

''Agnes,'' she said, ''I've been in the dumps.''

This took Agnes by surprise. She looked at her mother.
Could it be true?

''I've just felt so *dull*,'' said Mrs. Salter, ''I've just felt I
wanted to do something I *wanted* to do. Really *wanted*, you
know?''

''Well, why couldn't you?'' asked Agnes without hostility.

''Well, I can, I think,'' said Mrs. Salter, almost stammering
with caution and eagerness. ''But you know, almost anything
you want to do involves someone else. I wanted to do something I'd never done in my life, just because I felt like it. As

a sort of—well, not a joke exactly, but, well, something like a treasure hunt . . .''

Mrs. Salter could hear, on the brown mantelpiece, the count of the small ugly clock. Launched now, without shelter, she plunged her small strong hand into the depths of her straw bag and came up with the smooth greenness. She pulled off the rubber bands and spread on the table the crisp paper, like a deck of preposterous cards.

"It's ten thousand dollars," Mrs. Salter said. "I just wanted to give you these pieces of paper," she said. "For anything. For nothing. No plans. Just because I wanted to. I've never even seen a five hundred dollar bill," she offered.

"Well, neither have I," said Agnes in a neutral voice. "Just look at them. Who's that?"

"That's President Grover Cleveland," said Mrs. Salter. She picked up the bottle of dreadful sherry and refilled her tiny glass.

The silence scared her, and she said with real humility, "It's like a joke between us. A valentine. Or an Easter egg." She swallowed her sherry. "All right?" she asked. "This one crazy thing?"

Agnes' fingers reached toward the fan of green, and Mrs. Salter had a moment of pure exultation. She did not dare speak.

Agnes gathered the bills in a loose sweep, and then pushed them gently with the fingers of both hands into a neat and single heap. She raised her eyes to her mother's. She held out the compact pile, and Mrs. Salter saw her throat compress, as from an impediment.

Then she said, "Here. For goodness sake, take them."

Woe and a kind of rage began to simmer deep inside Mrs. Salter.

"You won't do this with me?" she said. "For no reason, you won't let me do this?"

Agnes dropped the little heap by Mrs. Salter's glass.

"It's out of the question," she said.

Something was rising, rising to Mrs. Salter's head. She got up and took the bills, and went into the little kitchen, where she opened the oven door. There were two cookie sheets inside, and she took one and carried it to the protective surface of the kitchen table. There was a half-empty box of kitchen matches by the sink, and she had one lit in an instant. She held the first bill delicately, letting the little yellow-bluish flame taste its corner and eat upward. As it writhed, curled, and flew to ash, she let it fall onto the cookie sheet. Three of the notes were dark powder by the time Agnes was at her shoulder.

"For God's sake, Mother," she said, and took her mother's elbow. Black with wicked rage, Mrs. Salter violently shook her off and lit the fourth note. "Don't touch me, Agnes," she said. "Don't touch me."

She found she could light one note from the other, and the cookie sheet was thick with ash.

"You're crazy," Agnes said, but she sounded somehow afraid, and she did not touch her mother again.

They stood close together, speechless. The room was thick with fury and exaltation. As the last note curled onto the blackened sheet, they stared at each other.

Then Agnes turned and bent down to the cupboard and came up with a small metal container. Without a glance at her mother, she began scraping the ashes from the cookie sheet into the little bowl. Carefully she scraped, but the heap in the bottom was very small.

She pushed the bowl at her mother. "Take this," she said. "Take this and go away."

Mrs. Salter took the little bowl and went into the living room. She picked up her straw bag and kept on, across the concrete porch, down the three steps to her car. She put her bag under her left arm, held the bowl in her left hand and opened her car door. Then she set the bowl carefully on the floor close to the emergency brake. She backed the car, and there was no one on the porch. The house looked still enough to be uninhabitated.

At home, she got out, forgetting her bag, but carrying the little bowl. She went through the living room and out to her glass-topped table, where her unwashed coffee cup still sat. She put the little bowl on the table and, bereft suddenly of strength, dropped onto a chair.

Noon hush was on the lawn. There wasn't a single bird to be seen. The flowers burned brightly in the border. From somewhere there came faintly the sound of a lawn mower.

The long accumulation of anger and some sense of unrepentant relief had given her, in exchange for what no longer existed, a sort of detached pause. She pushed the little bowl gently with her finger and suddenly she remembered that she intended to be cremated. She remembered, too, how a shocked survivor had kept repeating, after the cleansing ritual was accomplished, "But there was so *little!* How could there be so *little?*"

She looked at her hand, her arm, still firm in its curve. She moved her hand down her neck and over her breast. She tried to think about love, and anger, about the fragility of value, and to wonder about what she had done. Instead, she felt simply quiet.

The bowl could not stay there indefinitely by the stained coffee cup. She remembered now that someone had told her how ashes were good for the soil. Or was it bonemeal, at the flower's root? Both, she thought.

She took the bowl and walked over grass so green it seemed to give out light. At the border's edge, she set the bowl on the grass and went to the little tool shed by the kitchen steps for a trowel. She found the red-handled one and came back with it, kneeling by the border and staining her good cotton dress. There was so little ash she had to make a choice, and choosing to give to the rich, she emptied the bowl onto the earth at the root of the big rose-begonia, and began gently to stir it in with the trowel. The begonia seemed to have opened even wider, and it hung heavy with its own gorgeousness.

When the last of the ash was stirred into its soil, she sat back on her heels.

The sound of the mower had stopped. The distant burr of

the traffic made the lawn and garden seem more quiet. She had the strongest sense of dislocation. Before they were eaten by the small flame, what were the green slips of paper? Dresses? A deposit? Charity? A voyage? Before her eyes reality seemed slightly to skid.

But the strangest part was some kind of peace which had opened in the black anger of Agnes' kitchen; a sort of—what? Two women by the kitchen table, in some conspiracy of furious wonder.

A robin landed on the edge of the birdbath, peering about. Then into the water it went, splashing lavishly with a thutter of wings. It shook itself, and drank. Then it took off into the air.

Still Mrs. Salter sat on her heels. An intention was forming inside her, and the next moment she got up as though directed.

She went back to the little tool shed and looked around. There were several empty plastic flower pots of various sizes. None was what she needed. Then, further back, she saw the single terra cotta pot. She took that and went back to the flower bed.

On her knees, she leaned precariously over and began digging gingerly around the roots of the big rose-begonia. She thrust the trowel deep into the soil and bore down on the handle, feeling the give of earth and fibers. But she had to step right into the bed for the final act. When the big thing came up, trailing clots of earth and tendrils of root, she lowered it into the pot, clamping the soil down hard with her fingers.

She set out with it, over the lawn, and she could see its shadow in her shadow-hand as she crossed over the bright grass. At the tool shed spigot, she let a jet of water muddy the stalk and soil. She rinsed her hands in water lukewarm from the summer heat, and dried them on her ruined skirt. Then, carrying the pot, she went round the corner of the house and over the driveway.

In the car, she braced the pot against the brake, and then she began to back out as cautiously as though the car held brimming water.

When she went up the three steps to the concrete porch, reality came back with a rush, and she stood still, in embarrassed terror. At the same time, staring mesmerized at the begonia's stalk springing from its soil, she had a strange sly desire to smile, as at a lovely and secret jest. She hadn't yet moved, when Agnes opened the door.

They both stood still for a second, and then Agnes said, "Come in. Come in," and backed away, and Mrs. Salter went past her into the living room. Nowhere did she dare put the pot down, and she stood there holding it.

"If that's for me, give it to me," said Agnes, and she held out her hands.

The thick little sherry glasses were still on the coffee table. Agnes shoved them aside; one tilted and fell, and Mrs. Salter grabbed it just before it rolled over the edge. Agnes set the terra cotta pot in the middle of the table.

"It's so *big*," she said, almost admiringly. "That soil is so dark."

"Well, I've fed it," said Mrs. Salter.

"Look at all those buds," said Agnes. "Five."

"I *think* they'll open," Mrs. Salter said. "You never really know." She moved toward the door.

"Have you eaten anything?" asked Agnes.

"Oh yes, yes indeed," said Mrs. Salter

"You've ruined your dress," said Agnes.

Mrs. Salter knew this was a conversation without a past or a future, but at the moment it had power. They were joint witnesses.

"I have to go now," she said. "I'll see you soon."

At the door, Agnes said, "It really is very pretty. I'm glad you brought it."

As after passion, after struggle, a lovely lassitude bathed Mrs. Salter. Then as she went down the steps, Agnes called, "When it dies, you can have your pot back."

She was still leaning on the doorjamb when Mrs. Salter turned the car.

292   *Luba Tribe*

Anthony Watts

SAFARI NOTES

Today the bearers fled
taking whatever books were bequeathed me

A family of gibbons
perform linguistic feats in the branches

My digital watch went berserk
raced through a dozen matchstick puzzles
and puttered out

Couldn't find the compass
the map just came to pieces in my hands

The rain faceless as data

Gave up marking off the days
in my diary
day and night now indistinguishable

Somewhere out there . . .
                              the Lost Tribe

whose dialect I came to purify

Kioko Nagase

蒼いものさびしいあけ方

蒼いものさびしいあけ方のケゼリンの海に
遠く尖光の塔が立った。
「あれは何じゃい」
「あれは何じゃい」
ふなばたに集って無垢な漁夫たちがそれをながめた。

その時ふと心はかき乱され嘔吐を感じ
しかし瞬間に消えたそれが何であったかはついに気づかなかった。
今までの生涯に彼らが熱情をこめて求めたもの
それは波涛の裡に飛鳥のようにすばやく生きた魚群を追うことのみ
己れも同じく鰭をもって追うことのみ

その時運命の灰はしずかにしずかに上空を渡って来て
ひっそりと彼等の上に降って来た
みるものない海上に霏々として――。
一目みたものを石にする
あのメジュサの首こそ光の塔であった。

故郷へ帰って来た漁夫は
次第につめたく凍えはじめた
陸へあがった魚さながら――
彼らの求めたものはすべて永久に彼らを去った。

Kioko Nagase

A BLUE AND DREARY DAWN

At dawn, a blue and dreary dawn,
Far away in the South Pacific,
A spire of light stood erect.
"What's that?"
"What's there?"
Innocent fishermen on the boat gazed at it.

It was when they were confused and nauseated;
But none of them perceived it—that flash!
All they had so far wished for fervently
Was only to hunt for fish in the sea as swiftly as birds,
To hunt for fish with fins, as swiftly as fish.

It was when the Death Ash drifted gradually across
     the sky
And fell silently upon the fishermen,
Ceaselessly upon their private sea.
It was the head of Medusa—that spire of light!—
That turned whoever looked at it into a stone!

Back home, the fishermen
Began to freeze little by little
Just as fish on the land freeze;
All they had gone after deserted them forever.

—Translated from the Japanese by Kiyoko Miura

Vasile Poenaru

A FEAST WINE

How shall you stop this falling of stars—
The festive beginning of the school year,
Starched shirts, freshly ironed ties,
A feast wine bubbling in your eyes
And behind the tables, the silence with rotten soles
The headmaster's speech adjusted like a Fortran
$\qquad\qquad\qquad\qquad\qquad$ program . . .
Here are your children, you would take them all in your
$\qquad\qquad\qquad\qquad$ palms, a dawn of butterflies,
You would take them, wings on your back, you would flee
$\qquad\qquad\qquad\qquad\qquad$ into the forest—
What hiding can you offer, your heart is merely an eye
$\qquad\qquad\qquad\qquad\qquad\qquad$ of light,
The darkness gnaws at the detour mindlessly.
The parents carry their pride on their heads
Like a shattering baldness.
The school is blossomed like a gallows.
The students take pride in striding up the steps.

The universe starts as from a kind of sleep.
All want to put their hands on you, to pull you by
                                   the coat,
To convince themselves that you are alive and theirs—
They press their textbooks to their chests it is a cruel
                                   autumn how
Shall you raise
So much falling of stars.

                    —*Translated from the Rumanian by Thomas C. Carlson*

298   *Anonymous*

Yannis Ritsos

IN NAUSICAA'S HOUSE

When she returned in the evening from the river to
    the seaport
where the ships' masts touched the grape vines covering
    the balconies
her own brothers came out of the palace and unhitched
    the mules,
took down the laundered clothes from the cart, and carried
    them inside—
dry, smelling of sun, laurel, soap—
time now for the servants to light the lamps
and lay out supper. The daughter of the house
was radiant tonight with a new kind of beauty, agitated,
    trembling,
afraid her brothers might notice that the laundry was light,
that a suit of clothes was missing. Of course nobody
    noticed a thing.
    The stranger
had remained outside the watered garden, alone. When he
    showed himself
only Arete recognized the clothing of her son Laodamas
on the stranger's body when he dropped to his knees
    before her,
and immediately she felt him to be her son.
"Rise," she said, and motioned him to take the best seat
next to the pillar where Demodocos had hung his guitar.

—*Translated from the Greek by Edmund and Mary Keeley*

Yannis Ritsos

ΝΑΥΣΙΚΑ

Σβῆσε τὸ λύχνο, γριὰ Εὐρυμέδουσα, τί κάνεις τόσην
    ὥρα;
Μήτε πεινάω, σοῦ λέω, μήτε νυστάζω. Τὸ μόνο ποὺ
    θέλω
εἶναι νὰ κλείσω τὰ μάτια μου. Ρίξε μου μιὰ κουβέρτα
    ἀκόμα.
Καὶ τί ποὺ κάνει ζέστη; Ἐγὼ κρυώνω. Ὁλόγυμνο
    τὸν εἶδα, νένα,
δίπλα στὰ σκοῖνα, κ' εἶχε φύκια στὰ μαλλιά του.
    Ἄλλο δὲ θέλω
μονάχα νὰ τοῦ βγάλω ἕνα πρὸς ἕνα τὰ μικρὰ χαλίκια
ποὖχαν κολλήσει στὶς γυμνὲς πατοῦσες του καὶ νὰ
    τοῦ βάλω
ἐτοῦτο τὸ λουλούδι, ποὺ κρατῶ στὸν κόρφο μου, στὰ
    δυό του δάχτυλα
κεῖ ποὺ χωρίζουν ἀπὸ τὸ λουρὶ τοῦ σάνταλου. Τώρα,
κοιμᾶται δίπλα, σκεπασμένος μὲ τὰ κόκκινα σκουτιά μου.

Yannis Ritsos

NAUSICAA

Blow out the lamp, Eurymedusa, old woman, why are
    you taking so long?
I told you I'm not hungry, not sleepy either. The only
    thing I want
is to shut my eyes. Let me have another blanket.
What if it's hot in here. I feel cold. Nurse, he was stark
    naked when I saw him,
near the terebinth trees, and he had seaweed in his hair.
I want nothing more in this world
than to remove, one by one, the little pebbles
that stuck to the bare soles of his feet
and to put this flower I'm holding against my breast
    between his toes,
there where the sandal's thong divides them. Now
he's asleep next door, under the red wool covers I wove.

—*Translated from the Greek by Edmund and Mary Keeley*

Robert Sabatier

LA RUE FROIDE

Étais-je espace? Il poussait des murailles
Contre mon corps. Étais-je oiseau? La terre
En s'éloignant m'initiait au vol.
Étais-je fleuve? Auprès de moi la rive
Me dédiait ses arbres verdoyants.

Étais-je mort? Un vieux poisson funèbre
Me parcourait des échines aux reins.
Étais-je vif? Il poussait tant de fleurs
Sur mon ami—ce corps écartelé.

En ce temps-là, je dormais pour survivre
Dans une barque entre terre et soleil.
De chaque livre, il partait un bruit d'ailes
Et chaque mot détruisait son lecteur.

Robert Sabatier

THE COLD STREET

Was I space? High walls pressed
Against my body. Was I a bird? Retreating
Earth initiated me to flight.
Was I a river? Alongside me the riverbank
Endowed me with its lush green trees.

Was I dead? An ancient funerary fish
Coursed through me along the small of my back.
Was I quick? So many flowers grew
On my friend, this quartered body.

In those days, to survive I slept
In a ship between the earth and the sun.
From each book there rose a susurrus of wings,
Each word destroyed its reader.

—Translated from the French by Eric Sellin

Robert Sabatier

LES LUNETTES

J'étais un livre. On effeuillait mes pages
Pour découvrir des signes, des empreintes.
Or, je rêvais des archives terrestres
Ou d'un feu noir, mais chacun me lisait.

Des doigts mouillés, des feuillets et des notes
Sur tout mon corps, et même cette plante
Se desséchant entre mes dents. La mordre
Fut mon désir tout le long d'un hiver.

Déchirez-moi. Je suis autre que Bible,
Autre que vers d'un poème fardé
Car je suis chair, et livre est la parure
Où je me cache. Et nul ne trouvera
Le seul secret que je cache en mes pages.

Il faut me lire avec les yeux des morts.

Robert Sabatier

SPECTACLES

I was a book. People flipped my pages
In search of signs, in search of prints.
But then, I dreamed of terrestrial archives
Or of a black fire, but everyone read me.

Damp fingers, book pages and notes
On all my body, and even this plant
Withering between my teeth. To bite it
Was my sole desire one whole winter.

Tear me up! I am other than Bible,
Other than lines in an artificial poem,
For I am flesh, and the book is the exterior
Behind which I hide. And no one will find
The only secret I hide in my pages.

You must read me with the eyes of the dead.

—*Translated from the French by Eric Sellin*

Courtesy of San Diego Museum of Art

306   *Anonymous*

Syed Shamsul Huq

TO LIVE THE FANTASY

A peaceful, small town. But the tea shop where the local young men congregated opened onto the main road to Dhaka. Inside, constant clamor. Each table had its own topic of conversation. And words were hurled from one table in the direction of another. High-pitched music, blaring from a cassette. Waiters, constantly hassled. The owner's thunderous roaring. A veritable stream—truck, bus, and scooter—flowed through the street. Horns blaring. And when the wind rose, there arose a creaking, croaking wait through bamboo growing behind the shop.

But they could be heard.

His voice lowered, Badsha spoke just two little words. But they could clearly be heard.

"I'm going."

He'd not expected them to be noticed amidst that din. He had voiced them merely as an experiment, assuming that none of his friends would hear him. And he wasn't going to say them a second time.

Even he was startled. He seemed to recoil once he'd spoken those words. Who could have anticipated that mid-stream, in the current of noise inside and out, there would appear suddenly such an island of silence? Who'd have thought that upon that island his pronouncement, like a lone tree, would stand tall?

For a moment Badsha wondered whether the sudden lull the moment he spoke just happened. Or, did his declaration create that silence?

Be that as it may, he was rather pleased. The reaction proved even more astounding than he had anticipated.

Jalil's political opinions just hung there, half hoisted.

Samad's waving hand of objection turned to stone.

Jhumka, that maturing young thing from the loan-office neighborhood—her name, which for Ashraf and Abdul Momen had metamorphosed into a butterfly, now fluttered away.

The new poem that marched sprightly from Syamalendu's pen stumbled, along with the spelling of "suffering."

Kaci, senior amongst them, had been dunking a cookie in his tea. Soggy, it disintegrated in his hand.

The inspiration seemed to take hold of Badsha. Shaking off the tentative quality in his voice of a moment ago, he now reiterated full-throated, entranced, "Yes, I'm going."

His companions, somewhat taken aback, stared at him. Within these two everyday words they all of a sudden discovered something unexpected, quite possibly incomprehensible.

Because of his age, perhaps, it was Kaci who first stirred.

"What do you mean, you're going?"

Badsha cast a dreamy glance towards Kaci, but offered no explanation.

Pausing momentarily, Kaci again questioned, "What do you mean by you're going? Where're you going?"

No reply came. Actually, Badsha hadn't really thought about it any further. Or rather, he had thought about it, but not thought it through clearly. At that precise moment his common sense yet prevailed. He could still have said, "nowhere," he was going nowhere, that is to say, what people mean when they say "going"—away, far, to great expectations, to bigger and better things, no, it was not that sort of "going." Yes, he could still take it all back. So what if he took it back? These friends, to a man, would give a hoot and a holler, no more.

But he said nothing. Just remained quiet.

Every one of those present who looked into his eyes perceived sunlight from some faraway world. Sunlight in whose warmth man's dreams become visible, tangible.

Slowly, but steadily, Badsha came to sense a sort of power. He felt himself somehow profoundly removed, far distant. He seemed astride some towering pinnacle. And this exhilaration he was not ready to relinquish. He'd never realized such a thrill could ever be his. He hadn't passed his exams. In one after another attempt at earning a living he'd been a failure. Unsuccessful in love, embarrassed by a hoarse voice when he'd tried to learn to sing, even in this realm of tea shop small talk he was no rajah but merely part of someone else's retinue. Now, instantaneously, he found all his psychic fatigue, his feelings of inferiority fading. He sensed himself the center of everything.

Badsha spoke again. "I'm going soon."

Syamalendu retorted derisively, and as he spoke resumed his writing, "He's probably going to Dhaka. Where else would he go?"

Badsha shook his head. Momentarily, to his mind's eye. Dhaka beckoned, but he ignored that and once again, only more forcefully, shook his head. Syamalendu's eyes were upon his work. So Badsha said aloud, "No, I'm not going to Dhaka."

Syamalendu looked up, his brow now furrowed.

With a slap on the table, Jalil asked, "Then where is it you're going? Why all the mystery?"

"So he tells us something or other," added Samad. "He's probably headed to Jessore to take in a movie during the Eed holidays."

A burst of laughter erupted. The awe of a moment earlier had been sliced to bits by levity's blade. It was then that Badsha stiffened. But on the spur of the moment he couldn't quite figure out what to say. With jaws firmly set, he sat there, eyes fixed upon the table.

"That's right. What else could it be?" In this manner Abdul

Momen tried to resolve the matter and turn attention back toward Jhumka. Ashraf was Jhumka's neighbor, and he had a real crush on Jhumka's elder sister. Whenever these two friends got together, the conversation always found its way to that matter. And because of that, they'd become real chum-buddies for some time now.

Badsha had no interest in Jhumka or her sister, not in any-one really, yet he felt envious of Ashraf and Abdul Momen.

Suddenly Badsha leapt to his feet and shouted, "Just watch. You'll find out when I go."

No one had ever seen Badsha so agitated. He had made somewhat of a name for himself as the most calm, controlled of fellows. And one doesn't toss away such a reputation for no good reason. Kaci grabbed hold of his hand and sat him down.

"Hey, hey—what's going on with you guys, Badsha? Sit down, sit down."

Kaci shouted to the waiter to bring Badsha a cup of tea.

"No, I don't want any tea. I've got a bunch of work to do. I got to get a lot of things arranged. Got to go now."

"All right. Aren't you going to say where you're going?"

Badsha wished he could say something that would leave them speechless, now and forever more. But nothing suitable came to mind. Or rather, what did enter his head was impos-sible to utter—at least from his perspective impossible—because he just didn't find the nerve to blurt it out. He merely sat there silent. But sitting silent seemed to him another mark of defeat. And he felt as though whatever he was fantasizing would be found out, if he just sat there silently. So he huffed and puffed, trying to act as though he were fuming with rage.

His tea arrived. Kaci had to importune him a time or two more to drink it. While he sipped, a terror seized him. Why, he thought, had he said those things at all? Things had been going on as they were for a long time now. For a long time he'd been unemployed. For a long time he'd drifted aimlessly. For a long time he'd listened to the carping and scolding at home. He's seen his tea-shop comrades fall away, one by one—to get married, take a job, move to some other town.

Had his father that very morning not thrown a brass tumbler at him and not uttered that disgusting doggerel, would he have gone on sitting there mum in the tea shop, then finally blurt out "I'm going"?

His father's obscenity still now rang in his ears:

> I dreamt my finger fair blue skies did bore;
> I woke to find it lodged in my back door.

Badsha finished his tea, wiped his mouth, and stood up.

From behind, Ashraf couldn't control his urge to goad. "Badsha, you going to the Middle East?" At the tea shop's entrance, Badsha came to a sudden halt. He seemed to see refulgent before him a regal throne swathed in gold. Turning his head he replied, "You'll find out when I go."

Those primed by Ashraf's jibe for another burst of laughter were caught off balance.

"Yes, I'm going to the Middle East."

Badsha paused there not a moment longer. But he didn't go home. Instead, that day he spent a considerable amount of time wandering aimlessly. The sky, trees, dwellings, the long stretch of road which curved past a stand of bamboo, tube-wells, jute warehouses, two date palms intertwined, the dilapidated Hindu temple out in the field—all of these seemed gradually to take cognizance of him. As though they were bidding him good-bye. As though he were seeing them for the last time. As though somehow he'd become a stranger, not of that place.

No sooner had he set foot in his house that evening than his widowed sister came running up to him.

"Are you really going to the Arab lands?"

Badsha made no reply.

His sister took hold of his hand and spoke again, "Is it true?" Later, as she served him his evening meal of rice etc. she added, "When did you first decide? We had no idea! Your friends came by looking for you."

Badsha smiled weakly. Then again his fantasy took hold. Again he turned secretive.

This sister, widowed with four kids—back home and living off her father. She was constantly depressed, from a sense of shame. Now that she could see a ray of hope, she got very excited.

"That's great! Many people have become rich going to the Arab lands. And with your intelligence—you're a strong young man—you'll make thousands of takas in no time. Then you're going to have to bring me something, however."

"What? Tell me."

"You'll do it?

"Tell me what do you want."

"A sewing machine. Then you'll see, you folks won't have to keep supporting me. I'll do just fine, sewing and such. And when Khokan grows up—you'll be able to take him to the Arab lands, won't you?"

"Why shouldn't I? But let me get there first."

Khokan slept in the outside room with Badsha. That night, Khokan asked, "Uncle, will you buy me a plane? A real big sort of plane?"

"Plane? Do you have any idea how much a plane costs? Millions and millions of takas."

"No, no, a toy plane, with batteries. I saw one at Abu's house the other day."

Enthusiastically Khokan described the plane. Abu's father had been in Dubai for the last two years. He'd returned several days ago for the Eed holidays.

It occurred to Badsha that since the subject had come up, why not pay a visit to Abu's father. Perhaps he might actually suggest some means for getting to the Middle East.

The next day he went to see Abu's dad. But how could he broach the subject—in the meantime, the man had already come to know, from who knows whom, that Badsha was going.

For some unknown reason Abu's father did not seem particularly pleased. His brow knit, he said in a voice full of concern, "So you're going. Well and good. There are many who are going. I myself went. But sticking it out, that's the tough part."

"How do you mean?"

"You've got to work day and night there. If you don't show up for work, they expel you. And whatever else you might do or have done, they tolerate no inattentiveness on the job."

Badsha assured him, he would throw himself into his work. He hadn't foreseen that the intended purpose of his visit to Abu's father would be turned inside out in this fashion. He just wanted to get up and leave.

Abu's father resumed, "And then there's another thing. It's tough living there. You're not going to find real friends there. Idle chit-chat, conversation will not be so easy to come by. You can't be sure you'll even find any Bengalis where you're headed. Where are you going, by the way?"

Badsha plunged into the shoreless sea.

"The Middle East."

"You realize, don't you, that's not just one tiny locale?"

Gamely, Badsha proclaimed, "Abu Dhabi."

Abu's father's brow knit once again. "Hmmm, of course I don't keep up with the latest in Abu Dhabi. What sort of job there?"

Now he was in a bind. What answer could he give?

"You're here through Eed?" responded Badsha. "I'll discuss this further with you later."

He didn't stop by the tea shop that day. Who knew, were his friends sitting around asking questions? Instead, Badsha sauntered casually through the bazaar. But even there a few people called out to him, tugged at his hand, inquired about his going to Arabia.

To some he gave a brief "yes," to others he just nodded and kept moving. He could feel upon his back the arrows of jealousy from some, the pounding fists of envious sighs from others. He considered himself a winner. And the feeling made him giddy.

A couple of days later he happened upon Jhumka and her

big sister. The girls were about to enter a shoe store to purchase something for Eed, when their eyes and Badsha's met. This day the girls did not avert their eyes, did not cock their proud heads and turn away. Instead, the two of them gazed for a time in Badsha's direction. Between themselves they exchanged a few words. Badsha was surprised, for somehow they seemed rather plain to him today.

Around the house, also, his value of a sudden shot up. The father who used to scold him daily, even he now, from his sickbed, shouted to the rest of the household to treat him nice, to see to his meals—for, after all, how many more days was he to be here, and when a few days hence he will have left for the Arab lands, the house was going to seem so empty. In the meantime, he even called Badsha over one day and, stroking his head and back, explained that all the chiding and chastising he'd done had been with Badsha's best interests in mind. He told Badsha's mother twenty-four times a day, "It's because I threw the brass tumbler that day that the boy developed resolve, and now, just look, he's really done something. You're not to lack for anything anymore. This dirt-floored, split-bamboo-walled home of yours shall be rebuilt of brick. Badsha's going to bring in electricity. Electric lights shall shine. You'll be able to enjoy the breezes of a fan. You'll get to watch television, just like at Abu's house. Moreover, gold is cheap in the Arab countries. You've been after me my entire life for gold jewelry; your son's now going to satisfy your every whim."

No, no. This time Badsha would have to make the effort. He'd fallen into a trap of his own devising and now searched for a way of escape. He borrowed money from his sister for a trip to Dhaka. There he learned afresh what he already knew. One couldn't arrange to go to the Arab countries for less than twenty to twenty-five thousand takas. Badsha was well aware that he couldn't scrape together two or three thousand takas even, let alone twenty to twenty-five. In Dhaka he noted that many had sold their land in order to be able to go. But Badsha's family didn't have any land. Their household ran with the help of his two elder brothers plus father's pension. Nor did the brothers do such a booming business that they could afford to contribute so great a sum.

On the contrary, the day the second eldest brother heard Badsha was going to Arabia he came by to say that, obviously, their father must have some funds stashed away, otherwise where did so much money for Badsha come from. And he left informing them that it might not be possible for him to keep sending them money, month after month.

Badsha hadn't considered that particular angle. He felt bad about it. Why had he brought up the matter in the first place. And now, because of him, the family's means of support might be cut off? Badsha failed to see any way of rectifying the situation.

And in fact, the following month that elder brother did excuse himself from giving money. When Badsha returned home he heard his father, who had for so many days praised his second son, ranting and raving against him. "He'll see, he'll see. It's not long now till Badsha'll be sending money back from Arabia, till the room will come alive with new things— then he'll see, then he'll come around. Well, come on, come around then, you bastard!"

Badsha went outside. He took a walk through his favorite field. The streets in town frightened him. Familiar faces seemed to chase him away. He didn't want to run into anyone.

Then one day he did run into someone. Jhumka's younger brother. At least Badsha had nothing to fear from him. He wouldn't harass him with questions about his precise destination, the nature of his employment, the date of his departure. In an effort to gain some human companionship while at the same time avoiding human beings, Badsha now raised his hand and motioned for him to come near.

The boy was overjoyed. With eyes sparkling, he approached.

"Are you calling me?"

"Yes, you. You're Jhumka's brother, right?"

"Yes, I'm her younger brother. I've got three other brothers."

Seated atop a culvert, watching trucks and buses careering by along the main road, Badsha spoke with the lad. Just little things. Ordinary things. Concerning school. Sports. At one point he asked about Jhumka, too. "Didn't I see her that day at the shoe store?" From the boy he learned, because the shoes were too expensive she didn't buy them. "I guess your sister's not happy about that," volunteered Badsha. "Just think, if she marries well, if your brother-in-law, for instance, takes a job in the Middle East, your worries would be over, wouldn't they?"

A mere couple of weeks later something most unbelievable happened. That same boy pressed a folded piece of paper in Badsha's hand and dashed off. Even before unfolding it Badsha sensed a most subtle, sweet scent. Of what exactly, he couldn't quite make out. In his chest there commenced an unbearable pounding.

A letter, written by Jhumka. Though he read and reread it, he seemed incapable of comprehending what it said. His eyes invariably slipped off the letters. A single line obliterated all others, blazing forth—"Will you remember us when you go abroad?"

What did it mean? What did Jhumka wish to say?

Though he understood full well, he yet seemed unable to understand. Though he got it, it somehow remained beyond his grasp. The whole day this was all he read. Aside, in secret, how many, many times he read that very letter! Time and again he set off in the direction of the loan office. Each time he turned about and came back.

Jhumka's face hovered as a tiny happiness before his eyes. Hour by hour it grew larger. Quickly it grew. Any sweet fragrance he felt was somehow part of Jhumka. With any joy there existed a hidden link to Jhumka, so Badsha came to believe.

Then one day he got up the nerve to go to the loan-office neighborhood. He passed in front of Jhumka's residence. Then retraced his steps. Then again he walked by.

He felt sorry for Abdul Momen that day he caught sight of

him from afar in the bazaar. Constantly Jhumka's letter in his shirt pocket sang to him, "Will you remember us when you go abroad?"

Quite suddenly Badsha came to realize that now nothing oppressed him, nothing really bothered him—not his father's keen-eyed constant staring, nor his mother's endless, silent questioning, nor his brother's mean-heartedness, nor his widowed sister's sewing machine, nor Khokan's coveted toy.

Once more he found the courage to mix and mingle, to be with friends, to return to the tea shop on the main road. Then one afternon he realized from where within himself that strength now came—he realized, that is, when from a distance he caught sight of Jhumka, and when she made her eyes dance most wondrously before she hid her face within the rickshaw's canopy.

He stepped into the tea shop.

Syamalendu was reciting his poetry aloud; Ashraf and Abdul Momen were observing the flight of a butterfly; Jalil, at the next table, was holding forth on preconditions for a non-exploitive society; Samad, to himself, was drafting his rebuttal; it was just then that Badsha came in and pulled up a chair.

"You fellows are really carrying on, I see!"

The sound of his voice once again startled everybody. They all were well aware their Badsha had, since they last saw him, made great strides. But some out of envy, some from contempt wished to outshine his presence there.

When Kaci inquired, "Well Mr. Badsha, when's it going to be?" he didn't understand that Kaci wanted to know the date of his departure for the Middle East. He sensed the quickening pace of that dream within his chest, as though all knew about Jhumka, and it was their wedding date that Kaci wished to know.

Badsha, embarrassed, could say simply, "We'll see, Kaci, we'll see. You'll all come to know."

—Translated from the Bengali by Clinton B. Seely

318   *Arthur Rothstein*

Merryn Williams

HOUND OF THE BASKERVILLES

Sooner or later, I know, he is going to get here.
Daylight, I pretend he's insubstantial
(though I have glared into his blazing eyes, and found
a black hair of his in my washbasin).
But at night, bolting doors and sealing windows,
I hear his howl, distinct and coming closer.
I throw steaks and mutton chops to slow the creature
    down,
light fires to keep him at a distance.

It's never the people you think will come to grief
who succumb to his horrid fascination.
They looked like the rest of us; things were going well
the moment before they stepped off the escalator

and went out, as far as they could get from those lights,
to where a railway runs through open country,
sleep-walking over damp earth and bog-cotton
that glimmers white beneath a dusky clouded sky.

And it's no good my denying his reality
or shutting out the moors behind thick curtains. He is there
in the broken bulb at the top of the stair,
the envelope of five dried orange pips,
and in the empty room where the chat-show goes on,
with its bursts of pre-recorded laughter.

Cahit Külebi

IZIN

Izin alır gelirsem
Güleceksin sevincinden,
Sabahları erken kalkacağız.
Sobamızı yakacağız,
Saçların güzel olacak tütünümün renginden
Ellerin çay kokacak
Gün doğacak sesinden

Cahit Külebi

HOME LEAVE

If I take leave and come,
You will laugh with delight.
We will get up early in the morning,
We will light our fire,
Your hair will be more beautiful
  than the color of my tobacco.
Your hands will smell of tea
And the sun will rise
  through your voice.

—Translated from the Turkish by Özcan Yalim,
William A. Fielder, Dionis Coffin Riggs

Cahıt Külebi

Kamyonlar kavun tasır ve ben
Boyuna onu düşünürdüm,
Kamyonlar kavun taşır ve ben
Boyuna onu düşünürdüm,
Niksarda evimizdeyken
Küçük bir serçekadar hürdüm.

Sonra âlem degişiverdi
Ayrı su, ayrı hava, ayrı toprak.
Sonra âlem değisiverdi
Ayrı su, ayrı hava, ayrı toprak.
Mevsimler ne çabuk geçiverdi
Unutmak, unutmak, unutmak.

Anladım bu şehir başkadır'
Herkes beni aldattı gitti,
Anladım bu şehir başkadır
Herkes beni aldattı gitti,
Yine kamyonlar kavun taşır,
Fakat içimde şarkı bitti.

Cahit Külebi

ISTANBUL

The trucks used to carry melons, and I
Used to think of her continually.
The trucks used to carry melons, and I
Used to think of her continually.
When I was in our house at Niksar
I was free as a little sparrow.

Then my world changed suddenly:
Other water, other air, other soil.
Then my world changed suddenly:
Other water, other air, other soil.
How quickly the seasons passed
To make me forget, forget, forget.

I discovered that this city was different,
Everybody had always deceived me.
I discovered that this city was different,
Everybody had always deceived me.
The trucks continue to carry melons
But the song within me is stilled.

—Translated from the Turkish by Özcan Yalim,
William A. Fielder, Dionis Coffin Riggs

Courtesy of San Diego Museum of Art

324   *Seiko*

Gu Cheng

EARLY SPRING

1

The morose sky hangs back:
Will there be snowflakes? or raindrops?

The muddy river flows fast:
Is it seeking? or escaping?

Far from here lovers are parting:
A prologue? or epilogue?

—Translated from the Chinese by Edward Morin
and Dennis Ding

Gu Cheng

一 代 人

黑夜给了我黑色的眼睛，
我却用它寻找光明。

（原载《》星星》1980年第 3 期）

顾城　1956年秋生于北京。1963年入小学，1969年随父"下放"到山东，1974年返京。1977年开始发表作品。

Gu Cheng

A GENERATION

Dark night endowed me with dark eyes
Yet with them I seek light

Note: During the Cultural Revolution, writers were told not to write about the "darkness" of life in Chinese society. This dark side included feelings of personal melancholy which, if expressed, could put a damper on public morale.

Translated from the Chinese
by Edward Morin and Dennis Ding

Tommy Olofsson

Som en trogen hund kommer mörkret,
och kvällskylan söker mig med fuktig nos.
Stjärnorna skäller visserligen inte, men

om någon väntar sig att världen ska visa sig
vara ett stort djur, är detta rätt tidpunkt
att sitta på en sten och vänta,

vänta på att stjärnorna visar sina tänder
och att himlen avslöjar sin jägareblick.
Någon rycker i kopplet. Jag måste gå nu.

Tommy Olofsson

ON LEASH

Like a faithful dog the dark comes up
and the cool of evening nuzzles me with a
wet nose. I know the stars don't bark, but

if anyone thinks the world will turn out
to be a vast animal, this is the right time
to sit on a stone and wait . . .

wait for the stars to show their teeth
and the sky to reveal its hunter's eye.
Someone's tugging at the leash. I have to go now.

—Translated from the Swedish by Jean Pearson

Tommy Olofsson

Under en glödande diskus för länge sedan kastad
deltar jag, tätt förföljd av min egen skugga,
som både son och far i den stora stafetten.

I sömnen tänker jag ofta att skuggan är besegrad,
men i gryningen dyker den upp vid min sida
som ett egendomligt mätinstrument eller tecken

som tyder på att det inte finns någon seger att få.
Inte för någon av oss, och inte för den okände atlet,
inte ens för honom, som en gång slungade solen ut i
	mörket.

Tommy Olofsson

RELAY RACER

Under a glowing discus hurled a long time ago
I take part in the great relay race as both son
and father, stride for stride with my own shadow.

In sleep I often think the shadow is beaten
but at dawn he turns up again at my side
like a strange measuring wheel or a sign

that signals there is no victory to be won.
Not by any of us, not by the unknown athlete,
not even by him who once flung the sun out
into darkness.

—Translated from the Swedish by Jean Pearson

332   *Utagawa Toyokuni*

Chiyo Uno

CONFESSIONS OF LOVE

From the next day, I stopped going to the second floor of the boxmaker's house. Once I walked out of the police station, the oppression which had clung to me like a fog completely lifted. I myself had difficulty fathoming the stupidity that had possessed me until as late as the previous day. By then I was convinced that Tsuyuko was definitely not in the Yotsuya house, that she and the old woman were locked up somewhere far away, but I could think of nothing else to do but wait for my next opportunity to locate her.

For four or five days, I was at the mercy of my nerves since I stayed shut up at home. Then one night my wife came up to my second floor room with a telegram.

"Telegram for you." She pointed her hard, unmoving face toward me and then immediately went downstairs. My wife and I had been living that way for about six months, waiting for our attorney to send the divorce papers. In some way we had even become used to those living arrangements. I silently read the telegram:

HAKONE GŌRA TANIGUCHI ESTATE   TSUYUKO

This was the entire message. Tsuyuko was telling me where she was. I read it again. Just as I had thought, Tsuyuko was confined in an estate owned by someone named Taniguchi in

Gōra. Along with the news came the peculiar conviction that I had known this for some time. As soon as I got up the next morning, I would go to meet her, I decided. Settling upon this plan made me forget the long period of suffering I had just endured for it was as if warm, peaceful waters had been poured over me.

"I'll go early tomorrow morning," I whispered to myself, holding the telegram in my hand. Then a fear that was like a severe thirst came surging up into my throat. Had she sent me a telegram so late at night because a new crisis had arisen and she desperately needed me? It was possible that she had waited for a convenient chance to contact me, but suddenly had an emergency on her hands and could not wait any longer. Since it was exceedingly difficult to sit still I checked my watch, which showed just past 11:00, and calculated that if I hurried, I could catch the last train to Odawara which left after midnight. Nothing more was required to get me to put on my hat and rush to Tokyo Station.

A strong wind howled through the night as if about to bear off the platform roof, and after the train arrived at Yokohama, the wind mixed with the rain, creating a fierce, whipping downpour. By the time I reached Odawara, the storm had become severe with floods sweeping across the utter blackness of that city. The agents of the hotels who had come to meet the train all claimed that it was probably impossible to go to Gōra in that rain. Maybe they said such things to get me to stay at their hotels or perhaps I actually was mad to insist on going to the mountains in that violent storm. Still, since my mind was made up, I gave one of the men money and asked him to get me a taxi. He came back almost immediately with a driver from the garage in front of the station.

"There are no roads," the driver informed me as soon as we started to talk. In the morning he might be able to help, but at night it was so dangerous that we'd almost certainly crash.

"Why don't you take me as far as you can?" At such times I keep only my immediate goal in mind and expect that my singlemindedness will stifle all objections. "Just turn back once the road gives out. You get the car and I'll give you all my money. I'll pay you whatever you say."

Another young driver in a raincoat came out of the same garage.

"You say that you want to go to Gōra, Sir?"

"To the Taniguchi estate."

The young driver went back into the garage and came out with a convertible. It was on the tip of my tongue to ask him whether this convertible was the only car he had, but I was afraid that if I complained, he might not take me. I opened the door and soon we were driving away. Someone in the shop had probably forced him to take the worst car they had. As we journeyed along the muddy road, the rain, like sticks hurled by the squall, pelted my cheeks through the gaps in the convertible top. I raised my coat collar, listening to the fearful wind rising and falling across the dark night. Tree branches were also breaking and tree trunks splitting apart. By the mountain, there was more of a savagely flowing river than a road, with huge rocks tumbling down into the muddy waters.

"Sir . . ." The driver tried to tell me something but his words got lost in the wind and I couldn't hear very well. He was probably trying to get me to give up going any higher.

I shouted at him to continue. "It's all right! Just a bit more!"

"Taniguchi-san's house is the only one on top of the hill. I'll have to stop the car below the cliff."

"I understand. You just go as far as you can. I'll walk the rest of the way."

Perhaps if I had known more about Hakone, I might have given up on that mountain, but since I had been living abroad for so long, I had never been to places that most people had visited at least once. In addition, whenever my situation becomes difficult, I tend to feel even more determined about overcoming all obstacles. That raging weather actually goaded me on. The car almost turned over several times driving through piles of falling rocks and broken branches. The ripped hood made a frightening noise, flapping in the wind, while the rain, mixed with earth and sand, soaked the seats, beating at us from the side. Several times it seemed as if we were going to be buried in the rain and when a big tree broke like a pencil and was washed away completely, there was a sound, like the very roaring of the earth, which echoed into the valley.

"Sir, I will only go this far." The driver finally stopped his car.

The face of the young driver shone like a soldier in the car headlights and the rain ran down his face as I silently got out. No light from any estate was visible, but a steep road in front led up a tall cliff. Deciding to take that path, I went along for a bit until I vaguely made out a house at the top of a steep hill which was definitely the Taniguchi estate. Built in a simple cottage style, it was surrounded by a low fence.

I found myself suddenly turning around to watch the headlights flickering through the darkness as the car crawled down low in its descent from the mountain. A thought, like a flash of light, told me that it must be past 2 a.m. I used both my hands to fumble along the wooden fence, going around the outside several times, but of course found no sign of anyone being awake. Since the gate was open, I went into the garden and then managed to make my way through the small pines to the back. I groped along the exterior of the building, still searching, circling the whole house once or twice, but I had not yet been able to catch any glimpse of what was happening inside.

I hid myself for a little while behind a storage shed, while the rain against the tall water tank beside me pounded like drumbeats. Only then did I realize that my body, my hat, my coat, my shirt, my socks, were completely soaked, but in that sea of darkness with the astounding, terrifying wind and rain, I could only let out several great breaths to rejoice at my safe arrival.

I made another round with my chest against the house and discovered a faint light coming from a window hidden by some tall larches. As I approached that window, I gave no thought to who might be inside or what I would say if I actually discovered someone. Since the moment I had begun my journey at Tokyo Station and then been pitched about in that car, my sole preoccupation had been my need to see Tsuyuko—and that, like a raging hunger inside me, took precedence over all my other thoughts and allowed me to consider no other idea.

I can't say precisely why, but I sensed that she might be inside and that stirred wild plans about how I would, despite the rain, shout out to Tsuyuko if she were there, ask her to come out, and together we would run away. I pressed my cheek against the window and looked into the room through the small space between the curtains. In the light from the small lamp on the night table, I could make out that it was Tsuyuko indeed lying on the bed reading a book with her back to the window.

"Tsuyuko! Tsuyuko! Tsuyuko!" I called out to her but I couldn't even hear my own voice since it was carried off in the wind and the rain. I ran over to a window close to the bed on the north side and saw Tsuyuko's white hand as she held the book, and her cheek, like a child's in profile when it sank into the pillow. But closer inspection was impossible for I was suddenly drenched by the rain pelting down on the glass.

"Tsuyuko! Tsuyuko!" I called out again, but of course she didn't get up.

At that moment, I heard a noisy conversation out on the road beneath the cliff and gradually some people approached the house. I instinctively flew from the window, hiding under the small pine trees behind me. Since rain mixed with stones and small branches painfully hit against my face, shoulders, and back, it seemed wise to just surrender to the rain. I sat very still without breathing, while some people entered the garden. Four or five men in straw raincoats came near the trees where I was hidden. They were carrying lanterns as well as a large black object. My heart started to pound as I tried to understand why they had come there in the middle of the night. Suddenly a tremendous wind blew up and the light from their lamps fluttered, leaving me exposed for a moment in that flash of brightness. I came leaping out from those trees since I saw immediately that I should present myself before they discovered me.

"What's happened?" I asked before they had a chance to ask me the same thing.

They were carrying a young boy in a raincoat who, perhaps because he was drunk, had his head bent down like a dead man.

"He's a fool," one of the men declared, "driving in this rain."

They had been on emergency duty up on the mountain, and were approaching the bridge below when a gruesome roar made them look up, only to see the cliff give way. Simultaneously a car dashed by with its headlights on, getting caught up in the falling cliff and turning over. Although some went running out to help, it was already too late, for the car had been smashed like a toy and the driver hurled from the car, pinned beneath the rocks, almost dead. He had been rescued finally and since this Taniguchi estate on the hill was the only place available in the neighborhood, they had brought him over temporarily, despite the inconvenience this would cause. Was it the car I had come in? I was struck with terror as I looked at that young man's face—and indeed the man was so pale that he could have been a different person, yet he was definitely the driver who had brought me there. As I remembered how he had shone like a soldier when I had parted from him and how the rain had run down his face, I became so overwrought that I momentarily forgot about my own situation and how I had come sneaking into a stranger's garden.

Eventually I made some foolish remarks to these strangers about what a tragedy this was, but since there was no escaping the conviction that I had killed this man, I could not get myself to look them in the eye.

"Who are you anyway?" one of othe men thought of asking.

With a start, I regained my composure and at least had the presence of mind to instantly explain that I lived a way off and, having lost my bearings, found myself in this garden. I went on to say that since karma must have been behind this meeting, I wanted to help them care for the boy. I spoke these words very coolly, and, fortunately no one doubted my sincerity as I moved ahead of the men and went around to the entranceway. With the help of the lanterns, I could see the front of the house which looked like a mountain retreat, constructed of stone. The sturdy door had been made from logs.

"Anyone up?" I knocked hard at that door, "Excuse me, is anyone up?"

A small light went on inside. Evidently someone was awake and had lit a candle. The flickering light approached and when the door was opened, a white-haired old man came out, listened to us explain why we had come, and then went back into the house, only to come out again and invite us in.

We were led into a room next to the entranceway, apparently a sitting room. It was a big room, simply decorated, and the injured man was laid on the couch in the corner. They took off his straw raincoat and beneath was a jacket of the same khaki color. His gaiters probably meant membership in the town's youth group. We asked the old man to bring in some firewood and gradually, when a fire was started in the fireplace, the flames illumined the wounded man's pale face. Outside, the blood had been washed away by the rain, but in the room I could see it gushing out from the wound at the base of his head. The white of his fractured skull was visible between the torn shreds of flesh.

"We should call the doctor. Do you have a phone?"

"There's no use calling. After an avalanche like that, there won't be any roads, even to Odawara."

Much whispered discussion followed about how there were back roads, but those were more dangerous. Even if someone went out to get medical help, the wounded man probably would not survive until the doctor could get there. An old woman, who must have been the wife of the old man, also came in bringing towels and cotton cloth which she placed on his wounds, but these were quickly soaked with blood. I joined the others and went about opening the buttons on his shirt, trying to help remove his clothes. I took off the shoes which had stuck to his body as hard as plaster, then removed his socks and shuddered at the sight of his feet—white as paper and cold as ice. For a long time I stared at that young man's mouth, hanging wide open and jerking from spasms, and at his chest heaving restlessly beneath his dirty white shirt.

"He's finished," someone muttered.

Was this boy going to die? Was he going to die there, just like a dog, helpless, in this strange house where they couldn't even get a doctor? Because he had driven me? The men stopped trying to help him further and an eerie silence ensued while we waited the few moments until he died.

Outside the wind howled continuously and we could hear the crashing trees, forming a huge black shadow as they collapsed. The rain washed over the window frames and I started believing I had always been gazing at the wind, the rain, the flame burning in the fireplace, and the events in the room. For some moments I became convinced that there could be nothing more natural than for me to be among these people. But then I became cold and a chill ran down my spine as if I had been doused in cold water. I started shivering and heard my teeth chattering.

"He's gone." That sounded like the old man's murmur.

'So this is what has happened,' I thought, 'That boy is going to die.' Gathering every ounce of my strength I carefully observed the open mouth of the young driver who was lying down on the couch, no longer supported by anyone. When suddenly his neck fell from the cushion, I had to cover my face with both my hands.

"Old man, bring the candle. . . ."

While such phrases floated through the air around me, I believe I saw the candle being placed at the dead man's pillow and the small flickering flame. I next felt hot, as if my whole body were on fire. "Maybe I'll light a candle too," I said to myself, and was lifting my head to request one of the old man, when the door to the next room opened slightly and I saw the slender Tsuyuko standing there in a red striped housecoat.

I next fainted into unconsciousness.

I came down with an acute case of pneumonia from being out in that rain for so long. I heard later that I didn't open my eyes for two days. When I did awaken, I was lying on a bed near a sunny window, with a doctor in a white coat sitting by my pillow and listening to my chest with a stethoscope. "How are you? Have you come to?" I knew that the doctor had seen me open my eyes and was questioning me, but just as I was about to answer, the white of his coat actually seeped across the entire surface of my eyes, making me suddenly so tired that I went back to sleep.

About two days passed before I woke up to savor warm sunshine pouring in from that window to the bed and across the whole room. A child again, sleeping in the sunshine, I found Tsuyuko standing before me, pulling the window curtain. I had seen that bright purple kimono she wore on many occasions and tried to smile at her but was very tired and went back to sleep. When I opened my eyes once more to see Tsuyuko, sitting there as usual, her presence seemed completely natural, as did the sight of myself in this bed.

Tsuyuko looked very serious. "Did you sleep well?"

"This room is nice and warm." I stared at her long eyelashes.

"Oh, no!"

Her voice shrill, Tsuyuko flushed scarlet from fear as she leapt up to make sure no one had come in behind her. "Be quiet! Nobody knows that it's you."

And then an old man did hoarsely call out her name several times from another part of the house.

Tsuyuko answered that distant voice, quickly leaving my side to wait at the sliding door. "Don't say anything." She looked back at me, holding a finger to her lips, and once again called out, "Grandfather, our guest has awakened. He can talk."

342   *Literary Olympians II*

I found out later that this Taniguchi estate belonged to Tsuyuko's grandparents on her mother's side. After leaving me at her house that morning, Tsuyuko had been summarily sent to this place.

"Grandfather . . ."

Her voice shocked me into recalling that night of the savage wind and rain as, for a moment, the memories flashed like lightning through my mind: How I had sneaked into the garden unannounced and the men had carried in the wounded driver, how all of us had entered the house, attempted to help him, and how he had soon died. I had lost consciousness, driven by my panic and my guilt, because I had been out in the rain for so long. A sense of chaos and confusion swept over me when I suspected that the grandfather she called must have been the old fellow who had brought firewood, towels and candles for the wounded man. It makes no difference what happens, just relax, everything will eventually work out, I thought, forcing myself into calm as I waited. As it turned out, the well-bred old gentleman who came into the room with his long white beard and warm smile did not resemble the elderly man I had seen before.

"Oh, you've come to?" he asked.

"Please forgive me for causing you so much trouble." Barely able to speak, I was aware of the bright sun and the pale red color it shed upon the old man's slightly drooping eyelids, but I just couldn't lift my eyes. The old man put his cold hand on my forehead.

"Your temperature seems to have gone down. Way up here in the mountains, there hasn't been much we could do to help you." He spoke slowly, apparently remembering something when he asked, "Also we don't know your name and so we have not informed anyone about what happened. I heard that you live in the mountains a distance from here, but when I made inquiries, no one knew anything about you. Of course this was all so sudden and so it's perfectly natural that we are late about getting the facts out. Where is it that you live?"

This was not an interrogation, I told myself, but rather his way of apologizing for neglecting to inform anyone of my illness. Relieved, I remembered those men who had brought in the driver that night and how they had asked me where I was from. To evade the question, I'd said the first thing that had come into my mind, that I lived further up the mountain. I couldn't very well stick to that story and so I felt trapped, but was there actually any reason to worry? If they eventually discovered who I was, well, that would be the end of it, I thought, and, deciding to feign ignorance until then, I calmly answered him.

"I'm from Tokyo."

"Tokyo? And what is your name?"

This question was perfectly natural but I felt cornered and, taking a deep breath in, foolishly replied, "Saijō Sanjirō, I'm a musician."

I definitely should not have chosen 'Saijō' since this was Tsuyuko's family name, but I realized what I had done only after I had made that announcement and closed my lips.

"Saijō-san, is it?" The old man did not look suspicious. "That's curious. We have a close relation with that same name. Well, it must be some karmic relation. In any case, let us send a telegram to your family."

"No." I quickly interrupted him, and blurted out whatever came into my mind, trying to smooth things over by telling him that my real home was in a very southern part of Kyūshū and I'd hate to have my relatives rush over because of my illness. Also, I went on, since my residence in Tokyo was only a temporary home while I was studying, four or five days' absence would probably not seem alarming to anyone there.

The old man shifted to other matters but then returned to the same subject, asking why I had come so late at night during that terrible storm. He had probably decided to inquire about certain things as soon as I woke up, but I had come to the end of my tether. In struggling for ways to get around his questions about my background I had become drenched in sweat and was at a loss for more clever replies. Since my fever made me tire quickly, I fortunately could, part out of real exhaustion, part mere show, bury my face in the pillow and close my eyes

"Grandfather, you leave him alone," Tsuyuko told him, "You shouldn't tire him out with your questions when he has just regained consciousness."

"You're right. That was inconsiderate of me."

I heard them talking as I dropped off to sleep. I had to trust Tsuyuko's clever ploy, but even so it was lucky that my peculiar illness made me fall off to sleep so easily. I next woke up the same day at dusk to find Tsuyuko sitting at the head of my bed. Seeing me open my eyes, she whispered, "My grandparents have gone for a walk."

They apparently went for a walk at the same time every morning and evening leaving only the old servant couple in the house. I smiled at Tsuyuko with my eyes, conveying all my thoughts and feelings. Bathed in the dim light from the window, the thick eyelashes on her half-opened eyes cast shadows upon her cheeks like the eaves of a building. The play of soft shadows about her lips and chin were indescribably beautiful, but since I still had a fever, my mad starving love for her lay dormant and only a quiet happiness overflowed in me like water.

"Thank you for what you did before. Does your grandfather know who I am now?"

"No, and I can't understand why he hasn't realized yet. It's quite funny."

Tsuyuko's laughing, playful eyes enticed me. Feeling tranquil once more, I entertained wicked ideas. Of course, I'd deceive them all, I thought, sensing that perhaps I could escape from the guilt and panic that had plagued me while I was unconscious. To see if this was indeed true, I started questioning Tsuyuko.

"Do you know how I got here that night?"

"I know." Tsuyuko gazed at me with that same playful look as before. "I know. I know about everything."

"Do you know that I was in that car?"

"Yes."

"That the car turned over during the ride back?"

"Yes."

I gradually became bolder, not fully understanding the change in my attitude. Although the wretchedness I had felt about killing that driver should have never left me, by then I felt completely unconcerned about the entire issue. A fresh burst of daring in my heart convinced me that whether or not the car bringing me there had had an accident on the way back, it was truly no business of mine.

"Why is it that no one else has realized this?" I asked her, "Anyone who came from the Odawara garage would surely know."

The garage people would have certainly remembered me shouting about where I wanted to go, but maybe my voice had been swallowed up in the storm and only the dead driver had heard me. Tsuyuko told me that the next morning, the investigators and people coming for the body arrived, but since I had already been carried into another room, no one saw me and no one connected me to that driver. She then showed me a page of the local paper and I found an article only three lines long in the local news section which said that a certain person from a certain garage had brought a passenger to Gōra in that fierce storm and so on. While I was sleeping the whole matter had been neatly settled. In this house I had become Saijō Sanjirō, the musician, a man completely ignorant of that accident. Only God knew about me, I thought, as I raised a shout of joy in my heart. The divine protection of a wicked god had surely helped my love escape those dangers.

Tsuyuko's grandmother and grandfather often came to visit my sickroom, but they did not try to question me as before and my health gradually improved as if thin sheets of paper were being peeled off, one by one. Tsuyuko usually sat silently at the head of my bed and when the old couple went out for their morning and evening walk, we warily burst into talk, like lovers who had been playing hide and seek. This game definitely stimulated us and also, because we were so pressed, needing to discuss everything quickly, we spoke of the most urgent matters, particularly our secret flight from that estate.

"It's all grandfather's fault," Tsuyuko complained, "He said he'd do whatever I wanted. But after he brought me here, he just forgot all his promises. I suppose he's afraid of my father. I couldn't wait any longer and sent you that telegram."

With a speed that made me dizzy, I thought of our life together after we escaped. I worried more about how this must not end in a repeat of the bitter experience after the Kabuki, than I savored other pleasurable daydreams. We should go to Osaka because there I had an old friend, the head of a famous revue, who would find me some work. In the direst instance I could always play the piano in his orchestra or become a comic. And as for my family in Tokyo, I would ask the lawyer to make the final arrangements for my divorce after things calmed down somewhat. This final item, bringing with it a businesslike quality, came to my mind only out of a feeling of obligation to Tsuyuko.

Once we decided to wait until I recovered and was able to walk a bit, Tsuyuko stopped coming to my sickroom so that it would seem as if we rarely spoke to each other. Sometimes I could hear Tsuyuko calling her grandparents from the parlor beyond or I would be able to catch the sound of her sandals as she walked outside my room. Laying there alone, I could always sense which room Tsuyuko was in. I had never felt so at peace.

"Is it all right if I come in?" Tsuyuko would ask, sticking her head through the half-opened door. We waited for her grandparents to go for their stroll so that I could secretly practice my walking. I held on to Tsuyuko's shoulder with one hand, starting to walk gingerly around the bed. After about five days I was generally able to walk on my own and we decided on the next morning for our escape.

"I'm really nervous." Tsuyuko put both her hands on her heart.

After the old people went out on their walk, Tsuyuko would

leave first by the mountain road in back and a bit later I would take the short cut to the bottom of the cliff, eventually meeting her at the last stop of the bus which went into town. If all went well, our bus would have almost arrived at Odawara by the time her grandparents returned.

Reaching out to take Tsuyuko's hands from her breast, I gazed at the flower vase which always held a single fresh flower, at the window from which the ice bag I had been using until two days previously hung stretched with air, at the larches outside and the far rising sky peeking through the sparse branches. And as my eyes studied the familiar scenery I understood what a great betrayal it was to flee with Tsuyuko.

"Why, I suppose even a thief has a better character than I do. But then I might have done something worse."

"I wish you wouldn't talk like that."

"But, really, I don't know what lengths I might go to after this. . . ." Although I tried to sound humorous, the words fell flat and my expression must have stiffened for Tsuyuko pulled her body from me.

"They've come back."

A bell sounded and a cane clattered across the stones in front, signalling the old couple's return.

"Well then, until tomorrow." Tsuyuko murmured this while standing at the door longer than usual. We didn't realize that those words would mark our farewell.

That night I couldn't sleep and in my anxiety about the next day and the events to follow I became even more wide awake. If I didn't sleep, I'd probably have a fever the next day, but the more I tried to sleep, the more parched my eyes felt and then my body, still not fully recovered, responded to suggestion, for I gradually became hot all over. As I lay there on the bed, it seemed as if I were going to rise up and float off. I tried to relax by telling myself that if I couldn't sleep, I couldn't sleep and not to worry over it since sleep was not an absolute necessity.

Gradually the light dawned outside and I heard the water being drawn from the tank, probably by the old maidservant who had awakened. I gave up trying to sleep, deciding to make myself comfortable, at least until the time came, and lay in absolute quiet. Soon it was almost eight o'clock, the time we had decided upon, and I got out of bed and went to sit on the chair. But I couldn't remain still from my worry about whether Tsuyuko was just then stealing out the back door and hurrying down the mountain path or whether she was at the bus stop with her little suitcase, waiting for me. Rising softly, I went to the bureau to take out my socks and the shirt which had been dried and put away. When I started dressing I didn't feel as sick as I had feared.

I checked outside for a moment, saw that no one was there and went to put my shoes on in the entranceway. I walked from the sunroom to the veranda, stepping down into the garden, but suddenly, perhaps because I had gone into that bright sunny veranda, I became dizzy and tripped, falling down in a heap on the brick floor. The maidservant had by then come in through the back door with a Western-style vegetable basket, probably just returned from her morning shopping, and, as the dizziness overcame me, I saw her run over to me, shouting.

"Oh, Saijō-san, you've got your shoes on."

'This is the end,' I thought, 'They've found me.' Cold sweat began pouring from both my armpits and I lost consciousness.

When I came to, I was back in bed in the same room as before, my mind in a state of confusion and filled only with garbled thoughts about the morning's failed flight. I was there, but what had happened to Tsuyuko? I tried to get my bearings by listening for sounds from the rooms, but, perhaps reflecting the feverish state of my imagination, I could not hear anyone. Soon the door squeaked open to reveal the old maidservant standing beside and smiling weakly.

"Have you awakened?" she asked.

"Yes."

I said nothing after that, waiting for her to explain or for Tsuyuko herself to appear. But while the servant came to my room from time to time to look after me in many kind ways, she always purposely avoided the topic I most wanted to discuss. Tsuyuko, whom I kept expecting, did not come at all, nor did I hear the coughing of the old man who used to talk to me sometimes through the window as he tended the garden morning and evening. Soon I couldn't bear to wait any longer and asked the servant about Tsuyuko.

"The young lady went back to Tokyo with her grandparents that day around noon." Only she, her husband and I remained in the estate.

Tsuyuko went back to Tokyo that day around noon? Then she had been handed over to her father? My strength gone, I closed my eyes while the servant tried to console me.

"But don't worry, any day now a friend of yours from Tokyo will be coming to get you."

"A friend?"

"Yes. A friend of yours will be coming. As soon as you get well, you'll be able to go home with him."

A friend was coming to get me? I didn't know what she meant although I of course realized that much had transpired while I was unconscious. They know everything, I thought, as I gave up my fight in the unbearable chill of that big silent house.

I wanted to return to Tokyo as fast as possible since I felt I had fallen naked into a ravine and could not escape the gloom that enveloped me for several days. But my body gradually got better, in complete contrast to my bleak mood. We should have waited a few more days before trying to flee, I thought, at least until I recovered to this extent, then, even if I had lost a night's sleep I might have avoided such an ignominious failure. It was no pleasure to look at the walking stick I had taken out that morning and which was resting against the foot board of my bed. The whole episode seemed part of the distant past.

One morning I was surprised to hear a car stop on the road beneath the cliff and further shocked when a small man dressed in a formal *hakama* was led into my room by the servant. This was my senior colleague and old friend, the artist Kusumoto. My mind had only started to wonder about why Kusumoto was there, when the answer became clear to me and I understood that more had been discovered by Tsuyuko's family than I had earlier imagined.

"Hello!" Kusumoto's friendly smile was his most memorable trait and he brought it forth as he looked at me, even then laughing sheepishly at himself for coming in such formal clothes, in a *hakama*. What a friendly, warm smile! In an instant my gloom vanished and I returned his greeting.

"So how are things . . . ?" He opened the window and looked out at the scenery. "It's good that you got better fast. What a nice place. I'd like to relax here for two or three days myself." Then he whispered in my ear, "What do you think? What about going back to Tokyo with me? In about an hour there's a car coming to pick us up."

We at last left the estate. Later Kusumoto told me that the maidservant who had discovered me collapsed on the veranda had left her husband in charge, then raced off to find the old couple out on their walk. It was not hard for them to understand the truth once they realized that Tsuyuko could not be found and that I, even though ill, had dressed and was about to go off. Suspecting what our plans were, they split up to search for Tsuyuko who was discovered standing with her back against a post at the bus stop near the bridge at the foot of the mountain. Since Tsuyuko had probably not been able to offer any defense against her grandfather's very reasonable, very just probings of her intentions, she was, without further discussion, obliged to return with them to Tokyo. I, not to mention Kusumoto, didn't have any idea about what had happened to Tsuyuko after that, but the very idea that she had been confined under much stricter surveillance than before made me curse myself for my powerlessness.

"But tell me, how did you know I was here?"

"How?" Kusumoto laughed, an evasive look on his face. "A letter came from Yotsuya."

After receiving this letter he had gone to the Saijō house right away and a man, obviously a servant, had come out to tell him in detail about the events in Gōra, finally requesting that Kusumoto pick me up. I filled with shame imagining how shabbily Kusumoto must have been received at the Saijō's because of his connection to me, although he himself said nothing about that.

Once again, I remained in my house and began my life of spending days without a word to my wife. I didn't go out at all and, as much as possible, tried to keep Tsuyuko from my mind, but this proved impossible. My love became like the snake shut up in its hole during the winter months—it continued to burn but showed no signs of life. Occasionally Kusumoto came over to visit, seemingly relieved to find me returned to my domestic routine.

"You look as if you've settled down," he told me one day, as he handed over a sealed letter from Tsuyuko. He said that when we were about to leave the Gōra estate, the maidservant had called him over for a private word and told him to give me the letter after I returned to Tokyo.

Once alone, I quickly broke the seal. On the very morning of our trouble, Tsuyuko had stolen away from her grandparents and in an obvious rush had written that letter. The style, so rough and nervous that I could feel her anger rising up from her writing, showed the hard battle she had waged with her emotions. The rough words also proclaimed tremendous desperation and sadness:

This is the end. It's good-bye now. You'd better make the same decision for yourself also. Please decide this. From today on, Tsuyuko does not belong to you any more. Tsuyuko is Tsuyuko and you are you. You are alone. Please forgive me for writing such a cruel thing, but if I did not think this way, I know exactly what would happen. I am a bad woman. If I were there, your life would just be completely destroyed. Do you understand this? You mustn't think about wanting us to be together. Now we two are nothing. Nothing. From today on, even I will be able to forget all about you.

I was so stunned by the letter that my mind went blank and so I just singled out certain words, making no effort to comprehend what was written there.

I am afraid for you. You say that you don't know what lengths you will go to next, but I know what a person like you will do. You will gradually go further and further down into the bottom of a pit. Even though this is not what I want, I would be the one to send you rushing down there. I don't exactly know why that would happen but the more we think that we want to be together, the more impossible it is for the two of us. We are digging our own holes. Do you understand? That's what I am afraid of. Do you know what will happen now? We will both die. But I am not afraid of dying. I am afraid of what will happen before. You do understand this, don't you? You see how it has gradually become impossible? You see, don't you, Jōji? But don't think that I am a coward. I must get things to stop here and go no further. I am all right. I am all right. I can say good-bye. Good-bye. I am going to America on the ship Tatsuta Maru, on November 4th. It's good-bye to everything. Please don't come searching for me any more.

I read the letter again. Maybe because I had read it quickly I had misunderstood what she meant? Or perhaps there were hidden messages which were not obvious at first? But I had misread nothing. My mind rose, then fell in enormous distress as the events of that morning came surging back. Tsuyuko had certainly waited for me at the bus stop at the foot of the hill to make our escape. Could her feelings have undergone such a complete change in the one or two hours between when her

grandparents had found her and made her return with them
to Tokyo? And what had caused this transformation? Every
answer I could think of wounded me like a battery of arrows.

Perhaps Tsuyuko had never wanted to flee. Maybe after talking with me every day, she simply couldn't get out of it and
had gone against her own inclinations in agreeing with my escape plans. Was she then breathing a sigh of relief at getting
away from me? That fiasco on the day of the Kabuki had probably shown her how incompetent I was regarding practical
matters. Maybe she had agreed to flee just on a whim, but had
soon lost interest. I kept on going over and over these possibilities, but remained unconvinced by each and every one of
them.

Perhaps she had just been forced to write this letter under
her grandparents' surveillance? And even if this letter correctly
reflected her emotional state, I could not bear to have her
leave feeling like this. I won't let you go to America, I
whispered in my heart to Tsuyuko whose whereabouts were
a complete mystery to me. Then I remembered hearing Tsuyuko talk about a cousin her mother had wanted her to marry,
a man who worked for the New York branch of Mitsubishi. Yet
I found myself insisting that she was just lying, to distance herself from me, when she claimed that she was going to America. Even so, with this one letter, Tsuyuko had succeeded in
camouflaging her true state of mind. The very words she had
written in this letter rang false. Was the Tsuyuko I knew a complete fabrication? I wanted to find out about this, I wanted to
meet Tsuyuko and get her to talk for herself.

For the second time, just as I had done a month ago, I became utterly undone by my search for Tsuyuko. An objective
observer would have concluded that I had taken leave of my
senses for I went to ask Oyae of the Yūyūtei in Shimbashi to
call Tsuyuko's house and make up some lie about why she
was calling. I would loiter about the front of Tsuyuko's house
in Yotsuya until late at night, waiting for a car to return and
then question the driver about what was happening in the

house. I spent my days in activities that accomplished nothing, and even I myself was not completely aware of what it was I was doing.

But since my search turned up nothing, it dawned on me that maybe she really was going off to America and that she at least wanted to see me at the dock for a polite, distant goodbye. There was no other way to explain why she had informed me about her departure in her letter. Since this was my last hope, I had to wait for November 4th, the day the *Tatsuta Maru* would be sailing.

It was a clear, cold morning. I called the ship office several times the week before, and took a train to the pier somewhat earlier than necessary. When I arrived at Yokohama, the ship was waiting, having already completed preparations for departure. The pier and the deck teemed with people, but I made my way through the crowd and went up into the ship, finding no trace of Tsuyuko though I searched from the first class promenade to the middle deck, from the salon to the restaurant. When they talk about a person's eyes getting bloodshot from a desperate search, that was my state as I stood in those crowds wracked by immense violence in my soul: No matter where Tsuyuko was hidden, I had to locate her. I found the ships' head purser and had him show me the list of passengers, but didn't see the name Saijō Tsuyuko anywhere.

"Do you have her request for a reservation?" I asked.

"No. We didn't receive a request," the head purser answered brusquely.

Soon the gong rang requesting that the visitors disembark. Jostled about within this scene of countless partings, I descended alone to the wharf. The departing ship's steam whistle sounded as if it was going to break the air apart.

"Banzai. . . ."

"Sayonara. . . ."

Numerous cries mixed with the music coming from the ship since people wanted to leave nothing unsaid in that brief moment. It was apparent to me why the music was playing on the ship: Every note cried out, 'Hurry up and find me!'

I careened every which way through the streamers, thinking that even if Tsuyuko were hidden inside there, her mother and father or grandmother and grandfather or that aunt I had seen at the Kabuki must have been among the crowd to see her off. This became my firm conviction, but perhaps because distress distorted my vision, I could not find them. The ship moved away from the shore so slowly that it didn't seem to be moving at all. The numerous streamers fluttered from the ship, and in a moment the people on the deck faded into the distance.

For a long while I stood and stared at the ship. Perhaps Tsuyuko had boarded under an assumed name in order to avoid me? It would have been easy for one young woman to hide among the crowds of that huge ship. Extremely depressed, I walked along the pier where already the crowds had thinned out. By then I was no longer assailed by the intense emotions that had gripped me when I read Tsuyuko's letter. Whatever happens will happen, I whispered, tears pouring down my cheeks as I pitied myself for my own hopeless inability to fight in the world.

After that I stayed shut up in my house and when Tsuyuko came floating up into my mind, I don't know why but I was convinced she was still in Japan. I just sensed she was still in the country, though I couldn't say where. Maybe this was merely a way to improve my spirits, but at last I decided to go out on the streets and look for her.

One day I was on a street corner in Surugadai going toward Meiji University, when I saw a girl with her hair hanging down loose who looked like Tsuyuko from the back. I was so astounded that I ran after her, about to call out. She must have heard my footsteps, since the girl stopped and looked back. No wonder I'd thought she was Tsuyuko, for she was the girl who'd been playing the piano in that room facing the back garden of the Yotsuya house. Her narrow shoulders and the play of shadows around her eyes were definitely just like Tsuyuko, but on her pale lips I saw a faintly childish and haughty smile. Perhaps it was only my state of mind at the time but the smile also seemed to speak of understanding and compassion. As I stared at her, I could hear that Chopin melody she had played each night. My disappointment was soon mixed with a kind of happiness: I had at least been able to meet a relative of Tsuyuko's on this street corner.

"Just a moment," I called out to her, "Excuse me, but aren't you Saijō-san's daughter?"

She silently looked at my face and since her eyes told me that she knew who I was I boldly asked her about Tsuyuko. "She never left, did she?"

"No, you're wrong, she left," she answered clearly. "She left on the *Tatsuta Maru.*"

"*Tatsuta Maru?* But I went to the ship."

A shrewd, adult expression came to the girl's eyes. "My sister left from Kobe." She then turned at the corner coffee shop and went off.

Her departing figure left me stunned. What did this mean? Did Tsuyuko leave from Kobe because she was afraid that I would pursue her? I felt like squatting down right there on that windy street. That was how much Tsuyuko was afraid of me? That was how much she wanted to get away from me? Was I supposed to believe that Tsuyuko, who just that morning I had felt sure was still somewhere in Japan, had that same Tsuyuko already arrived in America, been welcomed by her cousin and at that very moment cozily rode with him on the train to New York? The conversation had also made me unavoidably aware of the contempt and disgust Tsuyuko's family felt toward me.

The anguish grew and controlling it was out of the question. Of course, I didn't want to let this matter rest, but frankly, what choice did I have? Only one recourse remained: I would most likely fritter away the strength which still remained in me, the strength I had been drawing on to keep up the memory of the Tsuyuko I had lost.

—Translated from the Japanese by Phyllis Birnbaum

Roger Elkin

OMAHA BEACH

Seagulls cry alert: Mine. Mine.
Wave after wave assaults the shoreline.
Polished shells push explosively through sand.

Crabs founder like grounded tanks, or move
Amphibious and armoured, sideways and back.

There are carapaces and skulls, limbs and bones
Where they've gone over the top.

Starfish surrender arms for the cross of Lorraine.

Above, the sky is forget-me-not-blue.

And, beneath feet, the surf is whispering
Vergissmeinnicht.

Roger Elkin

CROW

Knows where he is going
Even if wind wishes pushing otherwise.

Knows wind will wear itself out
So keeps himself by feigning defeat.
Allows a glancing swipe, a sliding back,
A slight, slow
Dive
Only to rise up, and on, across.
Soars easily.
Glides perfection.

Since before the beginning there's been
Plenty of rehearsal time.

Where leaves, aflame, kamikaze down
He holds more resolutely;
Where rain drowns itself in its own pools
He floats to safety;
Where wind blows out its own brains
He's more headstrong, level-headed.

Not even threats of immolation—
Tumbled drenched spun-down—
Deter him.

Fear slides off his slipping wings
As lying on air, letting wind work for him,
Allotting weight between spread fingered-wings,
Balanced out from beak to tail,
He leans, he leans
Then lifts
And traffics arrowing on.

Blown on, is blown in.
Has advantage.
Was born here
Always to arrive.

Knows only continuing,
Knows where he's going.

360 *Hans Hofman*

Yan-yi

IN AN AIRPLANE

Ascending, I leave noisy earth behind,
Ascending, I pass through sea clouds and mountain clouds.
Ascending, I meet the tranquil blue sky,
Ascending, I enter high altitudes.
High altitudes are merely empty space.
My heart falls back to the busy, disordered human world.
The upper air is fresh, without pollution,
Yet indifferent as ice, without human warmth.
There is endless isolation and quiet,
Yet no disgusting jealousy or deception.
Although thinking isn't prohibited,
There is no heart-to-heart talk with friends.
No path strewn with flowers for me to walk,
No fertile fields on which to use a plow or sickle.
A safety belt binds me to the seat,
Willfully stifling my feelings like a jail cell.
Let me go back to the ground where
Grief, such as it is, claims half of life;
The other half is cheerful laughter, fiery hope
Surpassing what's in the sky, more beautiful than dreams.

—Translated from the Chinese by Edward Morin and Dennis Ding

Octavio Paz

ÁRBOL ADENTRO

Creció en mi frente un árbol,
Creció hacia dentro.
Sus raíces son venas,
nervios sus ramas,
sus confusos follajes pensamientos.
Tus miradas lo encienden
y sus frutos de sombra
son naranjas de sangre,
son granadas de lumbre.
                              Amanece
en la noche del cuerpo.
Allá adentro, en mi frente,
el árbol habla.
                    Acércate, ¿lo oyes?

Octavio Paz

A TREE WITHIN

A tree grew inside my head.
A tree grew in.
Its roots are veins,
its branches nerves,
thoughts its tangled foliage.
Your glance sets it on fire,
and its fruits of shade
are blood oranges
and pomegranates of flame.
                              Day breaks
in the body's night.
There, within, inside my head,
the tree speaks.
                    Come closer—can you hear it?

—Translated from the Spanish by Eliot Weinberger

Octavio Paz

PROEMA

A veces la poesía es el vértigo de los cuerpos y el vértigo
de la dicha y el vértigo de la muerte;

el paseo con los ojos cerrados al borde del despeñadero
y la verbena en los jardines submarinos;

la risa que incendia los preceptos y los santos manda-
mientos;

el descenso de las palabras paracaídas sobre los arenales
de la página;

la desesperación que se embarca en un barco de papel y
atraviesa,

durante cuarenta noches y cuarenta días, el mar de la
angustia nocturna y el pedregal de la angustia diurna;

la idolatría al yo y la execración al yo y la disipación del
yo;

la degollación de los epítetos, el entierro de los espejos;

la recolección de los pronombres acabados de cortar en
el jardín de Epicuro y en el de Netzahualcoyotl;

el solo de flauta en la terraza de la memoria y el baile
de llamas en la cueva del pensamiento;

PROEM

At times poetry is the vertigo of bodies and the vertigo of speech and the vertigo of death;

the walk with eyes closed along the edge of the cliff, and the verbena in submarine gardens;

the laughter that sets on fire the rules and the holy commandments;

the descent of parachuting words onto the sands of the page;

the despair that boards a paper boat and crosses,

for forty nights and forty days, the night-sorrow sea and the day-sorrow desert;

the idolatry of the self and the desecration of the self and the dissipation of the self;

the beheading of epithets, the burial of mirrors;

the recollection of pronouns freshly cut in the garden of Epicurus, and the garden of Netzahualcoyotl;

the flute solo on the terrace of memory and the dance of flames in the cave of thought;

las migraciones de miríadas de verbos, alas y garras, semillas y manos;

los substantivos óseos y llenos de raíces, plantados en las ondulaciones del lenguaje;

el amor a lo nunca visto y el amor a lo nunca oído y el amor a lo nunca dicho; el amor al amor.

Sílabas semillas.

the migrations of millions of verbs, wings and claws, seeds and hands;

the nouns, bony and full of roots, planted on the waves of language;

the love unseen and the love unheard and the love un-said: the love in love.

Syllables seeds.

—*Translated from the Spanish by Eliot Weinberger*

Eugene Dubnov

THE POLISH SHIP

Late one afternoon in April, shortly after school had finished, Vladimir's friend Sergei phoned to tell him about the arrival of a new ship in the harbor and to suggest that they go and greet it. "Greeting" foreign ships was an old tradition of theirs. Like all sixteen-year-old boys they dreamt of foreign lands; seeing strange ships and getting a glimpse of sailors from another country was their way of having a holiday abroad. Some holidays were better than others, as, for instance, when an English ship carrying one hundred and fifty English schoolgirls docked for two days in the harbor. Others, although also quite exciting, were not so exotic: all ships from Eastern Europe belonged to this category, as did today's ship from Poland.

In the two weeks that the ship stood in the harbor Vladimir became good friends with one of the sailors, a short tubby little man called Tadek. Toward the end of the ship's stay they would see each other every evening, and Vladimir would show him around the city. He did not speak any Polish, and Tadek knew very little Russian, but still they could understand each other because their languages were so similar. Sergei did not join them, as he had a friend of his own, tall and thin like a beanstick. He was almost twice as tall as Tadek; on the other hand, Tadek was almost twice as fat, and the two boys had endless arguments as to whose friend was superior.

The Polish ship was leaving on Monday morning, and Vladimir missed school in order to see it off and to say good-bye to his friend. Sergei did not come with him, as he was suffering from the chill he had caught down at the docks. There was a small crowd of about thirty people on the quay. The boy and the sailor warmly embraced each other and promised to write. Then Tadek gave him a packet of Polish cigarettes and smiled apologetically—he wanted to give Vladimir some keepsake from Poland, and the cigarettes were all he had.

Other sailors were already calling him from on board, and the shrill whistles of the boatswain carried from the deck. Tadek jokingly saluted to his friend and ran to join the crew. A minute later he was waving to Vladimir from over the rail of the ship. Everybody on shore was waving and shouting, and two girls standing by the side of Vladimir even had tears in their eyes. On the other side of the boy were two young men. They were standing uncomfortably close. "Excuse me," one of them suddenly said to Vladimir, "can I have a word with you?"

He gently took the boy by the arm and, with the second man closing in on the other flank, led him out of the crowd. Vladimir was surprised and vaguely alarmed; he even thought they might be local thugs. But thugs would never attack him in front of so many people, and besides, he had nothing of any value on him. Once out of the crowd, he stopped and asked them what they wanted. By now, both of them were holding him politely but quite firmly by the arms.

"We would like you to come with us to the harbor offices," the second man said, pointing to the building nearby.

"What for?" Vladimir asked.

"It won't take more than a minute," the other man assured him. "Just a little chat."

While saying this, they were already leading him towards the building. It would have been stupid to have started a fight, and besides, had they been thugs, the last place they would have chosen was the harbor building. So Vladimir obeyed.

They climbed one flight of stairs and brought him to a door at the end of a passage. Having unlocked the door, they pushed him in. The room was very small; it had no windows.

The man who had first approached Vladimir then spoke. "Turn out your pockets. We are members of the Young Communist League Brigade for Social Order."

"Why—what right have you . . ." Vladimir started.

"Do as you're told," the other man interrupted.

Vladimir fumbled in his pockets and produced a wallet, two passport-size photographs and the packet of Polish cigarettes. They went through his wallet and carefully examined its contents.

"Hmm. An Egyptian banknote. Just as we supposed. Who did you get this from?"

"Oh, this is Nefertiti!"

"From who?"

"She was the queen of Egypt."

"Don't try our patience too far!"

"Honest, she was. She lived in the fourteenth century B.C. That's her on the banknote."

His captors exchanged brief glances; then the bigger of the two said: "An Egyptian queen, eh? Foreign currency, foreign cigarettes, eh? Who did you get the banknote from?"

"Why, from Laima, our neighbor. Her Egyptian boy-friend gave it to her. He's on a course here."

"Go on. Why did she give it to you?"

"Because she had no use for it—that was before she got him to pay her in dollars. You see, it's not entirely clear whether the head belongs to Nefertiti or to one of her six daughters. But . . ."

"Dollars?! Just as we supposed."

The smaller man took a sheet of paper and made a few notes. Then he copied Vladimir's name and address from the passport in the wallet. "You may go now," he said, returning all but the cigarettes, the banknote and the two photographs. "You'll be hearing from us."

Vladimir walked back to the quay, feeling furious at this humiliation. The ship was still there. Tadek was standing on the deck, looking anxiously around.

"Where have you been?" he shouted. "Where did you go?"

"They took me away—they took your present from me!" Vladimir shouted back.

Everybody around turned to look at him, but he was oblivious of their stares.

"Who—who was it? I saw two people," Tadek's usually smiling face was now grave with concern.

"They were from the Brigade of Social Order," Vladimir said, straining to make himself heard.

"Those two behind you?" Tadek beckoned, as if over Vladimir's head. The boy turned round. The two of them were standing there looking very uncomfortable; by now everybody's attention was directed at them. They began to move slowly away, trying to mingle with the crowd.

"Yes, yes, it was them!" Vladimir shouted. "You there! Don't try to hide—let everyone see you!" Turning back to the ship, he once more addressed himself at the Polish sailor. "Tell your friends back home about what happened, and how innocent people like me are treated!" Tadek, looking very worried and gesticulating, opened his mouth, but whatever he was saying was drowned by the siren of the departing steamer.

Walking away from the quay, Vladimir couldn't help noticing his captors: they were standing aside by the edge of the embankment, watching him closely, with frozen faces.

His older sister was just about to leave when he opened the door of the flat where they lived together with three other families.

"Something incredible just happened," he said excitedly and told her about the incident on the quayside.

"You're an idiot! Do you want to ruin the whole family! Too bad father is away. As a Party member, his words would have carried some weight. But don't tell mother anything. She'll only worry. Go immediately to Alexander and tell him everything.

He'll know what to do. Wait—I'd better make sure you go there straightaway."

She picked up the telephone receiver and dialed the number of the family's closest friend.

"It's Vera. I've got a little idiot here for you who wants to ruin his family. Can you set his brain straight? Yes, the cretin's coming right away."

Alexander sadly shook his head when he heard the boy's story. Alexander had once been married to the daughter of a high-ranking Party official and knew how the system worked. Vladimir liked him because he was always full of jokes.

"Your sister was right. You *are* a retarded youth. That theatrical display of righteousness on the quay was very stupid, and why drag poor Laima into it? She must have worked hard to earn her dollars. But let's get down to business. They will undoubtedly contact your school for a rundown on your character. Who is your form-master?"

"Daniil Petrovich Knyazhnin—he's just great. He teaches literature. Last time he told us about Alexei Tolstoy—you know, he wrote that thing called "Bread," just to please the Party. Daniil Petrovich was laughing at how he portrayed one leader as parading with his sabre, and another one as waving from the steps of the train. He's the youngest teacher there—he just came last year. Before him we had this horrible old bat who always read her notes straight from the textbook . . ."

"Sounds just the job," Alexander said, motioning the boy to be quiet. "Go to him first thing tomorrow morning and tell him what happened. And don't forget, ask him to mention in his report, in addition to the usual praise, two things. First, that you are emotionally rather unstable, and second, that you are a very disorderly and absent-minded boy."

Vladimir thought for a second and then beamed.

"Yeah, got it. Well, I'm with you on the first one, anyway. But what's this absent-minded business meant to mean?"

"My dear boy," said Alexander and chucked Vladimir under the chin. "all will be revealed in due course. Just run along now—and make sure you read up the classics of Marxism-Leninism, not forgetting, of course, our constitution. Yes, yes, my child, our Soviet constitution which is, as everyone knows"—and at this point Alexander addressed the ceiling—"the most democratic in the world. Come back to me as soon as you've received the summons. In the meantime I will draft for you an explanatory letter—one should be well-equipped when going to an interrogation."

Daniil Petrovich's lesson happened to be third on the time-table the next day. After the lesson Vladimir came up to him and asked if they could have a word together. They remained in the classroom during the break when the room was empty. Vladimir told his teacher about yesterday's episode.

"Yes, I know. This is old news already. A gentleman called round yesterday afternoon, and I have just sent off your written report."

"But how could you? How did you know what to say?" Vladimir nearly cried in despair.

"Don't worry," Daniil Petrovich smiled, "I wrote all the right things. I said that you are a good and conscientious pupil and take an active part in all the right extra-curricular activities. I also said that you are very excitable and rather scatter-brained."

"That's incredible," Vladimir exclaimed, "that's exactly what Alexander said you should write. He's the friend I mentioned who told me to come and see you. Have you been discussing it behind my back?"

"These are the thoughts," Daniil Petrovich loftily said, "which distinguish our new type of Soviet man from any other in the history of mankind."

Vladimir didn't quite understand what this meant, but not wanting to appear a fool in front of his teacher, he pressed the point no further. Instead he said: "Daniil Petrovich, but why is it so important that I should be scatter-brained? I'm not really, am I?"

"Why, didn't your friend tell you? Ask him. But I presume,

374   *Literary Olympians II*

judging from your lack of interest in that other regrettable quality of yours, that you are already aware of the role over-
excitability is destined to play?''

"I think I am—it's meant to explain why I said what I did on
the quay?''

"An answer worthy of my best pupil. We were lucky to have
that infantile ailment on your school medical card. I mentioned
it in my report. It is known often to have undesirable side-
effects on one's emotional stability.''

"You mean . . . you mean my—what's it called—leningitis?
But the doctors said it had no after-effects on me whatsoever!''

"Meningitis," Daniil Petrovich corrected him with a smile.
"It comes from the Greek word meaning a membrane. But, of
course, the knowledge of foreign influences in our language
is not to be encouraged in a Soviet schoolboy. Meningitis is
an inflammation of the membranes investing the brain.
Whether it had any effect on you or not is immaterial. What
matters is that we can use it. You must promise me, though,
never to be so imprudent in future. It's also for my sake—as
your form-master, I bear a lot of responsibility for you.''

Four days later, fishing with his hand for letters in the deep
tin mail-box, Vladimir brought out a white sheet of paper
folded in half and stapled. He was asked to come to the City
Young Communist League Headquarters for a conversation
with the Secretary of the League, the day after tomorrow.

"A Secretary, is it? Hm . . . hmm . . . We have seen such
secretaries," Alexander was chuckling to himself. "My young
demented friend, could you perchance inform us as to the true
identity of this so-called Secretary?'' He was relishing every
moment of his role-playing.

"It is . . . it is . . .'' Vladimir desperately searched for an
answer, "not a Secretary. It is somebody else.''

"Well done," the older man said patronizingly, "that was
clear from my question, I should have thought.''

"Will it be, perhaps, some security man?''

"Much better. We're getting there. I'd place my money on
some reasonably high-ranking KGB official. Well, now it's

about time to act out the scene. Leave the room and come in when I call you."

Vladimir excitedly hurried into the corridor, closing the door behind him. Half a minute later a strange dry voice, bearing only a vague resemblance to that of Alexander, called him from within the room.

"You can come in now!"

Alexander was sitting behind a table, examining a thick file of documents. "Sit down," he said, motioning the boy to a chair close to the table. "You know, I am sure, why we asked you to come. We have here a testimony from the two young members of the Social Order Brigade who apprehended you and a report from your school. I have also now read your statement; you seem to be an intelligent young man. We'll have a little discussion in a minute. But first let me tell you who I really am. I am not the Secretary of the Young Communist League."

At this point Alexander broke off and looked at the boy questioningly. Vladimir didn't know what to say; there was an awkward silence which was finally broken by Alexander's loud groans.

"Have you fallen asleep, or something?" he asked Vladimir in a sarcastic tone.

"Why—what was I supposed to do?"

" 'What was I supposed to do?'—just listen to him! O *sancta simplicitas!* You were supposed to express surprise! Are you capable of doing that, or is it too much to ask?"

"But why should I be surprised? . . . Wait . . . I see . . . I'm not meant to know who he really is—I'm meant to think he's the Secretary. And I have to play along with him."

Alexander's face relaxed into a satisfied smile.

"Good. These people do not like it when their masks are removed. If they choose to reveal their identity, they must do it themselves. But let us go on . . ."

"Where were you on the night of March the 12th, when the Swedish ship docked here? Didn't you go out with your friend Sergei?"

"The Swedish ship . . .er . . . yes, I remember! We did go out that night—we went to the quay. As I explained in my letter, my friend and I have this rather silly custom of greeting ships. Both our fathers were sailors, you know—must be in the blood."

"All this sounds fine, but why, why, I wonder, this interest in things foreign? Egyptian queens, Swedish ships?"

"It's not just Swedish—there was also that Polish ship, and last year one from East Germany. These are not really foreign—they are like ours, they are brotherly countries. And anyway, all those ships are good for us—they bring us a lot of trade. As Pushkin said: 'All the flags will be our guests.' Trade is also good for world peace—you know, our country is the most peace-loving in the world."

The eyes of the man behind the table became distant. "Peaceful co-existence with capitalist countries is only temporary," he said. "Our ultimate aim is to destroy them. Didn't you learn this at school?"

"We did, we did!" Vladimir quickly retorted. "But Lenin also says that the capitalists will themselves sell us the rope which we'll hang them with—so we must trade with them."

"This is true . . . You seem to be a good Soviet boy . . . But I still cannot understand why you shouted all those things you did on the quayside. That was very bad—to abuse those fine young men bravely serving their motherland and to shame your country before our Polish guests. Why did you do this?"

"I don't know." Vladimir seemed to be at a loss as to how to reply. "I really don't know. I was so angry—the way they dragged me off like that—like a criminal when I didn't do anything wrong. I was only seeing off my Polish friend—and he invited me to come to Warsaw and to see all the new factories and housing estates there. And they searched me and confiscated his farewell present. I just lost my head, I was so angry. And they wouldn't believe a single word I said. I really didn't know what I was doing. I get like this sometimes—you can ask my parents."

His questioner looked briefly at the open file before him and nodded, almost imperceptibly.

"Yes, yes . . . I see . . . It's clear to me now that you are not what we thought you might be. We thought you might be . . . but it's no longer important . . . Nor am I, for that matter, what you thought I was. You thought I was the Secretary of the Young Communist League. But this is who I am."

He slowly drew from his breast pocket a small identity card with the letters *KGB* on it and brought it close to Vladimir's eyes, while not removing his burrowing stare from the boy's face.

Vladimir gasped in astonishment, "I thought . . . I thought you were . . ." he began to stutter. The hard steely eyes finally relented.

"Now that you know I represent the Committee of State Security I can be open with you. Let us forget this unfortunate episode. Your father is a Party member with a faultless record. We would like to offer you the opportunity of helping us. Your school record refers to your intelligence, your wide interests and the active part you play in the school's ideological activities. You could be of great use to us. You could start by working together with those two young comrades who apprehended you. You should forgive them, by the way: to err is human. Afterwards you would have the chance to move to more responsible tasks. You *are*, perhaps, a little rash, but you will, I am sure, grow out of this."

Vladimir's face beamed with gratitude. "It is a great honor. Thank you very much."

And then, as if he had suddenly remembered something, the smile slid down off his face.

"But . . . but . . . I don't know if I am suitable for such demanding work. My mind is like a sieve—I keep forgetting things, I always lose everything, and I'm always bringing the wrong exercise book to school. Everybody laughs at me. And last time I threw out my exam answers instead of the rough work sheets. I really think that I am not totally useless—and my teachers say that in humanities, which don't require that much discipline and thoroughness, I might go far. But in the kind of work you are mentioning I will—I may just ruin everything, muddle everything up and then everyone will be angry with me and you'll throw me out.''

The KGB officer again looked down at his file, thoughtfully drumming his fingertips on the table.

''I see,'' he said slowly and stood up. Vladimir thought he looked slightly disappointed.

''Well, well, perhaps you are right. Maybe when you are older we could meet again and discuss it. In the meantime you can collect the things confiscated from you downstairs in the offices of the Social Order Brigade. You won't get your photographs back because they have been used in the file which we have already opened on you. Once a file is opened, there is nothing we can do about it.''

He walked over to the boy and stretched out his hand. Vladimir shook it with enthusiasm and thanked him.

The officials from whom Vladimir was supposed to reclaim the cigarettes and the banknote turned out to be the two men from the quayside.

''The officer upstairs has told me to collect the things you took from me,'' Vladimir said in a matter-of-fact tone. The men from the Brigade looked at each other, and one of them cleared his throat uneasily.

''Here they are,'' he said, opening the upper drawer in the table. ''No hard feelings. You could help us, you know, become one of us.''

''Your superior has already broached the subject with me,'' Vladimir said with as much contempt in his voice as he could muster, and walked out.

Half an hour later he was reliving the whole scene before Alexander's table. Alexander chastised him for his incautious and self-indulgent behavior towards the two men—''the whelps in the kennels of the regime,'' as he called them.

—Translated from the Russian by Chris Newman

Larry Rubin

ON REACHING THE AGE AT WHICH
MY FATHER DIED

Is there any solid earth beyond
This point? The edge of the world, it seems,
Only air and dragons. Clutching his years,
I clothe my skinny bones with memories—
Tales of a sailor under age, oats
So wild the harvest fills my vacant fields,
The haunted classroom after final bells.
But now his charts are done, no lines remain
To point his course, just spokes of spider thread
I fling through blind surmise, zero space.

380 *Tu Zho*

Li Qi

ICE CARVINGS

Ice carvings look strikingly
Beautiful because a warm heart
Molded them
In harsh Northern cold.

It seems I came to know this
By the caress and courage
Of harsh winter. Soft water
Can stand up robustly too.
And life's miracle emerges
Through a variety of postures.

These melt when spring comes,
Melt without a sigh
After having stood so proudly.
Happily they come into being;
Happily they accept departure.

Let the north
Carve me likewise—
Carve me into a lively fawn
Into a cheerful fish
Into a peacock or a swallow.
Even though I disappear
One day, I disappear
Into spring's smile.

—*Translated from the Chinese by Edward Morin
and Dennis Ding*

Fou'ad Rifqah

THE FORTUNE TELLER

She points to a star
that shows you your other shadow.
You see in a single poem
the fact of God, the fact of earth
and everything between the two.

You see a dove
that sleeps like any vagabond
in crevices or rides the lightning
until it rests in a blue cloud
moored on its own seas.

You seek a new map.

—Translated from the Arabic by Samuel Hazo

Fou'ad Rifqah

THE ULTIMATE DISTANCE

You will not travel
the ultimate distance
nor witness the harvest.
Snow barricades your door,
and your silent fence confines
no more than poetry.

There are seasons in your body's cells—
seasons and gleaming shores.

Soon they will vanish
as will the sign that followed you
from towers to mountains
where you explored temples in ruins
and noon's high wound.

You will spend tonight here.
The stars will keep their distance.
You will not witness the harvest.
Snow barricades your door,
and your silent fence confines
no more than poetry.

It is enough to know
that there remains an ultimate distance
like a thread from here
to anywhere.

—*Translated from the Arabic by Samuel Hazo*

William Stafford

EXPERIMENTS

Part of the cost, we knew, was the pain,
but the budget didn't show that,
and when the animals whined we closed
their door quietly so the accountants
could finish their work and go home.

I wish I didn't know how the universe
runs. I whine now and then when the door
opens or the wind carries what is out there
too near the room where my comfort is.

William Stafford

DISPOSAL

Paste her picture back of the mirror
and close it. Let landscape be
the focus of whatever the next scene is—
that's a face you can try to forget, and the weather
visits often this time of year.

You can throw her furniture out. Let the rain
decide what to keep and what to dissolve
or slash into bits, a ritual forgetting
that the world makes happen in its own way
from this time on, outside or in.

Now slowly release her name. It spins
miles long like a thread along the wind.

388   *Max Herman Pechstein*

Juan José Hernández

THE ROOMER

Before the bedroom mirror, Herminia made the finishing touches. She straightened the wide belt which set off her slender figure and knotted a kerchief in a turban about her head. Then she went to the kitchen and set the water on for maté.

It was Sunday. Her husband and daughter had gone out early. As usual, they would take a walk around the square and downtown streets before meeting her at mother-in-law's.

Herminia hated these family dinners at which she scarcely ate a bite, despite the insistence of Doña Rita, who jokingly called her sylph or predicted anemia in no time. Her frugality offended her mother-in-law, who gave special care to the menu on such occasions. Aware of that, Herminia drank bitter maté—it took her appetite away.

While the water was heating, she brought in some aprons she had hung out to dry. She was without a maid and must iron them when she came home. Every other day she changed Graciela's apron for another of dazzling whiteness, starched stiff as cardboard. Sometimes her daughter complained—the stiffness kept her from moving naturally. But the girl would end by giving in just as she had with her school hairdo—at first Graciela would whine when she tied the bow which drew her hair so taut that her face looked oriental.

Herminia had no luck with maids; they worked long enough to save a few dollars and then left her in the lurch. It was not

true, as Doña Rita insinuated, that she intimidated them with
her exacting nature. Exacting indeed! She was not about to put
up with certain of their abuses—having the radio on at all
hours or entertaining their dates at the front door. However,
she did give them permission to attend a sewing class or the
novena and advised them to look after their teeth, often ruined
from sucking sugarcane. Ingratitude and stealing a blouse or
a pair of silk stockings were almost always the pay she received
for her zeal. If it weren't for ironing aprons, she would have
taken the GIRL WANTED sign out of the window.

Except for cooking, doing her own housework didn't bother
Herminia. A daily food delivery service, enough for her and
her daughter, had ended the cooking problem. Besides, her
husband, who worked in a refinery, came home only on
weekends.

Doña Rita even now never tired of repeating that the delivery service foods were indigestible and made from leftovers.
You're a lazy thing, she told her. Anyone would think cooking up a little stew for you and your daughter took brains. Herminia shrugged at the reproach: *Her* house, where she kept
the blinds down to keep dust and flies out, was not contami-
nated by the odor of grease which pervaded Doña Rita's house
and even her clothes. Her own smelled of cleanliness and floor
wax.

Herminia remembered, as if it were a nightmare, her first
months of marriage. At José's request she had agreed to Doña
Rita's teaching her some of her special dishes. When she got
to her ragout of viscera, she was close to fainting from horror.
Come, help me with the innards, her mother-in-law had said
after uncovering a pan of congealed blood. Unable to control
herself, Herminia hurried to the bathroom to dampen her
hands with cologne.

At that time Herminia had determined to make her mother-
in-law like her, but her efforts were fruitless. Unlike her sisters-
in-law, who praised the woman's proverbial temptations, a
silent hatred took possession of her when her mother-in-law,
who had just had breakfast, gave way to her desire for a slice

of watermelon or a bunch of grapes. She could not avoid closing her eyes at the moment when Doña Rita twisted a chicken's neck, and the draining of the viscera nauseated her. So she used her pregnancy as an excuse to end her cooking classes. These oh-so-delicate modern mothers, Doña Rita had said, smiling.

But she did not smile when she saw her granddaughter for the first time in the hospital. Convinced that it would be a boy (it was a tradition in the family), Doña Rita had knitted blue blankets and booties. It's going to be determined, like me, she commented after putting her glasses on to observe the newborn closely, carefully. As for its clothes, they didn't matter: Doña Rita would keep them in boxes in mothballs for the next one, which surely would be a boy. Herminia dared not disillusion her at the time—there wouldn't be another: So the hospital doctor had told her.

Eight years had gone by and Graciela was the living image of her grandmother—not only physically, Herminia thought, but also in her inherited cunning and gluttony. Often, when her daughter was in school, Herminia went over her room thoroughly, looking for candy which Graciela sometimes hid under her pillow or on top of the wardrobes, candy she'd bought with money from her piggy bank. Besides, like her grandmother, Graciela was enchanted with animals. Already on several occasions she'd had to forbid her accepting the gift of one of the dogs Doña Rita had raised; they trailed after her when shopping, they followed her single file across the patio, they stuck their noses between the rungs of the balcony when she went out for fresh air afternoons.

Who else would dream of calling a male dog Jazmín and a female Azucena, Herminia mused. She would never allow animals in her house, least of all one of Doña Rita's mongrels in which the mixture of breeds produced monsters. Was there anything uglier than a dachshund crossed with a Pomeranian? Graciela, however, preferred to play with a dog instead of those dolls Herminia had had from infancy, which had adorned her own room until the day she had got her degree and married José. They were fine dolls, in perfect shape, with real hair. Herminia sewed exquisite dresses for them and made corkscrew curls with a curling iron while Graciela sat by, stubbornly indifferent.

Herminia brewed another maté. The herb, without sugar, retained its strong flavor. Although the kettle was half empty, the maté was still fragrant and foamy. She thought it must be after one, they were expecting her for dinner. José, no doubt, would be staving off hunger with salami and cheese tidbits. Doña Rita, with her farsighted glasses, would spy the hour on the dining room clock; Graciela, taking advantage of being late, would pet a puppy, unscolded. No, she'd never let her daughter bring a dog to this house. Graciela could indulge herself—go on, as she had till now, scorning her precious dolls. And what of the habit Graciela had developed of hugging and kissing her again and again for no reason at all? What nonsense! The bigger the girl gets, the more unbearable!

And as so often, Herminia asked herself again what she had in common with her daughter, that girl so devoid of charm. To top it off, when Graciela had lost her first teeth, two enormous replacements had appeared, exactly like those which made Doña Rita's smile look like a weasel's. She had the impression that Graciela's birth had been a cheat. Through her daughter it was not she, Herminia, who had been perpetuated, but Doña Rita and the whole tribe of obedient males who venerated her—a tyrant of a mother with a heavy dark down on her upper lip. Could it be that with the years I'll become masculine, she'd say maliciously. What a problem if the dead should come to life!

Doña Rita had been a widow since her youth. When her sons married and she was left alone, she did not wish to leave her own home to live with any of them, nor did she accept any financial help from them. The modest pension her husband had left was enough for her to live on. Nonetheless, a few days ago she had told Herminia her plan to rent a room. I've rooms to spare, she'd said, and a few dollars would come in handy at the end of the month.

Except for José, who worked in the sugar refinery ware-house, Doña Rita's sons lived in Buenos Aires, but every year at Christmas they visited with their families and stayed at their mother's house. Doña Rita seized the opportunity to tyrannize her daughters-in-law, who had to wait on her day and night, and put them to work preparing those meals which their husbands longed for and which they never managed to duplicate in their own homes. The result was different without Mama's touch.

The behavior of grown men, who vied for Doña Rita's love and nostalgically evoked the time they had lived under the same roof, struck Herminia as ridiculous. She and her sisters-in-law were strangers to that happy past, the fortune of paradise enjoyed exclusively by Doña Rita and her single sons, but they had to submit. They had enough simply by being her sons' wives, a privilege, according to Doña Rita. Herminia thought perhaps that might be true for her sisters-in-law, who were common women without any education. In her case it was precisely the opposite—with all goodwill she would have dumped her husband back into Doña Rita's lap.

Despite everything, it was a continual relief that José worked in the country. Only on weekends must she share her bed with him, a discomfort because of his corpulence. To shift to twin beds would have shocked Doña Rita, who preserved her own bed as if it were a relic: there she had given birth to her four sons; there her husband had breathed his last; there too she would close her own eyes, obedient to the call of the earth. I already feel that the earth is calling me, she would say emphatically. But Herminia did not believe in that mysterious call. The woman would live to be more than a hundred, like the tortoise.

Meanwhile, every weekend Herminia repeated her wifely role with no enthusiasm: She waited for José to come home from the refinery; they went to a movie, then for a snack—or took a walk and windowshopped downtown. After, arm in arm, they walked back to their neighborhood along pleasant streets lined with orange trees. José, the heat as an excuse, drank a bottle of cold beer before bed while she, removing her makeup, suspiciously noted the invader's objects on the shelf of the medicine chest—the razor, the still wet brush, hair lotion. Then, in the shadows of the room, she waited frigidly for him to possess her, although at times tears of humiliation burst forth when her husband plunked down beside her and at once fell into a deep sleep. Herminia remained on the edge of the bed, wide awake, listening to his savage snores. Was it possible that he had a lover at the refinery? Her mother-in-law had insinuated as much, almost with pride. José with his lady-killer's ways at work.

Herminia brewed her last maté. Before leaving, she looked at herself again in the bedroom mirror. She raised her brows, satisfied with her image. Her beauty in dress and her disdainful dieting accentuated Doña Rita's sloppiness and voraciousness.

They had lunch on the patio, under the foliage of an avocado tree, which softened the violent noon glare. At one end of the table Doña Rita, with a fan, kept the flies from alighting on the dish of empanadas.

"Eat another, José. There are more. And you, Herminia, won't you try just one little one?"

She refused the offer. With the heat a little salad was preferable, or boiled rice.

"I didn't put much hot stuff in them. Try one. It won't kill you."

"They're fantastic," José said. "Chalk one more up for me if you don't mind."

"Don't stop, José. That's what they're for—to eat," Doña Rita said. Then, flagging her fan: "What heat! Surely the weather's going to change."

José sliced lemons, which he added to the pitcher of wine, sugar and ice. When he tried to fill Herminia's glass, she quickly capped it with her hand. Sangría, instead of quenching her thirst, seemed to increase it. Nothing like a simple glass of water to cool you off. Doña Rita and José, who were drinking sangría endlessly, were suffocating, steeped in sweat.

Not a leaf was stirring on the avocado tree. Stretched out on the patio tile, the dogs named for flowers were dozing in the shade of fern and palms whose roots threatened to break out of the great pots they were planted in. From the unpainted walls hung shelves of conserves and decorative plants, which reminded Herminia of the bungalows in the suburbs.

What was she doing on this patio, dressed so impeccably? She glanced at her mother-in-law; she had stopped worrying about the flies. She had her robe half-opened and was fanning her breasts, which spilled out of her bodice. Graciela, with an expression of rapture, was savoring a plate of homemade sweets which Doña Rita had prepared especially for her. José, his shirt opened to his navel, went on eating; between empanadas he rubbed his round, hairy belly. She wished she had never married him.

Almost gratefully, Herminia thought of the unknown woman who must liberate her. She was incapable of that passionate abandon José was seeking in her body, which he had intended to win with caresses and words, which at first left her indifferent and now exasperated her. But she would go on being his wife. She could conceal her humiliation. Only his repugnance was unconquerable, a stain which saturated everything, which she stubbornly tried to remove when she cleaned, almost to exhaustion, the floors of the house, the bronze door knocker.

"Mama, give me some soda," Graciela said.

But Herminia ignored her.

"Herminia, your daughter wants some soda," Doña Rita said.

"She's old enough now to wait on herself," she answered, bored.

It was then that Graciela, wanting to reach for the soda siphon, knocked over the pitcher of sangría. Herminia leaped up from her chair. Too late. Her dress was ruined. She had all she could do not to slap Graciela, who threw herself into Doña Rita's arms for protection.

"Be happy!" Doña Rita exclaimed as she wet the tips of her

fingers with the spilled wine and traced a cross on Graciela's forehead and her own. And José said:

"It's nothing, Herminia. You're not going to cry, are you?"

She's going to lose him. José is good, but a man's a man and temptations abound. He's patient enough with Herminia. It'd be tough on anybody to come home to such a death mask after working all day. Why should she live so bitter? There are plenty who'd love to have her luck. She's got everything she needs—a lovely house, French Provincial furniture, as people who have it call it, clothes to give away. I don't understand it—so much living room furniture with pillows, so much primping and she never has company or goes anywhere. Really, she hit the jackpot when she married José. Now she's annoyed she can't find a maid. As if she needed one. With only one child she could certainly get along without anybody's help. Be glad she's not too stupid. What would it be like if she had to contend with four in a row, like mine, who once one got sick, all got the same thing. Not to mention the work to feed four mouths? Though I was alone, I never complained.

Girls to hire there are piles of. What happens is she ends by intimidating them with her mania for waxing and polishing even the leaves of the plants. That's too much. The same with the child's aprons. Every other day a clean one. Stiff as a board. And hair drawn back slick so nobody will notice she's cute. What's she want? Who'd he turn to? Fortunately not to her, who may be blonde but tasteless as an asparagus. And what airs! Anybody would say that diploma she has framed in the hall is out of this world. She's all diploma, but can't fry an egg. Every day more wrinkled, skinnier. What pleasure can a man have with a woman who's all skin and bones? Poor José. He's smart to have a good time with somebody else. Why should he go without, a good provider and good-looking as he is?

I told him if she's pregnant, bring her to live with me. I've rooms to spare. This time, God willing, we'll count on a boy.

—Translated from the Spanish by H. E. Francis

Juan José Hernández

THE HEIR

So shall the king greatly desire
thy beauty: for he is thy Lord;
and worship thou him.
—Psalms 45, 11

All of us knew his reputation as an energetic, domineering man. Although justified, his reputation alone doesn't explain that respect, mixed admiration and fear, which Grandfather's presence inspired. As for the rest, how can you measure a storm? or lightning which blinds and destroys? I, who grew up at his side, can bear witness to his greatness.

A moment ago my aunt Leocadia suggested that we ought to send for a priest. The truth is Grandfather was never very religious, but I believe if he were well enough, he would approve of that measure out of respect for tradition. It was wise, however, not to be too quick to call the priest. Until his collapse my grandfather's good health had been as proverbial as his bad character. An improvement was not improbable. My aunt, incredulous, raised her brows, sighed deeply. "There's no hope," she said dryly. Then she put on her glasses, opened the *Anchor of Salvation* she carried with her, and from a page marked by a withered flower read aloud, "Let, O Lord, my body be trampled on, consumed by worms and reduced to dust in punishment for the pride with which I preferred my caprices and pleasures to Your most holy will." Such were the gloomy, allusive words my aunt read in her devotional beside the bed of the dying.

My aunt Leocadia, Aparicio and I were the only ones to accompany Grandfather in his sorrowful passing. With very good judgment, my aunt hid the gravity of the situation from her sisters: it was better not to give those heartless women the chance to reconcile themselves to Grandfather. As for Aparicio, what a marvelous example of gratitude to someone who always considered him one of the family! At the risk of falsifying reality (Aparicio was Grandfather's attendant or, if you prefer, his confidant), I never cease to wonder at the cynicism of my aunt, who used to call him, if I remember right, bloody Chink, savage idiot, not to mention other insulting names. Now she treats him with a certain deference; she chats with him and even accepts cups of herbs he prepares to calm her nerves.

I brought my dress uniform home from the Academy. I consider it my duty to wear it on this solemn occasion. On the side it will be amusing to aggravate my relatives' hate. They don't forgive me for being able to finish my studies in the capital, thanks to Grandfather's generosity. I am, without the shadow of a doubt, his chosen grandson, the only one called to carry on his name.

Grandfather's illness helped my aunt Leocadia to disguise as filial sacrifice something much less noble which she'd coveted since I was a child: to situate herself in this house and satisfy her curiosity freely. On pretext of airing the rooms, she violated the room with my grandfather's collection of arms and patriotic medals; she removed the tiger-skin rug ("a breeding ground for moths," she said) and hung it on a line out back, causing all hell to break loose in the chicken coop. She also removed the hero's portrait from the study and replaced it with a painted plaster Sacred Heart. I preferred to overlook my aunt's disrespectful behavior. It would be useless to dispute with her, protest. I knew her arguments beforehand: "No one's going to keep me from doing my duty as a daughter and a Christian." Didn't she know how little sympathy my grandfather felt for the women in the family? Those who know the details of his life will have no choice but to justify him.

By a cruel irony of fate, Grandfather's marriage only produced women: nine daughters, nine successive failures without giving birth to the longed-for scion. I imagine Grandfather's disenchantment each time at the town clerk's when he had to debase the imagined name of his successor by adding an ''a.'' My aunts Eduarda, Justa, Tomasa, Leocadia, Calixta, Augusta, Roberta and Argentina carry in their names the traces of Grandfather's inconsolable frustration. The exception was my mother, who was the youngest, Artemisa.

It is probable that my grandfather's insistence on having a male heir may have impressed on the face and character of my aunts certain austere characteristics which distinguish them from the general run of women but which, exaggerated in my aunt Leocadia, predisposed her to widowhood and mysticism. In fact, neither gargling with egg yolks and honey nor careful plucking of her eyebrows managed to soften her voice or confer femininity on her gaze.

My mother, on the other hand, was a woman of great beauty. I have a vague recollection of her face, but on Grandfather's bureau there is a portrait of her: she is wearing an amazon's clothes and is mounted on a lively horse. She died in this very house when I was five. That misfortune upset Grandfather, who then asked for his retirement from the Army and at the same time decided to live apart from his family, ''refusing the consolation and company of his other daughters, all decently married,'' as my aunt Leocadia always says. Grandfather kept only Aparicio, ''a mental defective,'' according to my aunt, who encouraged his cruel tendencies.

I've often heard from her lips loaded phrases of the kind which refer to my situation as a natural son or condemn Grandfather's taste for fighting cocks. I'm convinced that my birth was the fruit of a plan elaborated by mutual agreement between my mother and Grandfather: from then on both refused to reveal the identity of the anonymous planter of the seed, with no concern for the void the family created about them or the evil suppositions they made, and still make, about that mysterious person. Who had been the amazon's seducer? The portrait of my mother, so sure and arrogant, holding the reins of the rampant sorrel with tight fist, does not fit the image of a seduced maiden.

The problem of my paternal origin doesn't bother me a bit. Grandfather, with his moral example and his financial support, made possible my joining a much greater family, which wears the same uniform and professes the same ideals. I'm ahead of all the students in my class. Actually, the sober, disciplined life which I had lived with Grandfather made my adjustment to the Academy's program easy.

What would have been my luck if Grandfather, yielding to family pressure, had trusted my upbringing to one of his daughters? It seems that when my mother died there was a meeting, which Grandfather left with a slam of the door. Haughty, my aunts argued afterward: that it was a blunder to educate an orphan without a woman's care; that Aparicio, despite his recognized efficiency in domestic tasks, would never take the place of a real housekeeper; and that I'd never learn anything worthwhile from a bad-tempered old man who was satisfied to raise killer cocks and considered it natural to express himself in grunts.

Experience has demonstrated the error of such assumptions. If it is certainly true that when I was seven I broke an arm obeying one of Grandfather's orders and then on another occasion got pneumonia from practicing gymnastics on the roof, these accidents do not negate the value of my exemplary training. On the contrary, by jumping off the wall I lost my fear of heights, and since that winter I've been immune to colds.

My aunt Leocadia was the only daughter who did not go along with the isolation dictated by the rest of the family; and she continued frequenting him, a valiant act, but not completely disinterested, if you consider that as a widow without resources she will inherit the desert expeditionary's pension.

To appease Grandfather, who was an enemy of bureaucratic dealings, my aunt dealt with those annoying business matters which Aparicio, because of his illiteracy, couldn't handle. At the beginning of each month Grandfather received her in his study, comfortably seated in a revolving chair which creaked under his weight; he offered her a cup of coffee; then they set his papers in order and put them in a black portfolio which, when opened, looked like an accordion. In Grandfather's presence my aunt adopted an innocent, girlish air—she bit her nails and blinked constantly.

I remember that once she came earlier than usual and pressed me with indiscreet questions concerning my meals, Grandfather's private life, and my familiarity with the catechism. I was wise to her malice and said that Aparicio gave me raw meat to eat, that Grandfather was visited by a pale woman with deeply shadowed eyes with whom he played cards, and that the only saint I knew was the one with the sword, enthroned beside a stuffed condor on a shelf in the study. My aunt gazed at me, stupefied. Before going into my grandfather's study, she begged me to keep our conversation secret and gave me a candy, which I spit out afterwards in the spittoon to avoid being an accomplice to her meanness. Despite being a child, I was clearly aware of the abyss which existed between my aunt's pedestrian imagination and my grandfather's world. Until this very day she maintains that the weapons of his collection and the medals are a pile of tin junk, the tiger skin the hide of a wildcat, and raising cocks a pastime.

That Grandfather, Aparicio and I could live harmoniously in an atmosphere of virile austerity and sane camaraderie was a fact that the family refused to admit. Grandfather's authority, the order and discipline he imposed, was the secret of our happy life together. Mornings, when Aparicio played reveille, I leaped out of my army cot, ran to shower in cold water, and after a frugal breakfast attended the raising of the flag on a mast which Grandfather had improvised by using an antenna from an old radio. Immediately after, I gave myself up to the pleasures of exercising in the presence of Grandfather, who marked time for my movements with a whip against his boot while Aparicio went back and forth between patio and kitchen brewing innumerable matés. With the sagacity of a cardplayer, Aparicio interpreted the slightest contraction in Grandfather's calm face: a slight raising of his brow meant the maté must be sweet; a very rapid wink of his right eye meant he preferred it bitter; if he bit his lower lip, then Aparicio trembled like a leaf—it announced his irrepressible anger.

Grandfather exercised his authority with the help of his metallic voice, which had a paralyzing effect on people. To dispute his orders or mull them over was impossible—you simply obeyed them without back talk. Aparicio, always a very simple man, had no need of those lethargies of the intelligence to obey him blindly. His few brains did not hinder him, however, from being a consummate master in training fighting cocks. In his hands those radiant birds were transformed into beasts.

Money from fighting cocks and his expeditionary's pension allowed Grandfather to live decently and save a modest capital with which he assured my study at the Academy. Serious, fat farmers, owners of farms or country houses in the vicinity, visited Gradfather's breeding ground; they argued about who would possess those slender creatures which, when fighting, became fused in vibrant flashes of fury and blood; they admired the richness of the plumage with its golden, bluish reflections, the vivid arched ruby of the crest, the spurs sharp as daggers.

The magnificent plumage of the males provoked envy among the females, who, not so favored by nature, picked their best feathers to pieces. To solve the problem Aparicio decided to mutilate them: with their beaks cut off, inoffensive and grotesque, the females were confined to fulfilling the functions of the species.

It's a pity Grandfather got sick just now when he was about to crown his work and attend my graduation ceremony at the end of the year. Perhaps the imminence of the journey impelled him to increase the number of bends he practiced daily to keep himself fit—and the collapse followed. Last Monday I received a telegram from my aunt Leocadia, telling me Grand-father had grown worse. I made the trip heartbroken at the unhappy notice. When I arrived I remained a long time beside my grandfather's bed, hoping he would recover consciousness. The light of the candle burning on the night table projected the quivering shadow of his majestic profile onto the wall. I held the candle close to his face: his brows, scowling severely, accented the leonine wrinkle between them. I couldn't repress a movement of fright when I saw he was biting his lower lip fiercely. What terrible insult was he preparing for Death? I noticed he had not gone gray. His hair and mustache were still thick, dark. Grandfather told me he owed that exemption to an infusion of bitter roots which he had drunk habitually at breakfast ever since the time of the Desert Campaign and that he had obtained the recipe from an Indian whom he had taken prisoner on the border of Paraguay.

As could be expected, the neighborhood, which had been following events anxiously since last night, noticed the arrival of the priest. I've ordered Aparicio to put the crossbar on the street door to stave off the most excited ones, who might try to enter, eager to be first to pay homage to Grandfather. The cocks, behind the house, do not sleep: now and then you can hear a harsh, grievous crowing. Mysteriously the expedition-ary sword fell from the wall. Something tense, threatening, hangs in the air. It would not surprise me if a shining sword descended from heaven to watch over Grandfather's mortal remains.

Respectful of hierarchies, the priest, an old acquaintance of my aunt Leocadia, greeted her with only a nod, then crossed the hall to join me in Grandfather's room. I think my bright uniform and my fortitude made the greatest impression on him.

While he was taking the instruments for the rites out of his bag, he asked about my studies at the Academy and showed concern for Aparicio's future: Would it be an inconvenience to transfer him to the parish?

Extreme unction produced an effect we did not expect: it intensified Grandfather's fury—he gnashed his teeth, purplish patches appeared on his cheeks, a strong quaking seized his body and vibrated the foundation of the house. The priest, my aunt and I had to lean against the headboard to keep from falling. Aparicio rolled on the floor, terrified. It was like the warning of the eruption of a volcano. Suddenly Grandfather became calm. There were a few minutes of silence charged with warnings like those which precede a catastrophe. Then Grandfather opened his flaming eyes, shook his tumultuous dark mane from one side to the other, and "Spit on God!" he roared powerfully, and died. His lifeless head, sunk in the pillow, already had the dignity of bronze.

That utterance, a phrase common in Grandfather's mouth while he was alive, still resounded in our ears when we decided to forget it and replace it with another, simple and patriotic, which posterity will remember.

I asked the priest and my aunt to leave me alone with Grandfather to lay him out properly. His expeditionary sergeant's uniform and the insignias of rank were kept in mothballs in a bureau drawer. When I took off his undershirt, I saw that he was wearing a locket with a golden curl in it, probably my mother's, the proud amazon my Grandfather loved. I noticed too the silverish trace of the scar from the lance wound in his right groin and the contrast between the very white hair there and his very dark head. I remembered that my aunt Leocadia had told me with a slur that Grandfather's famous hair prescription was La Carmela water pure and simple. On another occasion, with equal perspicacity, she managed to make Grandfather's glorious past dubious by insinuating that the scar on his right side was not the work of a chief with whom he had fought, but of a surgeon who operated on a strangulated hernia.

I ask myself who will benefit by my aunt Leocadia's campaign to discredit him. It doesn't bother me if she believes in the babbling tongue of San Juan Nepomuceno or in the miraculous blood of some saint who makes the dead trees whose trunk they had martyred him on burst into green again. I think her duty is to defend such errors as my duty is to exalt the memory of Grandfather, who after all was my real father, to weave a crown of laurels for his exploits, real or imaginary. What does that detail matter? A factual history interests only those who are ruled by common sense or a common morality—pacific, gregarious attributes which the mediocre boast of. Somebody like Grandfather does not let details stand in the way of his purpose: against deep-rooted prejudices he made me his heir.

Although my aunt Leocadia does not know it, the society of spiritual brethren which she serves is the reverse of that other which Grandfather gave me for a family. The violent possession of the present needs the alliance of the supernatural, which has never disdained expressing itself in an authoritarian language similar to ours. Knowledge has it that before the wrath of the All-Powerful Lord of the Armies, the only fitting thing is fear, obedience.

—Translated from the Spanish by H. E. Francis

406 *Ma Yuan*

Bei Dao

MANY YEARS

This is you
Tired by the shadows flying, this is you.
Sudden light, sudden dark,
I no longer walk in your direction.
Cold has turned me away, too.
Many years before the icebergs formed,
Fishes floated out of the water,
Then sank. Many years
Sent me careful through the slow moving night.
Lamplight gleams across the steel forks.
Many years, this loneliness,
This room with no timepiece, and people
Left still holding their keys.
Many years after
Blowing whistles in the thick fog,
The train on the bridge speeds by.
One after another season,
It started from a small station in the wild,
Waiting for every tree to blossom forth,
To bear fruit, many many years.

—Translated from the Chinese by Julia C. Lin and
Tan A. Lin

Margherita Guidacci

AL DOTTOR Z

Fissando il nostro pianeta lontano
con il tuo rozzo telescopio,
ci elargisci benevoli consigli:
"Siete nel mare, salvatevi a nuoto!"
Senza capire
che il mare che tu vedi da codesta distanza
è un increspato deserto di lava
raggelata su noi come sui morti
antichi del Vesuvio.
E tu insisti: "Perché restate immobili?
Poche bracciate e la riva è vicina!"
Insegneresti il volo
a una farfalla murata
in secoli d'ambra?

Margherita Guidacci

TO DOCTOR Z

Gazing at our far-off planet
with your rough telescope,
you lavish kindly advice upon us:
"You're in the sea,
swim and save yourselves!"
Not understanding that the sea
you perceive from that distance
is a rippling desert of lava
solidified on top of us as it is
on Vesuvius' ancient dead.
And you persist: "Why aren't you moving?
A few strokes and you'll reach shore!"
Would you counsel flying
to a moth walled up
in centuries of amber?

—Translated from the Italian by Ruth Feldman

Eugene J. McCarthy

BORYSTHENES AND KATIE

"Jim-Bill will bury that horse," said Clifton Clark
Of Katie, the old white mare.
No one in the country store did dare
Question or challenge Clifton's remark.

"She'll never be trucked to a slaughter house
To be shot, and skinned, and ground into meal,
Or having died a natural death, to a rendering plant,
To be boiled, and melted and distilled
To the essence of horse and beyond.
She'll not be fed to the hounds in the kennel
Or stripped of her hide and left in the pasture
For hogs and vultures and crows.
She'll not be cremated with brush fire and oil
Nor stuffed, moth-proofed and hung on a frame
Like Lee's horse, Traveler, of Civil War fame.

A horse like her is hard to find
And not to be treated as ordinary kind.
She never fell, or threw man, woman, or child.
Yet she set the pace for every ride.
She would jump what other horses refused,
But none but a fool, horse or man,
Would try when she turned aside."

She'll be buried there on the west hillside
Whole of body, with unmarked hide
Not crowded or jammed in a ditch,
But laid on her side in an ample grave,
Neck extended, legs stretched for a joyful run
With Borysthenes, Hadrian's hunter
Who some 2000 years ago, his epitaph states,

    "Galloped through plains
    And marshy meadows
    Past old Etruscan barrows
    And chased the Pannonian boars."
    Lived long, and then
    "With his legs unblemished
    Met his fate, appointed,
    And in the field was buried."

412   *Anonymous*

Ramapada Chowdhury

INDIA

The military signboard read: BF–332. In truth, it was no station at all—no platform, no ticket window. A small section on one side of the tracks had been fenced off with shiny new barbed wire. That was it, nothing more. Throughout the day none of the regular "up" or "down" trains stopped. Only one particular train used to halt there, arriving suddenly one morning. We alone—the five of us including our Bihari cook—would be informed ahead of time just when and on what day it was going to stop.

Though not a station, with no daily trains, still, by word of mouth among railway men, the place took on a name. And we too, from that, used to refer to it as "Anda-Halt."

Aṇḍā means egg. On the sloping foot of two rather squat hillocks which crowded up against Anda-Halt stood a Mahato village where chickens wandered freely, inside dwellings and out. Off a ways, quite a ways, in the open-air Saturday markets of Bhurkunda the Mahatos would go to sell those chickens or their eggs. And at times, a choice rooster tucked under arm, they might go there for cockfighting. It was for none of these reasons, however, that BF–332 got the nickname Anda-Halt.

Actually, we could care less about the Mahato village's eggs.

Our supplier had worked out an arrangement with the railway. He even had his own handcar which, flying a red flag, would come rattling down the tracks, halt to be unloaded, then leave again. What was unloaded were baskets and baskets of eggs. Bhagotilal, our Bihari cook, would hard-boil those eggs the night before they were to be served.

But it was not even for that reason that we got the name Anda-Halt. It came from the burgeoning mound of eggshells piling up just beyond the barbed wire, from that hill of eggshells that daily grew in size.

It was always our suspicion that the initial two letters of the BF–332 military code were not code at all but merely an abbreviation for "breakfast."

At that time there was a P.O.W. camp in Ramgarh. Italian prisoners-of-war were held there, encircled by barbed wire and bayonets. Now and then a trainload of them would be dispatched along our line to somewhere or other. Why and to where, none of us knew.

All we got was the notification that at dawn a train would be halting.

After perusing the supplier's communique and pointing to the egg baskets from the previous day, I said to Bhagotilal, "Three hundred thirty breakfasts."

Bhagotilal would count out six hundred sixty and a total of twenty-five extras—in case he'd selected any rotten ones. Then, when they had been boiled brick-hard, he along with our three coolies would shell them.

And the pile just beyond the barbed wire got higher and higher.

Early in the morning a train pulled in, and immediately, from both sides, military guards piled out of the cars. With fixed bayonets, they stood guard over the prisoners.

The foreign prisoners, dressed in their striped clothing, one by one got down from the train, over-sized mug and enameled plate in hand.

The three coolies, who functioned as servers, had made a table out of two large drums turned upside down. Single file, the prisoners one after another stepped forward and received their breakfast. One coolie poured the coffee, one handed out two pieces of bread, and the third supplied each man with two eggs. That was it. Then and there the prisoners would reboard their train. The khaki-short-sleeve-shirt-clad guard, the letters I. E. on his shoulders, would blow his whistle and wave his flag, and the train would depart.

None of the Mahato villagers came anywhere near. Way off in the fields, sowing millet, they would stand up and gaze somewhat bewildered in our direction.

After the train had left, we would leave Bhagotilal in charge of the tent and, on some days, head off toward the Mahato village to search out fresh vegetables. In that rocky soil on the hillside they planted mustard, eggplant, and *jhinge* squash.

There came a time when Anda-Halt was transformed virtually overnight into a regular "halt-station." The little area beside the tracks and enclosed by barbed wire had been built up with gravel into something of a platform.

Then, not just P.O.W.s, but from time to time military specials pulled in and stopped. Even gabardine-pant-wearing, wallet-stuffed-in-hip-pocketed American troop specials. The military police would get off the train and pace about, maybe joke a bit; and the soldiers, in that same way, lined up, mug and plate in hand, and one after another took their bread, eggs, and mugful of coffee. Then again each climbed back into his own compartment; the khaki-short-sleeve-shirt-clad guard blew his whistle and waved the flag; and I would run to the major in order to get his OK on the supply form.

The train left. To where, none of us ever came to know.

That day too an American troop train just like the others pulled in and halted. The three coolies were in the process of dispensing eggs, bread, and coffee. Bhagotilal was checking to see whether anyone would toss an egg because it was rotten or a slice of bread because he got the heel.

At just that moment my gaze drifted out beyond the barbed-wire enclosure.

Some distance from the barbed wire itself one of the Mahato

boys, wearing the typical loincloth, stood staring, eyes peeled back. It was the little fellow, a small chunk of metal tied round his belly with a string, that I'd seen one day go clambering up on the back of a baby water buffalo.

The lad just stared in awe at the train. Or maybe it was the red-complected American soldiers he gawked at.

One of those soldiers, catching sight of him, yelled out, "Hey," at which the loincloth-clad boy turned tail and scampered off toward the Mahato village. That brought laughter from a few of the American servicemen.

I figured the boy would never come back.

None of the Mahatos would come, none of them. They would keep on working out there in their fields—stand erect and just stare, from afar.

But when the train chugged in again and halted, I noticed the lad with the metal chunk tied round his waist standing beside the barbed wire. With him was another, slightly older boy. Around his neck from red string hung a zinc amulet. The day I had gone to Bhurkunda's outdoor market, I'd seen heaps of them piled up on the ground for sale; and mounds of vermilion powder; and other amulets, of copper and brass; and colored threads dangling from bamboo poles; and glass-bead necklaces. From time to time I'd observed a peddler, the dust stirred shin-high, a shoulderful of countless sticks of beads, walking from way-off toward the Mahato village.

The two boys, eyes wide, mouths agape, just stood there on the far side of the barbed wire, staring at the American soldiers. In the gaze of the young one from the first day there showed a bit of fear. Knees bent in readiness, were someone to cast a reproving glance, he'd bound off like a spotted deer.

I was busily going here and there with form in hand. If the opportunity arose, I made small talk pleasantly with the major. A soldier, standing in front of the door to his compartment and sipping coffee from his mug eyed the two boys, then said to the G.I. next to him, "Awful!"

It hadn't occurred to me. But here these people were, working their fields and their threshing floors; they hunted with slings or else with bow and arrow; they listened to their local singers; they drank their rice liquor; and sometimes, taut as a bowstring, they stood proud and defiant. Their loincloth-clad bodies were slender, quite dark, and rough. But that G.I. fellow's "awful" was like a poke in the ribs. I resented terribly those two boys.

One of the soldiers belted out some off-color song, and a couple of others laughed. Another, who had gulped down a mug of coffee, fixed his eyes on the coolie and told him to fill it up again. The guard came forward to see how much longer they were to be there. A Panjabi, he spoke with the major in that perfectly nasalized way.

Then the whistle blew; the flag waved; everybody scrambled back onto the train, even the military police with their wide, red arm bands.

With the train gone, there was once more that emptiness, just that barbed-wire fence, like cactus amidst the expanse of dust and sand.

Several days later, another train arrived. This time a P.O.W. train, Italian prisoners-of-war from Ramgarh once again being transferred somewhere. We never knew where, never wanted to know.

They wore the odd, striped clothing. No smiles across their faces. Constantly on both sides of their train were posted guards with rifles at the ready. I'd heard when last in Bhurkunda that one of them had slipped into the local dhuti and *pānjābi* garb and tried to escape, but had failed. Being Bengali, I was somewhat more apprehensive than the others.

Once the train left I noticed that just outside the barbed wire stood those two kids, a teenaged girl in a sari a bit too short, and two adult men who had left their work in the field. After the train pulled out, they exchanged words, smiled, and chattering like a mountain stream flowed off in the direction of the Mahato village.

One, two, five of them—one day I saw as many as ten of the Mahato villagers who had spotted the approaching train, leave their fields and start running. Maybe they saw the khaki color through the windows and understood. Each day two passenger trains would whiz by, just like the fleet mail trains. And daily one or two goods trains rattled past. At those times the Mahato villagers did not assemble, knowing it wouldn't stop!

One day I went and asked an old Mahato gentleman to send someone to our Anda-Halt tent to sell us vegetables and some fish—shrimp, *sarapuṇṭi*, or *maurlā*.

The old man smiled—"Not while we've got work to do in the fields."

That's why I stared in amazement. At the very dark-skinned, loincloth-wearing men, the short-sari-clad women. Only the old bare-chested Mahato gentleman wore a shoe, on one foot, a work shoe of sorts, made by the village watchman. They had gathered and were standing just beyond the barbed-wire fencing.

By that time the train had come to a halt. The American soldiers piled out pell-mell, lining up with mug and plate in hand.

Two hundred eighteen breakfasts readied at BF–332.

The days had begun to get a bit chilly. Mist ringed distant mountains like a muffler. The surrounding vegetation shone a dew-washed green.

From a Yankee soldier's voice there came an expression of awe.

Another, standing beside his compartment, gazed fixedly in the direction of that indigence on the far side of the barbed wire. Suddenly, he put his mug down on the footboard, his hand going to his hip pocket. From his wallet he took out a shiny half rupee piece and flung it in the direction of the Mahatos.

They, for their part, stood there and gawked dumbfounded at the soldier, then stared at the shiny eight anna piece on the gravel in amongst the barbed wire, then glanced at one another, then continued just to stare blankly, confused.

When, after the train had left and I saw them silently turn and go, I called out, "The sahib gave you baksheesh. Take it."

Each looked at the other. Nobody came forward.

I picked up the eight anna coin and put it in the old Mahato's hand. He remained gazing at me, as though utterly dumb.
Then they all went away, without a sound. Not a word from
any of their lips.

I began to detest this contractual obligation of mine. No one
to keep me company. Not a single passenger train ever
stopped here. Only Bhagotilal and the three coolies. Lonely,
peopleless. The land was harsh and dry, so too the noon sky,
and my mind.

Even the Mahato villagers kept their distance. Now and again
I'd go buy vegetables or some tiny fish. They didn't come to
us to sell their produce, though they would walk to the Bhurkunda market, a distance of more than six miles.

For several days we got no news of any trains. All was quiet,
very quiet.

One day the little guy with the piece of metal tied round his
waist showed up and asked, "Won't the train come, mister?"

I laughed and said, "It'll come, it'll come."

And how can you blame the boy. Stumpy little hills, harsh,
dry fields—just to see a crowded country bus, one had to
tromp four miles through clumps of catechu brush. Each morning a passenger train flew by, not slowing down a bit. Nor did
the afternoon "down" stop, though we ourselves would come
running out of the tent in order to catch but a glimpse of the
blurred faces in windows. We'd be upset if we didn't see a
human being, didn't see some new face.

And so, when we heard that an American troop special was
due to arrive, we felt both put upon as well as much relieved.

Within a few days there first came the notice, followed a day
later by the military special. Out burst the G.I.'s; through the
line they went, taking their eggs, bread, and mugful of coffee.

All of a sudden I became aware of the crowd of Mahatos
gathered on the other side of the barbed-wire fence. Maybe
twenty strong, maybe thirty, who knew how many including
the knee-high wee ones. And there were the girls also, wearing their short, rustic saris, staring wide-eyed, naively. Upon
seeing them I felt somehow uneasy. I had felt even more un-

easy whenever Bhagotilal or the three serving coolies had wanted to go to the Mahato village.

There was no platform, merely gravel dumped alongside the track to build it up so as to make exiting and reboarding the train easier. The American soldiers paced back and forth, sipping on their coffee. A couple of them were staring hard at the dark-skinned folks from the village.

On an impulse, one of them went up to Bhagotilal, took out his wallet, extracted a two-rupee note, and asked, "Do you have any coins?" None of the soldiers ever wanted to carry around change. Before a shopkeeper or street-merchant or taxi-driver could return them their due, they'd say, "That's OK, that's OK." I saw it happen several times when I was in Ranchi.

With an anna here, two there, and some four-anna coins, Bhagotilal proceeded to make change. At just that time it came to my attention that from within the crowd on the other side of the barbed-wire barricade the little one with the iron object strung round his waist, giggling, had his hand extended, wanting something or other.

With no hesitation, that American soldier scooped up a handful of coins from Bhagotilal and hurled them in the direction of the Mahatos.

My supply form had been okayed, and the guard had sounded his whistle.

As the train began to move, I turned my gaze back toward the Mahatos.

They were still standing there, silent, just staring. Then, springing forward, the boy with the iron something round his waist and the fellow wearing the red string and zinc amulet about his neck pounced upon the coins strewn over the gravel, in between the strands of barbed wire.

At that moment the shoe-wearing Mahato elder rebuked them with a sharp reprimand. He did it so vociferously that even I started.

But the boys didn't heed his words. They both were picking up as many annas as possible. With mouths like two tender ears of shucked corn they grinned. The adults en masse were smiling.

The shoe-wearing elder, angered, spewed a stream of something in their language. And the grown men and women smiled even more broadly.

Grumbling to himself, the old Mahato gentleman headed off toward the village, alone. The other villagers went away chattering to each other, laughing merrily.

With their departure, once again there descended upon Anda-Halt a silent emptiness. From time to time I'd feel terribly depressed. Off in the distance the mountains, the mahua forests, the small spring lined with lime deposits out beyond the catechu brush, and the Mahatos' green fields. Soothing to the eyes, most soothing. Among all that, a dark-skinned, loin-clothed man.

But here, an American troop train would arrive from time to time, halt, take on eggs, bread, a mugful of coffee, and leave. The Mahato villagers would gather, lined up on the far side of the barbed-wire fencing—

"Sahib, baksheesh. Sahib, baksheesh!"

A chorus of many village voices shouting.

As I went to get the major's OK, I turned to look and was taken aback.

I saw not just the two boys but also two full-grown young men with their hands outstretched. Even a rather well-developed girl, in her short, rustic sari.

One day when I had gone to purchase vegetables, that very woman, smiling, asked me, "When is the train coming?"

Some days, for no reason at all, they would come as a group and just wait there, then go away.

By that time Americans, with three and four stripes on their sleeves, had taken handfuls of small coins out of their pockets and tossed them in their direction. They didn't wait for the train to leave but fell all over each other and over the coins. With the pushing and shoving as they darted in and out between the barbed strands, some legs and arms got scratched. Some tore their loincloths.

Once the train had departed, I observed them more closely. It struck me that half the Mahato village had assembled that day. A big smile on everybody's face; everyone got something. But though I searched hard, I didn't see that shoe-wearing old Mahato man. He'd not come. Despite his objection and reprimand that day, the two boys hadn't put down the coins. Perhaps that was why in anger he'd not come this time.

I felt good thinking about the old man standing in the field, working the soil by himself.

Our days—the five of us including the cook Bhagotilal—we passed our days in that tent at Anda-Halt somehow. From time to time a military supply train would come, stop, continue on. Mahato villagers would line up outside the barbed wire, extend a hand, and in unison shout, "Sahib, baksheesh, sahib, baksheesh."

Then one day I again caught sight of the old Mahato gentleman. Somedays, putting aside his work in the field and brushing the dust from his body, he would come hurriedly, angrily rebuking all of them. Because none listened to him, he would, with no other recourse, stand and stare through protesting eyes at his fellow villagers.

But no one paid any attention to him. Soldiers continued to dig into their pockets and, laughing heartily, fling fistfuls of coins. And the Mahato villagers continued to fall over themselves to get at that money, snatching and grabbing from one another, quarreling. The soldiers watched it all, amused.

Finally, for several days in a row I noted that the shoe-wearing Mahato elder had again stopped coming. I felt a sort of pride knowing the old Mahato, infuriated by the sight of them, had stayed away. Pride because, now and again, we too—Bhagotilal and I—felt just as irritated at their behavior. At heart, we were ashamed. Seeing their obvious poverty, the soldiers undoubtedly took them for beggars. And it made me sick at heart because of what they must have thought.

That day they were on the other side of the barbed wire shouting, "baksheesh, baksheesh." I was chatting with Janakinath, the guard in the khaki short-sleever shirt with I. E.

on the epaulets. An officer passed crisply by us, listening to their shouts. With a voice that sounded more like expectorating, he blurted out, "Bloody beggars."

Janakinath and I just looked at each other. Our faces turned black with insult. I couldn't even raise my head to gaze out in their direction. Inside I felt myself burn with rage.

Bloody beggars, bloody beggars.

All my fury became focused on the Mahatos. Even as the train pulled out, I, along with Bhagotilal, went over to drive them away. They, stuffing the coins into their loincloths, dashed off smiling.

The shame I felt because of them, however, I buried in a particular pride. That pride, as high as the mountains, appeared before my eyes in the form of the old Mahato man.

But that very day all the burning in my breast cooled.

I had gotten the news when I went to Bhurkunda to meet with our supplier.

Two of the coolies were pushing—actually kicking—the two drum-cum-tables out past Anda-Halt's barbed wire. And the third was in the process of striking our tent. Bhagotilal, giving the one drum a solid kick, followed up with, "Good riddance."

I was startled to hear all the whooping and hollering and turned to see Mahato villagers heading toward us on the run.

All I could do was stare at them in disbelief. Bhagotilal for some reason laughed out loud.

By this time they had all assembled on the far side of the barbed wire.

Almost simultaneously I heard the whistle and the other sounds of a train.

As I turned the other way, I caught sight of it as it came round the bend and hove into view, heading straight for Anda-Halt, khaki dress at every window.

We were a bit embarrassed; we were also surprised. Had they forgotten to notify us, the Bhurkunda office, that is? Or was what I had been told incorrect? The closer the train got, the louder that strange roaring noise grew. Not a noise, really, but singing. A little closer and it became apparent that the whole train, the soldiers which packed this train were singing in unison, at the top of their lungs.

Nonplussed, I glanced once at the train, then at the barbed-wire crowd. It was at that moment I spotted the old Mahato gentleman. In concert with the rest of them, the old man too had his hand stretched forward and was shouting, "Sahib, baksheesh, sahib, baksheesh!"

Like lunatics, like mendicants they shouted. They and that old Mahato man.

But the American troop train did not, as it had on other days, stop at Anda-Halt. Like the normal passenger train, it ignored Anda-Halt and sped on by. We knew, trains would halt here no more.

The train is now gone. The Mahato villagers, however, all became beggars. All these people who cultivated their fields—beggars all.

—Translated from the Bengali by Clinton B. Seely

Issam Mahfouz

WEARINESS IN THE EVENING OF JANUARY THIRTY-SECOND

At your door
I left everything—
the house-mermaids, the psalms,
the kites and paper boats.
I left everything at your door
when I left you
yesterday.

The deeper I go
the longer grow my hair and fingernails.
The deeper I go
the more often I see
your shadow behind me.

The earth revolves
like a winter or summer fruit.
Before my eyes, sun and autumn happen.
Before my eyes and the gold
of the whole world—
only you
with me.

Between you and me—a sign,
a theater on tour,
a silver sword,
a lost crow.
Between you and me—a rainbow.

Your lovers are many and cannot know me.
Your things are everywhere—
your trophies,
your medals,
your servants,
your shoe-shiners,
your plantations,
your compatriots,
your books,
your streets,
your statues.
I see them and forget them.

When demonstrations roar,
when armies are crushed,
when screams and words of justice fill the air,
I know you are near.

When there is weeping, when bread is trampled
and roads are deserted
and the Marseillaise begins,
I hear your voice

When I hear your voice,
when I hear the horns of hunters
I hear your silence.

When ships waver
and hotel sign-boards flash
and exports and imports cross
and throats are parched,
I glimpse your body.

When I undress before a mirror,
when I laugh or frown,
when I cover my hand with my hand,
when I drown in a mirror,
I see you.

When singing possesses me
on white evenings,
when I travel road after road,
I feel your breathing.

Even when I tire of talking
and the road is short,
I feel you behind me.

I lose you in days of work,
but still you find me.

I bury you in strolls
or in words
or in conversation,
but still you lift up your head.

I scatter you in laughter and gestures,
among plates of meat and vegetables,

among headlines and projects,
but still you appear before me.

I hide you among paper and letters,
I hold you in my arms
or between my lips.
Even in dreams
we wrestle the soft wrestle of lovers.

I crucify you with luck,
with all the numbers that lose and
win,
and you are near me.

I imprison you in safes
or in the boxes of my sorrow,
and still you escape.

I enter with you.
I exit with you,
and still you lead me on.

I betray you in public squares,
in cafes,
at the movies,
at celebrations,
in congregations,
inside shops and markets,
with people or without people.

I trade something for nothing,
and still you forgive me.

There is no way to escape,
no place, no time.
Even the planets are no refuge.

I stand on a summit.
Between the earth and myself,
there is space enough for murder.
Between the earth and myself,
there is time enough for hatred.
Between the earth and myself,
there is you.

Will you push me from the summit
with just a touch of your hand?
Will you push me?
Will you?

—Translated from the Arabic by Samuel Hazo

Dalton Trevisan

AN ANGEL IN HELL

Dad, I who hoped for a good marriage, here all I've got is grief. I left heaven and entered into hell. João's a real skinflint and I work from morning to night. Sunday I stay at home, it's really just like a shack, it doesn't even have no ceiling. Nice corn meal bread forget it, just refried beans real early in the morning, then straight for the fields.

Let me tell you, Dad, my life's nothing but tears. On my knees, I beg you, save me from this agony. It's shameful, a daughter of yours here in the sticks, with a stove that's nothing but smoke. I'm really sorry I got married, I'm so miserable I'm ready to die.

I was so deluded. The house belongs to my brother-in-law José, also the fields and the poor cow. What am I, a servant? Dad, for God's sake, save me, poor little me. Mom should throw her hands up to heaven. I can't wash clothes without a trough or a tub. I have to do my scrubbing in the wash basin and, what's more, draw water from a well sixty feet deep, the bucket is real heavy.

Oh, Dad, how awful that I got married. Now I see why Mom wanted it to be cousin André. I've fallen straight into hell. When it comes to work, João is like an overseer, where he is, the slave is right there, hand to the hoe. Is that a life?

I don't know if it's a sin, but I dream of cousin André. Daddy, João wants to stay here. José owes him and isn't paying up. João, the pig-head, is set on this valley in the boonies. Anyone who marries this young is a fool. Does cousin André still ask about me?

A cup with a broken handle, I'm forgotten off in a corner. The father has got to take his miserable daughter back. I'm really upset. Dad, do I have to clean out José's chamber pot? If only I had stayed at home and not gotten married. This I don't need. If at least it was a real house, this, the crumbiest shack in the world.

—*Translated from the Portugese by Alexis Levitin*

Courtesy of Santa Barbara Museum of Art

432   *Henri Riviere*

Janusz Anderman

THREE KINGS

Scales of rust cover the chain link fence. It separates the private garden plots from the crowd gathering outside.

On the mesh a few fistfuls of tulips hang wilted from last night's chill. On a wire that sticks out a faded picture sways in the short gusts of wind.

Inside the fence the lone silhouettes of gardeners stoop over as they rummage through the brush remaining from last year. At the slightest touch a cloud of dust rises from the dried stalks.

Bending over, the gardeners cast a sidelong glance at the crowd growing outside the fence. They are wary lest someone try stepping on their land. They look up with despair at the sky as they roll packing paper over their vegetable plots to protect the soil against radioactive fallout.

The crooked walls of the window-filled housing projects rise up between the gardens and downtown where the city is clashing and clanging with march music. On May Day it is like an Asian bazaar.

The people on the outside of the fence huddle together. The women whisper, point their fingers and for emphasis yank the bows of their babushkas tighter under their chins. A little to the side stand the men, serious expressions on their faces, shielding in their cupped hands a just lit cigarette. Emanating from their presence is a smell of alcohol and lack of sleep.

"I saw it plain as I see you."

"You saw it?"

"I did! I still can see it."

"In color?"

"Sure. Why not in color?"

"What kind of color?"

"What is this? An interrogation?" The first woman suddenly gets defensive.

"No. No. I'm only asking."

"Well—Don't you see it?"

"No. No, I don't. I was only wondering if you saw it in a certain color. . . ?"

"A certain color? What exactly are you driving at?" The woman's eyes narrow suspiciously. "Maybe you do see something."

"That's just it. I don't. My eyes are about ready to pop from my head and I still don't see a thing."

"That doesn't surprise me."

The crowd continues to wait on the trampled meadow. Around them is a network of molehills hard as concrete. The wind blows up scraps of paper which stick to the wire fence. Inside the fence stretch row after row of gardens and small sheds slapped together from old boards, tarpaper and plywood.

"*Bücher aus Polen,*" the crowd mouths, syllable by syllable, the inscription on a piece of cardboard tacked to the wall of an outbuilding.

"*Bücher,* that means it's German," several people aver. "That German stuff's good. It won't leak. They must have brought it back on a trip. That should be good to hold out the rain for a few years!"

"If them Russian atoms don't ruin it first, that is." They cock their heads to the side until their ears rest almost on their shoulders as they examine each shed with an expert eye.

The gardens touch on a brick cemetery wall over which can be seen a tangle of black tree limbs. The assembled crowd searches the branches with a nervous eye. "There, where that fork is in the tree, I see it!" "No, it's more over there, where that branch makes a semicircle. You can see the blue coat." "No, there above that shed—where it says *veritas* on the side. There it is. There is the miracle."

Meanwhile three old men stand far away on a sidewalk. A fast-moving parade fills the street, preventing them from reaching the other side. It is an impossible task, but they have no choice. They have a long way to go. They must soon reach the edge of town and some vegetable gardens which border on a red wall of uneven brick.

Women come down the street in brightly-striped aprons, their heads drowned in gas fumes. They are ringed by a group of morose gentlemen wearing polished boots. Everyone is doing a sort of dance step. But the folk band has yet to start up, and the procession moves down the street as if into the silence of outerspace. The only sound is the rustle of long skirts and petticoats. Then the loudspeakers above the crowd boom out: "The Siedlce Dancers are coming!" The hot as ever Siedlce Dancers. Men with two-day's stubble and red eyes execute their leaps and heel clicks in silence and with unbridled malice whirl their frightened partners from one side of their hips to the other.

"The trams and buses aren't running in the downtown area today," says one of the old men. "We'll have to make it to the miracle on foot."

"The trams will start again after the parade. We just have to get to the other side of the street. And then to the River."

"But we're cut off. They won't let us cross," says the eldest, his face turned black from the sun.

"How long can they keep this up?"

"Pretty long. They just don't stop. Maybe I'm seeing double, but it seems to me I've seen these soldiers march past before."

"Those women in the aprons also went by once."

"No, not those. The ones you saw were from Łomża. Also in aprons—so it's easy to confuse them."

"We're not going to get there on time. This parade will go on a couple hours easy. We won't make it. By the time we get there it'll be dark."

Back at the gardens the crowd scans the treetops through the wire mesh. They wait full of hope, but can't help gazing enviously at those who have already seen the miracle. The latter keep up a steady stream of conversation. They spew out details as if wanting to be assured they are not the victims of hallucination.

"It's a man's shape. An entire man."

"No, it's not a man. Just the head. A big, brightly-colored head."

"How can that be a head?"

"It's a head. A brightly-colored head."

"But a head can't appear by itself."

"What do you mean it can't?"

"It can't."

"Anything can appear if it wants to. If the head wants to appear by itself the head will appear by itself."

"A head can't appear. Only when the entire body appears can the head appear. Then okay."

"But where is it?" asks another.

"I see it. There where the branches make a kind of canopy. I see it plain as day. It's even moving."

"No, nothing's there at all. Maybe there's something moving inside your head."

From the glass walls of the apartment buildings people string out in groups across the meadow. They quicken their pace when they see the size of the crowd by the fence. The women break into a run, their purses flopping as they try and wipe the guilty smirks of disbelief off their faces. The crowd grows deeper.

"Maybe we can make a run for it," says one of the three old guys back at the parade.

"When there's a break—off we go."

"What do you mean break? They'll be stomping past till

doomsday. They don't even look where they're going. A parade like this sees nothing but itself. It just—"

A group of sweat-covered men sneak off from the parade. They hold the lines to a gigantic balloon which sways majestically above their heads. The men whisper excitedly. They wipe their faces and glance around until one of them comes up to the old men.

"Would you mind holding our balloon for a second, c'mrades? Just for a second? We have to, well, you know. . . . Pretty soon we must carry the balloon past the reviewing stand. If you could just take it off our hands for a split second," suggests the purple-faced man slyly. He sticks his hand inside his shirt and yanks it from his bulging neck.

Flustered, the old men exchange glances.

"How long would it be?"

"Just for a moment, and then. . . ."

"And you'll be back?" asks one old man suspiciously.

"You bet! We had to sign for this balloon. We have to return it after the parade. For years it has been carried past the reviewing stand. Sometimes at the head, sometimes buried somewhere in the middle, a kind of symbol. It was around even when Gierek was still party secretary, but a different route, maybe you remember. It was even in the parade earlier—under Uncle Gomułka. C'mon c'mrades, what do you say?"

"Well, we maybe could . . . It won't break loose, will it?"

"No way! It's only half full. Well, catch you later," the man adds heartily. "In a pinch you can always count on a Pole."

The old men take over the reins timidly. The balloon rocks, washed by the waves of army music. "Only be sure—" one old guy starts to say, but the departing men are suddenly obscured by a giant sleeve of red material which sweeps the old men with a hiss on their legs and shoulders. By the time the wind lifts the red fog from around them, the former balloon-holders are nowhere in sight—as if they have fallen from the face of the earth.

The balloon hovers obediently above the heads of the old men. The reins droop. The old men hold on without moving a muscle. As the balloon turns in place they crane their necks to read the inscription wrapping its belly: WE SALUTE THE PARTY CONGRESS WITH ALL OUR MIGHT.

An old woman with a canvas bag shields her left ear against the sharp wind. With tears in her eyes she looks at the out-buildings in the gardens, at the cemetery wall and the trees beyond. In desperation she turns to the assembled crowd."

"There's no figure of a man. No figure at all."

"No figure?" wonder the people in disbelief.

"No figure. Nothing has appeared to me at all."

"How can it not appear when it was on television. There was a figure then."

"Ah, television, television. On television all the figures in the world can appear, but nothing seems to want to appear to me."

"It has to appear," they reassure the disappointed woman.

"Maybe it's because of this radioactive wind. Maybe it got erased."

The crowd swells. Newcomers mill around uneasily. "Where is the miracle?" they ask, "where is the miracle?" "There, above that building. See the coat?" the local menfolk patiently point out in their threadbare jackets and upturned collars.

"What are we going to do with this balloon," worry the three old men. "Those other guys sure have made themselves scarce."

"They have to show up. After all, they signed for it. They have to get their deposit back."

"They won't come back. They just tricked us with this balloon."

"We sure can't take it to the gardens with us."

"Take it with us? On the tram?"

"Maybe we could give it to somebody?"

"But who would take it?"

Their words are drowned in the resounding and threatening

strains of parade songs. Only the cries of the announcer pierce through the uproar. The streets fill with an unruly band of students in vocational school caps. They are surrounded by a convoy of teachers who constantly count them, raising up on their toes and stretching their necks painfully. A few boys dodge the attentive gaze of their instructors and huddle near the curb, obviously plotting something. With deft little movements their fingers roll up the canvas flags on the flagpoles they have been carrying in the parade. They use the tips of the poles to fish around inside the grating to a storm sewer. Finally they let go. The red-shrouded poles drop to the sewer waters where they float like giant bobbers. Meanwhile the boys retreat to the sidewalk, squatting in the crowd to try and duck their chaperone's notice.

"Put on Radio Free Europe," says one of the students. "Maybe they'll give something about the cloud."

Another boy pulls a small transistor from his pocket. He twists the radio dial searching for voices amidst the static. Over the speaker comes a tête-à-tête between a man and woman. The boys bend down to listen. "There's only one way for a woman to have any privacy," says the man, "and that's to be a councilwoman. A councilwoman can be seen in a cafe with a fellow councilman and no one's the wiser. There's no room for gossip." "You jackass," chide the disappointed boys. "That's not Radio Free Europe!" The owner goes back to twisting the radio knob until he finally tunes in a broadcast of the parade. A gust of wind jerks the balloon. The old men hold on with all their strength, their fingers clinging to the slippery line.

"I just saw something. Another figure. More to the side. Over there above that shed. It gave off these golden waves of light. And it had chestnut-colored hair. Just like yours." The woman telling the story begins to finger the hair of the woman standing next to her. "Chestnut brown and hanging down to here." She slaps the woman between her shoulder blades. "He had a beard and a solemn look on his face. As if he was prepared for the worst. As if he knew what was in store. And there were those golden waves of light. No, wait, I said that already—''

''I saw the same thing. An entire figure stood in the branches. It was enough to take my breath away. I always—''

''I'm just not sure. Maybe in the evening I could see. But in the day I can't spot a thing. Maybe this radioactivity has affected my eyes—''

''I see it when it moves. Sometimes this way, sometimes that—''

From the windows of the apartment buildings people gaze out with binoculars. Sometimes they train them on the clumps of trees beyond the cemetery wall. Sometimes they point them at the sky from which sifts the silent, invisible dust of Chernobyl.

''O sirs! O veterans with the balloon,'' says a woman in a flowing coat as she rushes up to the three old men and fixes them with a vacant stare.

''Have you come for the balloon?'' they ask hopefully. ''Here it is. It's still in one piece.''

''Who cares about the balloon,'' says the woman in a huff. ''We have to go on the radio. We have to announce every hour about the peace conference the day after tomorrow. We have to bring this Chernobyl issue up in a full session of Parliament. We have to form a committee right away to broadcast the news hourly. A peace conference and a full session of Parliament. But I can't seem to come up with a committee.''

Dumbfounded the three old men look at the woman. With their hands behind their backs they hold onto the balloon.

''Yesterday I talked with a group from Cuba. They were full of understanding. So it's to be a full session of Parliament. And you can be part of the committee. You can represent the veterans.''

''But the police,'' says one old man uncertainly.

''Are you afraid of the police?''

''I am,'' the old man answers truthfully.

''But I'm not, and I'm only a woman.''

"Please don't be offended, but maybe you don't know life like I do. And besides, we don't have time. We have to get to Praga. To the vegetable gardens."

"What good is that? Travelling around in circles. If you go there you'll have to come back. I'm off right now to the hotel. We have two hotels at our disposal. I have to look up the delegation from Cuba. They will take part in the peace conference for sure. They promised. Very nice people. Very supportive. Here. Sign this declaration."

"I'm not signing anything," says an old man jerking the line of the balloon.

"Well, would you at least have some iodine you can give me," asks the woman disappointedly. "To offset the radiation?" But before they can reply she scoots off towards a group of steelworkers approaching in their traditional costumes.

"I look and look until my eyes fall out and still nothing," moans a woman who turns around from the fence in frustration. She suddenly walks up to a woman standing nearby and grabs a fistful of her white hair. "My, but isn't this fluffy! Beautiful," she says as she poofs the petrified woman's hair and bends her ears behind her head. "Fluffy as can be. It flies right through your fingers. For years I kept some lemon in a jar and washed my hair in it, but still my hair kept going thin. But yours is so beautiful. It's important to add a little spirits to the egg yolk to keep it from clotting and sticking on your hair. But now it's too late for that. Your hair will drop out from this cloud like nobody's business. Then we'll both be in the same boat."

"But I tell you I did see it," the other woman desperately defends herself. "And in general if someone believes in a miracle, he doesn't have to see it. He just has to believe he sees it."

"Maybe so, maybe not," says a thoughtful voice. "Nowadays the entire nation is distrustful. Used to be at a miracle that people'd lay face down on the bare ground with their arms stretched to the side like a cross. But now people don't know what they want."

"Because nowadays it's beyond people's understanding," say others diplomatically before turning back towards the brick wall.

"This will be the thirteenth miracle after the war," shouts one old man over the noise of the brass band. "My fingers are about to give out from holding this balloon."

"Thirteenth? Maybe this will be unlucky for the people waiting," says another old man pointing his chin off to the side.

"Thirteen. In '49 in Lubin. In '57 on Kossak Square in Krakow. In '58 in Chełmek," counts out the third.

"In '59 the steeple shone on the church in Muranów. The one that had just been painted," continues the second.

"In '65 in Zabłudowa a girl was the only witness. Her mother was arrested for false testimony."

"In '71 near Radzymin. In '74 in Piotrków Kujawski. In '75 in Wrocław."

"In '81 in Oleck."

"In '84 in Oław."

"Also in '84 in Karczew."

"Lately there's been a rash of them."

"And we've never been late. And now? With this balloon?"

Down the street snakes a file of young nurses in their white caps. The young women glance around uneasily and try to hide behind the backs of each other, prey to a continual nervous laugh they cannot control. Every few feet, at the command of their leader, the women change step, jumping in place as if seized by the hiccups.

A few yards from the old men a young guy comes to a halt, his right arm tucked under his left armpit. He sizes them up with a professional eye for a few moments, then whispers to the fellow next to him. "Some stockings for the little lady?" He wrinkles the cellophane under his jacket suggestively.

"Who has seen this miracle anyway," demand several members of the crowd and turn their exhausted eyes from the cemetery wall.

"What do you mean seen it? Everyone has seen it."

"I even have a snapshot."

"Could you please show it to us?"

"I don't have it with me. My sister has it. It's in color."

"If it's in color, then let's see it."

"I told you I don't have it. It's at my sister's. Close up you can't see much. But from far away it's clear as day. You just have to hold it out at arm's length. It's there in pink and blue."

"And maybe you're just getting carried away with this photograph of yours."

"As you wish," the woman sniffs. "But please don't make fun of miracles."

A noxious cloud hovers over the meadow. The people's eyes water. From the concrete walls of the apartment buildings reach the smells of cooking and the roar of tv sets broadcasting the parade.

A neighborhood cop wades through the meadow in the direction of the crowd. With his gloved right hand he supports the bottom of the duty satchel hanging from his right shoulder. The waves of noise from the transmitted parade push him along, not allowing a hitch in his slow but sure stride.

He goes up to the wall of backs and stops there undecided. He opens his mouth to say something but quickly closes it. He steps over to a nearby molehill and rakes it with the toe of his shoe. He bends down and slowly straightens up.

In his fingers he holds an inkpen covered with dried mud. He shakes off the dirt and looks around him to see if anybody is watching. He blows on the ball-point and sticks out his left palm to see if the pen writes. Only then does he pull off his left leather glove and start to scribble something on his naked hand.

He starts to speak, his eyes cemented to his palm as if he were reading an official announcement.

"People. Now why do you want to gather here for? Go on home. Otherwise there'll be trouble."

Those at the back of the crowd turn around and look at the lone figure standing opposite. They gaze at him blandly, without fear.

"People. There's nothing here. There never was. Ever since

I've been stationed here I've never seen a thing," the cop goes on uncertainly, his eyes still glued to his palm. "There's nothing going to appear over there."

"It doesn't appear to the sinful," carries a voice from the crowd.

"Or to the unrighteous," adds another.

A short hush falls. Then a murmur rumbles through the crowd, the voices growing stronger and more sure of themselves. People look at each other in amazement as if struck by a revelation.

"Miracles more likely appear to the unrighteous. The righteous don't need to be shown. Only the unrighteous. Maybe it will help them to change their ways."

"People. It's better to go home. Don't cluster in a group like this. Miracles don't appear at your beck and call," the neighborhood policeman says without conviction. He scrutinizes the crowns of the trees above the cemetery wall.

Meanwhile the hands of the old men are about to fall off. The gusts of wind and waves of marching music jerk the balloon this way and that.

One old man pulls a pack of filter cigarettes from his pocket and hands them to his friends. Each takes a cigarette with his free hand. Their heads bend down over the thin flames of a match. No one knows when the reins slip from their numbed hands. The balloon jumps up and to the side. A group of young girls with snare drums strapped to their waists pause with their sticks in mid-air. With wide-open eyes they trace the uncertain flight. Suddenly the wind grabs the balloon and twists it into a banner carried by two rail station workers. The skin of the balloon ruptures on the tip of one of the poles. A stream of air roars out and tears from the hands of the workers the entire banner with its slogan: "POLISH RAILWORKERS SAY NO TO AMERICAN MISSILES." The balloon starts to swerve in all directions, wreaking havoc with the nearby marchers.

Women squeal and hold down the ends of their rainbow dresses. The two railyard workers clamp their caps on top their heads as they bend down to gather from the asphalt twisted construction paper letters that have fallen from their toppled banner. Meanwhile the flaccid balloon quivers in the gutter like a jellyfish.

The space around the worried old men suddenly swarms with young officers. They surround the old men and grab their arms. The sound of barked commands and half-finished sentences floods the air. "Inciting the crowd." "Disturbing the May Day ceremony." The three old men can't understand. They look around helplessly as they are led off to a gray paddy wagon waiting unobtrusively off to the side.

"We have to get to the gardens," one starts to say but falls silent.

"You'll have your own gardens," says a derisive voice. "You'll each have your own garden to tend."

The three old men stand and look up at the gaping doors of the paddy wagon. They know it is too high for them to jump in unassisted. They want to say something, but their ears are filled with the brisk words of one of the officers.

"Well, hop into our discoteque. Who do you think you are? The three kings?"

—Translated from the Polish by Daniel Bourne

Yang Lian

海边的孩子

—— 一本新诗集的序言

我不知道那个孩子是谁
那个在海边做着快乐游戏的孩子
—— 沙土城堡和幻想的主人
　　　草帽遮住眼睛
　　　明朗地笑着
　　　和太阳一同漫步
我不知道那个孩子是谁……

他那衣襟前别着蓝色的手帕
蓝蓝的，象写上生活全部奥秘的睛空
—— 他的脸就是一个美丽的梦
　　　喃喃自语着
　　　一个人来到这世界的海滨
　　　为了与波涛谈话
我不知道那个孩子是谁……

我不知道那小篮子般的心里
是不是也盛着另外的回忆
—— 大海铺开淡淡的光芒
　　　把笑声藏进永恒的谜语
　　　可即使远处有暴风雨又怎样呢
　　　世界依然是值得孩子们笑的
我不知道那个孩子是谁……

Yang Lian

BOY BY THE SEA

I don't know who that boy is:
He's playing an intriguing game by the sea.
    He's owner of a sand castle and daydreams!
    A straw hat shading his eyes,
    he laughs robustly
    as he strolls together with the sun.
I don't know who that boy is.

The handkerchief pinned to his shirt front
is blue as the sky emblazoned with life's mysteries.
    His face is a beautiful dream
    as he whispers to himself.
    He has come to the world's beach
    to talk to the waves.
I don't know who that boy is.

I don't know whether his basket-like heart
contains other memories—
    an ocean overlaid with the rays of twilight,
    laughter hidden in an everlasting puzzle.
    Even though storms may hover near the horizon,
    the world deserves small children's laughter.
I don't know who that boy is.

—Translated from the Chinese by Edward Morin
and Dennis Ding

Maria Banus

FIRESC

tu tragi hăis eu trag cea
tu vii cu potop cu zgîltîieli
eu — cu logica si melancolia

ce mai cuplu facem o Doamne
ce-mperechere nefirească obscena
un tablou de rîs si de groază

dar ce splendid
cu ce artă dementa
sunt migălite detaiile.

Maria Banus

NOT BY DESIGN

You pull this way, I push that.
You, all frantic flood,
I, logic, static and sad.

What an unlikely pair, O God.
How unnatural, even obscene
this coupling of horror and farce.

But yet, how splendidly
the pieces, the details
of this demented art fit.

*—Translated from the Rumanian by
Diana Der Hovanessian and Maria Banus*

Ferreira Gullar

BICHO URBANO

Se disser que prefiro morar em Pirapemas
        ou em outra qualquer pequena cidade
        do país
        estou mentindo
ainda que lá se possa de manhã
lavar o rosto no orvalho
e o pão preserve aquele branco
sabor de alvorada

Não não quero viver em Pirapemas
Já me perdi
Como tantos outros brasileiros
me perdi, necessito
deste rebuliço de gente pelas ruas
e meu coração queima gasolina (da
comum)
            como qualquer outro motor urbano

A natureza me assusta.
Com seus matos sombrios suas águas
suas aves que são como aparições
me assusta quase tanto quanto
esse abismo
            de gases e de estrelas
aberto sob minha cabeça.

Ferreira Gullar

URBAN CREATURE

If I said I'd rather live in Pirapemas
    or in some other small town
    in the country
    I'd be lying
even though there it is possible
to wash one's face in the morning dew
and the bread doesn't lose that white
taste of dawn

No I don't want to live in Pirapemas
I'm already lost
Like so many other Brazilians
I'm lost, I need
this frenzy of people in the streets
and I have a heart that runs on gasoline
(low octane)
        just like other urban engines

Nature scares me.
With its shadowy woods its waters
its birds like apparitions
it scares me almost as much as
this abyss
     of gases and stars
wide open around my head.

—*Translated from the Portugese by Richard Zenith*

Ferreira Gullar

NÃO HÁ VAGAS

O preço do feijão
não cabe no poema. O preço
do arroz
não cabe no poema.
Não cabem no poema o gás
a luz o telefone
a sonegação
do leite
da carne
do açúcar
do pão

O funcionário público
não cabe no poema
com seu salário de fome
sua vida fechada
em arquivos.
Como não cabe no poema
o operário
que esmerila seu dia de aço
e carvão
nas oficinas escuras

Ferreira Gullar

NO OPENINGS

The price of beans
doesn't fit in the poem. The price
of rice
doesn't fit in the poem.
Electricity the telephone
gas don't fit in the poem
much less the warehouses
that hide
stockpiled milk
and meat
and sugar
and bread

Public servants
with their wages of hunger
their lives sealed
in files
don't fit in the poem.
Laborers
sanding away at their steel
and carbon workday
in gray factories
don't fit in the poem

—porque o poema, senhores,
  está fechado:
  "não há vagas"

Só cabe no poema
o homem sem estômago
a mulher de nuvens
a fruta sem preço

  O poema, senhores,
  não fede
  nem cheira

—because the poem, ladies and gentlemen,
   is closed: sealed shut:
   "no openings"

Only the stomachless man
the woman made of clouds
the fruit without a price
will fit in the poem

     The poem, ladies and gentlemen,
     doesn't smell
     fresh or foul.

     —Translated from the Portugese by Richard Zenith

Kirsti Simonsuuri

MATKA ARKTISILLE SEUDUILLE

Sumu vain syventää tätä autiutta.
En näe kuin ikkunaruudun, oman kuvan
näen kylman joka jäätää silmääni umpeen.
Muistan kun lapsena uskoin maailman
loppuvan Hammerfestiin, maan päätyvän rotkoon
jonka takan on vain sumu, näin uskuin.
Olen tullut pohjoiseen koska jokin
on minussa loppu, olen kuolemanväsynyt
kadottanut kompassini, sen neula ei koskaan
pysynyt hiljaa, se on hukkunut hankeen.
      Jos kuulisin sumun keskeltä
      laivan huudon, löytäisin taas suunnan.

Kirsti Simonsuuri

ARCTIC JOURNEY

Fog only makes this emptiness vaster.
What I see is the window, my own face,
cold congealing in my eyes is what I see.
I remember believing, when I was a child,
the world ended at Hammerfest,
the earth came to an abyss
and there was just fog beyond;
that's what I thought.
I've come north because something
in me is finished for good, I'm bone-weary,
compass gone—its needle constantly
wandered and was lost in the snow.
            If I could only hear a ship's horn hooting
            in the fog out there, I'd find my way.

—Translated from the Finnish by Jascha Kessler
and Kirsti Simonsuuri

458   *Camille Corot*

Andrei Voznesensky

UNKNOWN TERRAIN

Don't make bargains with daimons.
Promise nothing to the devil.
But don't give up your devotion
to their homeland,
the unknowable terrain, the same
mysterious and beloved land
that lies unmapped in
everyone's soul, guarded
by a dark woman whose eyes
are rimmed in black.
Yes, It is my motherland,
that unaccountable place
with geese flying over
its plains, geese which have
started an endless journey.
It is the unknowable mystery
whispering warnings
about dangers in its own pits.
The subconscious. The subconscious.

And when roaring daimons
tip you upside down and
ask finally "Is there anything
you need?" you answer, "Only
daylight. Only daily bread.
Black bread. Only one thing
more: access to my beloved
homeland, my subconscious."

—*Translated from the Russian by Diana Der Hovanessian*

C. Denis Pegge

MANDEVILLE'S RESTING PLACE

The country conquered Mandeville. He became content at last to lounge, to smoke his cheap powerful cigars and to muse for hours together on nothing at all. The slight gusts and dust-laden swirls of wind now and then arising came in that hot-house climate to be enough to discomfort and alarm him. Among other characteristics of a native, he acquired an oriental fatalism. Everything was reconcilable; it had to be. To return 'home' would have meant giving up the sustenance of the moment, and would have called for a tremendous effort. It did not, finally, seem to him in any way worthwhile. His earlier mental vitality and dreams—his schemes for architecture, for music, for doing something of worthiest kind, became altogether supplanted by a sensuous longing for luxury, for peace, for nothing but to be left alone.

At the fortieth year of his life Mandeville, the young idealist, the artist of good nature, sinking, drifting, had become irretrievably the degenerate—an outcast from his own kind, and yet himself a despiser of all natives and a firm believer in the superiority of his own race; a poor parched specimen; a drunkard, and given occasionally to fits of violence and acts of vice.

In the isolated tract of the Central Provinces of India, where in the first years of the twentieth century he lived, he was far, far away from any railway or city. The splendor of his position—in his own eyes—was not diluted by the presence of others of his own 'superior' race. The district was rich in bamboos. He had entered into partnership with a firm of Indian merchants. It was in bamboos he traded.

The jungle came right up to the neglected enclosure of his bungalow—which stood on relatively high ground between two tree-covered craggy hills.

To get himself carried—in a queer contraption slung from the shoulders of four coolies—to the top of one of these two hills, was his occasional recreation. At the top he would dismount, and—after perhaps kicking the leading coolie for slowness or clumsiness—would seat himself or lie back beneath one of the great slabs of rock or in the shadow of one of the trees; above everything, above even the tigers. For this hill with its iron-like rock and trees of bright foliage and flaming flower, was the lair of a pair of tigers, sometimes glimpsed, and he would have his carriers call out and beat gongs at one point in his customary route of ascent.

From the very flatness of the country that surrounded them those two hills rose like mountains. From the summit to which he was carried, Mandeville would look down over green still jungle of feathery-foliaged bamboo, tiger grass, scrub and trees stretching for miles and miles on every side.

Within this ocean of stretching wildness, where those two tiger hills rose like mountains, for several years now Mandeville had been marooned, isolated.

Nevertheless this once, this still lover of music, so hard so fast a lover of it that he had once thought of being a composer, was able to obtain for himself a sort of music. Since its invention he had possessed a phonograph, and recently had procured a gramophone of more modern kind; and his collection of records—accumulated over years—contained nothing that might not be termed 'good music.' At wide intervals, he would send for new records from a firm in Calcutta. Their arrival—months later—would be an outstanding event in his life.

He had trained his servant to work the gramophone. Frequently, after sun-down, his long chair placed in the open before his bungalow and facing the forest beyond the low railing of the small neglected compound, a whiskey peg at his elbow, he would lie back and listen.

And others heard. The sound of the gramophone would attract native villagers and passers-by, who moth-like out of the darkness would gather—and squat with his servants about the sides of his verandah and on the ground behind his chair. They would sit there marvelling at the sight of the instrument, and not a little enchanted by the noises it emitted. Nor did Mandeville ordinarily object to these unobtrusive listeners, who—were he in ill-humor or hopelessly drunk—at the first sign of his animosity would sheer off, as quietly as they had come.

It was while having his gramophone played one evening early in May that Mandeville gave forth to an outburst, a silent exhibition, which must have struck those obeisant squatting natives, accepting as they did Mandeville's singularity, even so, as singular.

That very day, a consignment of two or three new records had arrived. They bore well being listened to, over and over again. Each time they were played, Mandeville caught further harmonies and crosscurrents of sound; which enhanced his next hearing, leading him to the discovery of yet more. Most especially did the grandeur and solemnity of the pieces strike him amid the customary desolation of his life. Within that close environment of wildness, it was natural that Mandeville should have been especially susceptible—especially enriched and especially aroused by Music; by Art, which existing through man's creation is intrinsically and above all other things man's own.

He was a drab figure stretched out there as usual while listening on a long chair, his legs hitched over its extended long arms, his loose khaki shirt unbuttoned, his white drill trousers hitched over his shoulders by a pair of bracers, his feet in soiled canvas shoes; his deeply lined face tanned a dirty yellow, the head nearly bald; lying prone and still with his mouth open—no motion but his breath.

But his spirit, which lay as a rule surely as lifeless as did now the recumbent form of his body on the chair, the hearing of good music could bestir. Slowly and in a scarce perceptible gradation this evening as the music played, was his spirit stirred—into resurrection.

Very largely the process was brought about by the fact of his audience and his consciousness of it. He wondered, as he had wondered on similar occasions, what they must think of the Western music; while he stayed ignorant or forgetful of all oriental culture past and present, and saw the whole East as the barbaric jungle tract in which he lived. Must they not deem it exceedingly wonderful? Was it not for them as Cortez gazing upon a whole new world? Their initiation it seemed to him must be of such a kind.

Like the hum of a thousand alternators, the stridulation of crickets from the forests was an accompaniment to the music, a thrill that never ceased: intermittently also could be heard the churring of a night-jar, the hooting of an Indian owl or the distant wail of a jackal. Beyond dark masses of vegetation, the shape of the hill in front showed up against a palely illuminated space. The air was even now so warm that perspiration hung as a heavy dew on Mandeville's brow.

Europe and Scotland, his home, were as far and as strange as this almost comforting heat was familiar. However, he knew not of Europe as a myth and by hearsay, but by experience of his own, although now it seemed another life. This did not lessen, it increased the glamour in which he viewed it.

All men were white there.

He told them it, as they sat about him. They nodded—wondering and amazed.

Was not this country, being the chief nation in Europe, the very center of the world? Had they not sent out armies in the past? Was not the white man equal to a score of these? And there within that western continent they were all white—at so great a distance, it seemed to him a race of supermen. His first mutterings and thoughts had a trend. They were preliminaries. With such he began to build up for himself the form and body of what he loved.

From thinking of such material developments as railways, and now even aeroplanes, he went on to dwell upon the idea of scholarship and learning, of research both scientific and of the imagination. These, from his point and condition of observation, seemed higher and richer than they had ever before to him. Chiefly, indeed, on this evening it was the idea of activities belonging to that other realm of man's mind that possessed Mandeville, activities which were quite unheard of here, where the bare things of existence—where mere living, mere carrying on was all that occupied him.

What luxury! What a far cry!

'*Ai Admi!*' he exclaimed, 'Oh man! Oh men! This was my country, this was my land.'

For an interval he was silent in a grief that he had ever left it. Then he lifted his hand for another record. The etherial airs of a Bach 'contralto and chorus' sounded into the compound, into the still air of the night. He grew into elation even greater than before. Was not this glorious witness to the artistic activity of his civilisation, of then all men's civilisation?

With a surprising eagerness—though it was but a pretext, but one way of expressing his feelings—he began to tell his audience of the organisations of western society; how sensitive they were, and yet again of individual aspiration. He described where he came from fabulously, as fabulously as a narrator in a northern clime might have described India. The great nations had evolved. They were studying the laws of nature, and getting at the ultimate secrets of the world. These peoples had in the past sent out representatives, who had undergone hardship and risked death in their quest for new lands. This still continued. He told them of the strange countries of the polar regions, the ice, the vast fields of snow, the long twilit days and the eternal night.

When he went on to describe his own land, there entered into his talk a strain of the passionate love in which he held it, quite apart from his admiration and pride in the greatest ones of its people. As he spoke he pictured to himself—as well as to them those islands washed about by savage seas, bathed in lights subdued and soft—their hills with the lochs of the sea coming in, their pastures, their fields. In slow and fervid tones he attempted to explain how the glare of the sun, what was here the sun's merciless rays, was there chastened to a mere benevolence of delicate light and warmth; and how the stillness of the days here, was antipodal to the freshness and vigor of the North, of his hardy North.

Brought on time's drift a failure, Mandeville was not at this moment exactly conscious of his failure. His pride was of a kind enorme. He rose from his seat, even his body following his soul's resurrection. He indulged then in one last recitation of all that he was and all that he belonged to—an exultation, a eulogy, a hymn, a paean, spoken into the heated air. . . .

He told them of something far, unutterably far. Great, yes great; as these things were unknown. Activity, intense, predominant; where here was stagnation! Perception—keen as a knife! Endeavor! Strength! Purpose! Resolve! Courage! He waved his arms in some vague indication—beyond the trees—of that distant North.

The presence of the simple—uncomprehending—men who formed his audience associated him with the rigid frame of life, and so gave stability to his attitude. It was as if, as well as expanding a love, he was truly giving to them an explanation. Their presence had had a great effect upon him; for afterwards, when they had solemnly *salammed* him and gone one by one away and he stood there alone, there was in his heart nothing but regret.

A faint stir, like a human sigh, for a moment started all the trees of his compound into movement, then left the air warm, oppressive, still—as before. He began mechanically to undress, and at length—within the mosquito net—stretched himself out on the charpoy bed standing not far from the long chair on the hard ground, within the broad but stifling night, contained within the wildness, alone, stationary, encircling, all about.

It was alright—he thought—to go on living in this place so far removed from all he had described. After all, what was *he*? What did he matter? His life was a wasted thing. But when he died he would like to lie there where there was endeavor sharp as a knife, where men strove, where there was creation—this for his toil on earth, there for his eternal peace and knowing. He would make careful arrangements. He would make it clear where they should bury him. The bungalow could—he calculated—be made to cover the expenses of an embalmment. He turned over onto his side relieved, as though he had found the solution to a mighty problem.

Oscar Hahn

ESO SERIA TODO

Te estoy haciendo un destino aquí mismo
Lo estoy dibujando en las alas de un pájaro.
Lo estoy pintando en la pared de mi cuarto

Ahora el pájaro vuela con furia
ahora lanza su grito de guerra
y se dispara contra la pared

Sus plumas están flotando en el espacio
Sus plumas están mojándose en su sangre

Coje una y te escribe este poema

Oscar Hahn

THAT WILL BE ALL

Even here I am shaping fate
I am drawing it on a bird's wings
I am painting it on the wall of my room

The bird flying wildly now
lets loose its war-cry now
and shoots itself against the wall

Its feathers are floating in space
its feathers drenched with blood

Catching one it writes you this poem

—Translated from the Spanish by James Hoggard

Oscar Hahn

NINGUN LUGAR ESTA AQUI O ESTA AHI

Ningún lugar está aquí o está ahí
Todo lugar es proyectado desde adentro
Todo lugar es superpuesto en el espacio

Ahora estoy echando un lugar para afuera
estoy tratando de ponerlo encima de ahí
encima del espacio donde no estás
a ver si de tanto hacer fuerza si de tanto hacer fuerza
te apareces ahí sonriente otra vez

Aparécete ahí aparécete sin miedo
y desde afuera avanza hacia aquí
y haz harta fuerza harta fuerza
a ver si yo me aparezco otro vez si aparezco otra vez
si reaparecemos los dos tomados de la mano
en el espacio
          donde coinciden
               todos nuestros lugares

Oscar Hahn

PLACES ARE NEITHER HERE NOR THERE

Places are neither here nor there
Each place is projected from within
Each place is superimposed on space

I am now clearing a place outside
I am trying to lay it over there
on top of the space you're not in
to see if it's strong enough if it's strong enough
you appear there smiling again

Appear there appear without fear
and move from outside toward here
and try hard try hard
to see if I appear again if I appear again
if taken by the hand we both reappear
in the space
           where all our places
                       come together

—Translated from the Spanish by James Hoggard

Alain Bosquet

THE MUSTARD COLLECTOR

The hills between Fond du Lac and Prairie du Chien, the American said to himself, are reminiscent of both the spurs of the Rockies in Wyoming and those of the Ozarks in Arkansas. They were rich in maple trees and sycamores, but lacked the charm of an occasional nineteenth-century church or a crumbling wall. And his ultra-agreeable Polish host, a pianist turned into a gentleman-farmer, who had come to Wisconsin to escape from the perpetual displacement—like that of a suitcase in the baggage compartment of a derailing train—of a boundary line between the Oder and Vistula Rivers, was nursing a nostalgia of his own. These hills could not compare with the rolling hills of Silesia or even with the barely undulating stretches of now forever-lost Livnia, with the warmth of their purple sunsets.

The French visitor, on the other hand, had immunized himself against comparisons. There was grace, to his eyes, in the signs of glacial deposits, in the dark leaves of the trees and the shucks of corn, nonchalant as gloves carelessly dropped from a little countess's hand. Let the wind from the Winnipeg blow! He felt sublimely free before these new skies, fields and trees, which had no past and raised not his memory. Their grave yet lightly borne anonymity dispensed him from drawing any parallels. No need to think, for instance of Charente and its over-abundance of unforgotten Romanesque stones.

The Pole was thoughtful. He wanted to show the American that he had learned from this nation's hospitality, from its now deliberate now abrupt ways, that he had fallen in with the unspoken rules of the countryside—reasonableness, hard dealing, unquestioning faith—but appreciated also its qualities of enthusiasm and generosity. At the same time, his due regard must not pass for servile imitation. He would not restrain the outbursts—the cavalry charges—of his Slavic soul; he could vary his newly learned placidity with fiery vehemence. His house was a jarring fragment of Europe, rebuilt in a New World which he blessed for its fertility and for the welcome it extended to fugitives like himself. He wanted to live up, visibly, to his American neighbor, yes, and to his example. The Frenchman was amused, possessed not so much of principles as of curiosity. Plainly he was keeping his distance, warding off sentimentality and the promiscuous intimacy that is born of impeccable food and excellent wine.

"If I've come over here today," the American explained emphatically, "it's not only because Casimir's my friend; it's also, Monsieur, because I love the art and the life-style of France. It's a treat to meet you. French intellectuals don't come by every day. They know Wisconsin for its universities rather than for its countryside. They're not so wrong at that. The state has nothing special about it, and its animals are commonplace compared with Canadian bears and Minnesota beavers."

"But charm doesn't lie in the spectacular," said the Frenchman. "Our Polish friend's table is justly famous and I hope he'll also give us one of his inimitable performances of Chopin."

The Pole was pouring vodka, Cinzano and Amer Picon, stubbornly holding out against the suggestion of his wife, moved by courtesy, no doubt, rather than by slavish imitation, that he serve Bourbon old-fashioneds and dry martinis. The crackling sound of salted almonds did not prevent the smiling musician from soon obliging his pressing friends by playing the piano. A pupil of Paderewski, he had a nobly sculpted profile, a philosophical bald spot and the fingers of a thoroughbred. The notes came out, lightly and almost distractedly, velvety as hors d'oeurves that soothe the palate or, rather, prepare it for the masterpieces of the meal to come. The keys must have been tepid; he glided over them, seeming to elicit their nervous resistance and to announce a mad gallop to the horizon of sound.

After ecstatic praise, some of it sincere, they went to the dinner table. The American based his compliments on the pianist's frenzied perfection; the Frenchman thought out something more subtle, comparing their host's virtuosity to that of certain rare plants which he had seen burst into bloom within a few seconds, either in gardens along the Italian Lakes or else on the Pacific Coast between Honduras and Guatemala. He apologized for this hazardous comparison. It was permissible, wasn't it, to couple the pleasures of music with the delights of eyes and ears afforded by primitive nature?

Meanwhile, the pianist's wife saw to the working of the guests' lips and jaws and the muscles connecting the cheek to the pharynx. Her role was to display unfailing serenity. Her silence was punctuated by short interrogative phrases, innocent but appealing to discretion, in order that her husband should not pass from polite solicitude into overly demonstrative expression. The self-assured American, at ease with both his body and soul, reinforced by his solid past, by a present that he wouldn't have exchanged for any other and—such is the power of hope—by his vision of the future, tossed the ball to his own wife that she bolster his boasting. This disciplined procedure became the American wife. She was perceived as harboring an undiscriminating, imprecise, repetitive admiration for practically everything. There was appreciation of her warmheartedness toward her fellows, of the Basset hound running from one sofa to another, of the white wine, of the high ceiling, the caviar, lemon and toast, of picturesque France, and distant Poland, of America (which called for no adjective), of landscapes here and there, of the cute little forks, like those she had bought in Liverpool, Lyons, Livorno or some other European city. No, no; to pronounce those names was too risky.

The meat was red and juicy, separated from its crust by a layer of mushrooms, which aroused violent enthusiasm. The Pole, as good a chef as he was a pianist, called his recipe commonplace. All he had to do was to combine three kinds of mushrooms: morels, truffles and ceps, these last least, lest they give the dish the consistency of an overcooked snail. The sauce and the wines were the next to be praised. Now the movement of jaws became grave and solemn, slowed by the pleasure of the tongue and taste-buds, as they followed the unforgettable scent from the lips to the esophagus.

Suddenly the Pole disappeared into the kitchen and came back with a battalion of mustard pots painstakingly deployed on a lace-covered tray. As a true knight—Sobieski would have been proud—he laid out around the American pots of every size and description: earthenware, porcelain, glass, tin, precious wood, some of slender, almost Gothic shape, others round or in bizarre forms of Tyrolean hat, barrel, big-bellied coachman. Labels revealed places of origin. Only two came from the United States; three came from Poland and Finland; others had come a long way, from Hong Kong, Taiwan, Chile and Madagascar. With loving, almost maniacal care the American opened jar after jar, plunging a knife-blade and then scraping it on the rim of his plate, which soon began to look like an artist's palette, festooned with every shade of color between yellow and brown, including ochre and burnt sienna, enough hues to warm the heart of a Titian, a Rubens or a Velasques of gastronomy. Staring boldly—but with an obvious desire for admiration—the American proclaimed:

"Sir, there's no greater mustard expert in the world than myself. I'm the emperor, the tyrant, the unconditional lover! Mustard is the crown of civilization, and I collect it untiringly. A leg of lamb is only an excuse for the enjoyment of this divine food. My Polish friend knows my weakness, and this array does him honor. A while back—twenty-five years—I founded a group, a brotherhood, rather, of Lords of Mustard; I was elected its President. There are quite a few of us: Lord Mountbatten, the brother of the King of Sweden, the late Aga Khahn and the Maharajah of Lahore, who, at a banquet held in Melbourne, nearly beat me on my own ground: the blindfolded identification of the various types of this sacred substance.''

''It's the way, with wine, in my country,'' the Frenchman responded, half ironically. ''A legend, you might say. A wine-steward of reputation can identify a wine without tasting or even looking at it, by the noise made by the cork coming out of the neck of the bottle. But I'm no gourmet.''

''For a Frenchman, that's a crime. Guess why the banquet for princes and upstarts like myself was held in Australia, a continent so bleak and so backward in matters of cooking. Very special meat was needed to set off the mustards, forty-three of them, as I remember. Giant turtles, kangaroos and the duck-billed platypus were the big attractions. Well, we liked them well enough, but the big surprise was the prairie rabbit, an unattractive little creature, but one which, prepared with a tomato sauce, is tastier than woodcock or pheasant . . . Sir, your country has a place in history only for having produced the greatest of all mustards, Gray-Bourbon. The world's capital is Dijon.''

The Pole looked askance, as if a clown, and the Frenchman, conscious of presenting, willy-nilly, his three-thousand-mile-away country, did his best to take seriously the American's flattering remarks. As for the wives, they nodded approval, not out of conviction but simply because this attitude was expected of them.

''When we were married,'' the American went on, holding out to his young wife a chubby hand made ridiculous by little tufts of hair but manicured to perfection, which she seized with suspect eagerness (he could have been her father), ''I said to Pamela: 'The first thing is to travel, to broaden your horizons, to grab what the universe has to offer rather than to cling to commonplace unfulfilled desires.' Scottish castles have their place, I take off my hat to Westminster Abbey, there are no more beautiful paintings than those of the Prado and Venice is a jewel smelling of rats, but a jewel all the same. But there's nothing, sir, like France.''

"Really," asked the last of the Gauls, always ready to react to positive statements with a question mark, a euphemism, a deep doubt concealing a certain weariness and perhaps the realization that his country was no longer a great power. "Do we really deserve such admiration? Doesn't it crush us?"

"And so I didn't show Pamela museums, ancient walls, Notre-Dame, the Eiffel Tower, the Lido and the Folies Bergeres. We left those to the tourists. The man of the street's life-style, that's what's amazing and instructive to an amateur psychologist like myself.

"You went into the factories, did you?" said the Frenchman. "Wonderful! You talked with workers at Longwy and Saint-Etienne, with the stevedores of Saint-Nazaire? Few of my countrymen display such healthy curiosity."

"Sir, to live is to eat. A country is to be understood through its cooking, that's my standard. You can trust my experience as a sixty-year-old lawyer and traveler. You can't contradict that. Pamela agreed, and we made a classic pilgrimage."

"No Louvre, Mont Saint-Michel, Loire castles, no Aubervilliers of Tourcoing? Sir, you intrigue me. Don't tell me you went from one *bistrot* to another, and ate with truck drivers. Country pâté and a liter of red wine, or, on the coast of Brittany, clams and cider. There's a certain France for you; everyone gets the one he deserves."

"We left out all minor objects of curiosity and stuck to the one and only pilgrimage."

"With or without its artistic treasures, you might say that France shines for its variety: a corner of Beauce, a tiny harbor in Brittany, a vineyard in Roussillon, a moor covered with lavender, a landscape of Touraine with a peasant girl speaking the purest French, and almost dried-up Loire or a row of poplars overrun by holly . . ."

"It took us exactly thirteen days to visit the thirteen restaurants to which Michelin has given three stars. Pamela can tell you that I'm right. The spirit of France and the best of the Western world are to be found in those temples. I'm not speaking for the Haut Brions, the Mumms, I take them for granted. And the mustards, close to perfection . . . I verified the fact that no one knows them better than I."

The American wife picked up her cue, retelling her husband's stories, mixing up Burgundy and Bordeaux and detailing fabulous menus. Just as her servility had begun to irritate even the amiable Pole and the Frenchman, lazily indulgent from drinking, she launched into a list of things of which she had been deprived on the journey. Oh, if she could only see Autun, admire Tournus, rave over Moissac! This display of knowledge, gleaned, no doubt, from books, didn't sit well with her husband, although it inspired him to a self-satisfied declamation.

"The itinerary of our next trip is already planned, and Pamela will enjoy her Romanesque churches and ivory carvings, the things she studied at Princeton . . . We had a curious misadventure, you know. After a memorable meal at Point's at Vienne and a night infected by bedbugs in a hotel such as we haven't had at home for the last hundred years we set out joyfully on Sunday morning for Pere Bize's at Talloires. Just imagine! I'd never tasted a *chevalier trout* stuffed with carrots and goose-liver and grilled in port wine. I had a passionate desire for it. And then when we got there, we found it was the day of the week when the place was closed. Sadly, I told our chauffeur to take us to Baumaniere's at Les Baux . . . But let me tell you the best of all. Right after we were married . . . Pamela's my third and best wife—my first wife was a disaster, the second a bore wrapped up in tennis, golf, swimming and calorie-counting, as if losing weight were the goal of all humanity . . . Anyhow, I built a house in the country some twenty miles from here. We designed it ourselves, and Pamela sent for a decorator from London. You really must come see it. I allowed for a space of three cubic feet for mustards: the little gifts sent by my correspondents. Ah, that Maharajah of Lahore! If he were alive he'd surely have sent me a precious jar, decorated with emeralds and lapislazuli. And, wait . . . in order to build up reserve I wrote to Gray-Bourbon asking them to send me two hundred pounds. That's what I like about the French, young man; they've no sense of reality, and don't give a damn about business."

Thanks to the liquor and liqueurs the diners felt that they were somewhat confused and that the differences of their characters and sensibilities were wiped out. Well-being, after all, implies giving up our individual merits, relying on the judgment of others and letting them think for us. Stories stood out less clearly, and mingled one with another. Now, anything not completely understood was attributed to a programmatic and slightly apoplectic amiability, which needed no concrete expression. Cigars and cigarettes made floating smoke rings among the velvets and organdies and cradled the guests' minds, creating the illusion of a lightness, between white and violet. The Pole was waiting for someone to call him back to the piano and the Frenchman hoped that he would be spared further pledges of love to his country.

"Gray-Bourbon answered me with a stupid question: did I want the two hundred pounds in jars of one pound or four? So I had to explain: I had to save space for my *vosnes-romanee* and *chateau-yquem*: in short, I wanted the mustard in a single container. A month went by before I got a still more inept letter: the company, to its regret, had no container of this size."

"Excuse me, but you can get Gray-Bourbon in the States. Can't you?"

"Young man, you deserve the Legion of Honor (incidentally, you can see that I have it)! You're right, overwhelmingly right. They've two factories over here, one in New Jersey and the other in California. But there they cheat. They use American vinegar."

"Is there a real difference in the taste?"

"That's not the question. It's all wrong to mix French and American products."

"Really, sir?"

"I tell you, it's a matter of principle, especially if the two brands are the same. I answered with a cable that gave me a certain satisfaction: *'It's your problem.'* After that two or three months went by, and I said to myself that your country had hit the lower depths. So little feeling for business! On the other hand, I admired the company because it wouldn't change its ways for the sake of a Yankee millionaire.''

Coffee lent an agreeable smell to the confusion. A certain heaviness of words and gestures seemed to give way to more gracious impulses. Facial expressions shifted, looking, perhaps, for amenities beyond the pleasure of satisfied appetites. The men might have smothered the women with well-turned, exaggerated compliments, which the latter would blushingly reject in order to show that they were appreciated. Political events came into play, visible on frowning foreheads and eyebrows, in expressions that betrayed perplexity and confusion. The Pole's fingers tapped a spoon on the tablecloth. Weren't they going to ask for a taste of something more intoxicating than the Courvoisier and the Hine, for a piece by Chopin or Bach (John-Sebastian, naturally)?

''Well, just five days ago I received, via the Great Lakes, an enormous box with, inside, an authentic Greek amphora containing two hundred pounds of mustard. Just imagine my joy! I'm a bit screwy, but I've my head on my shoulders. 'Not such fools, those Frenchies,' I said to myself. 'But what the devil will they charge for the amphora?' I very nearly insulted the French nation! Yesterday, after a period of, yes, anxious, no, I mean delicious (I can't find the word for sheer emotion) waiting, I got the letter I'm going to read to you from the head of Gray Bourbon . . .''

The Frenchman couldn't fail to play his expected role and duly informed those present that the letter was written on very fine paper topped by a plum-colored, filigreed monogram in old-style manuscript letters, including certain *s's* that looked like *f's* without a cross-bar. He read the letter out loud, slowly, so as to echo the delight of the American, and with a somewhat artificial tone of voice, in order to match his hearers' outburst of laughter without really subscribing to them.

Dear Sir:

In the course of my long career I have never met anyone who so deeply appreciated mustard, particularly my own brand. Chance and some research have enabled me to learn very flattering things about the way you honor this product. Forgive any delay on the part of myself and my assistants and do me the favor of accepting this modest sample and its container, which I trust will not startle you by its incongruity. . .

There followed toasts to French friendship, Polish friendship, American friendship and friendship in general. They all exchanged confidences and seemed ready to tell a few risque stories. The Pole could no longer endure his failure to obtain the lion's share of attention. He rose, with a majestic yet unreproachful air as if he were on the Himalayan heights of inspiration and embraced the piano as a long-desired lover. Then, tenderly, ecstatically, gravely, with religious attentiveness, he soothed the awareness of all with a tearfully romantic melody.

"Only a Frenchman can make gestures so magnificent," the American proclaimed. "And France shall have its reward. I've not always been rich, believe me. I'm a self-made man. By the time I'd made my pile the Rembrandts and the Van Goghs had already been bought up. I had to be content with Monet—I've seventeen, I believe, and Degas—eleven and two drawings, lost, incidentally, some Seurats and a few minor things— Braque, Rouault, the Fauves. Anyhow, a hundred or so solid works. Pamela is taken care of . . . no, don't worry, I'm not the sort of American who discusses a widow's inheritance when she's around . . . I've been hesitating; I've friends among the curators of the Chicago Art Institute and my collection would fit in very well, in a room bearing my name . . . There's Philadelphia, too . . . But Monsieur Gray-Bourbon has caused me to make up my mind. It's definite—I'm leaving my paintings to the Louvre."

There was no need for music to soothe the savage breast; good manners prevailed. No one really listened to the Pole, but they vaguely heard his gallopades through marshes, infinite plains and dazzling sunrises. The wives wondered if they could talk about clothes, but finally decided to stay at the high level of their husbands. The Frenchman, after so much overwhelming praise, took hold of himself and recovered his skepticism. Prudently, almost tenderly, he asked the American:

"Excuse me, but do you know the mustard of Meaux?"

"What's that?"

"Meaux, the birthplace of Bossuet."

"No. It must be an infamous modern concoction, one of those mixtures . . ."

"On the contrary, it dates from the thirteenth century; it's a greenish-brown, with dark, almost black grains plainly visible."

The Pole stopped playing, as if resentful of this assault on his concentration. As for the American he mopped his forehead, while his cheeks went from white to purple to black (color of the plague) in turn. He opened his mouth and gulped, but could not get out a word. Indeed, he was positively ill. He didn't deserve this insult and couldn't see why anyone should commit a sacrilege in his presence. Then he regained his self-control, took a notebook out of his pocket and said, somewhat incoherently:

"A bit of a blow, Monsieur! I'm flying to San Francisco tomorrow. In three days I have to be in, yes, Montreal. If I send you, Pamela . . . yes, if you'd fly to buy it in Paris . . . No, the Hartfords are expecting us Saturday in Washington."

The Pole restored order, if not serenity. He multiplied his wiles, mobilizing Pergolesi, Schumann, Beethoven, Debussy, Couperin and Sibelius. But this array of geniuses could not reconcile two men who, in spite of all their polite phrases, considered themselves mortal enemies. There was talk of future meetings and other unforgettable dinners, but it did not ring true.

A week later the Frenchman, back in Paris, sent a beribboned jar of mustard from Meaux to the American. In acknowledgment he received the following cable:

"Thanks. Excellent! But Gray-Bourbon keeps its top rating. Negotiating with Louvre for bequest of my paintings."

—Translated from the French by Frances Frenaye

CONTRIBUTORS

ALICE ADAMS lives in San Francisco. Her stories have appeared in the *New Yorker* and in many magazines, journals and anthologies. They have been included in many editions of *Best American Short Stories* and *O. Henry Prize Stories*. In 1982 she won a Continuing Achievement Award from the O. Henry Awards. She is author of two collections of short stories and five novels; *Superior Women* is a recent title.

YEHUDA AMICHAI is a leading Israeli poet, novelist and dramatist; he has published ten volumes of poetry, as well as novels, short stories and plays. His themes concern love, death and war; among recent books are *The World Is a Room & Other Stories, Travels,* and *Selected Poetry.*

JANUSZ ANDERMAN is a Polish writer. His short stories appear regularly in *Puls* and in the spoken journal *Na Glos* held every month in Krakow; in the United States, they have appeared in *Triquarterly* and in other journals. He has also published a book of short stories, *Bez tchu (Lack of Oxygen),* collected in English under the title *Poland under Blacklight.*

CLAES ANDERSON is a physician within the field of psychiatry as well as a renowned pianist; he belongs to the minority in Finland writing in Swedish. He has served as editor-in-chief for the literary magazine, *FTB,* and as chairman of the Finnish-Swedish Writers Association. He is author of a dozen collections of poems, including *Genom sprickorna i vårt ansikte;* he has also written a novel and plays for the stage and for television.

ZOE ANGLESEY has published many of his own poems as well as translations, in such publications as *Ploughshares, Greenfield Review, Poetry East, Bloomsbury Review, Fiction International, Kauri, Oro Madre,* and *Massachusetts Review.* He has won fellowships from New York University and Writers Retreat, among others. He is also author of the book, *Something More than Force: Poems for Guatemala 1971–1982.*

WERNER ASPENSTRÖM is one of Sweden's most important poets; he has published twenty-one collections of his work, including *Litania* and *Dikter under träden*. He is a member of the Swedish Academy, and has won numerous literary awards. His work has been translated throughout Europe.

ETELVINA ASTRADA, born to an Argentine father and a German mother, grew up in Argentina, now lives in Spain. Her poetry in translation has been published in *Nimrod, Chelsea, Chariton Review, International Poetry Review, Letras Femininas,* and *Massachusetts Review.* Her books include *Autobiografía con Gatillo, Muerte Arrebatada,* a final selection for the Casa de las Américas de Cuba prize, and *Libro de Mal Amor.*

MARIA BANUS is a leading Rumanian poet. She has been publishing poems, plays and prose for decades; in 1950 she won the State Prize. Her works include *Portrait of Fayun, Everyone and Something, Forbidden Magic,* and *From the Chronicle of Those Years.*

HELEN BAROLINI lives in Scarborough, New York. Her stories, translations, reviews, essays and poetry have appeared in *Kenyon* Review, *Paris Review, New York Review of Books, Antioch Review,* and elsewhere. For her work, she has won an American Book Award from the Before Columbus Foundation and a creative writing grant from the National Endowment for the Arts. She has translated many books from Italian into English; she originated and compiled *The Dream Book: An Anthology of Writings by Italian American Women.* She has published the novels, *Umbertina* and *Love in the Middle Ages.*

MARIA BENNETT is not only a fine translator, but a poet. She has published in *Stone Country.*

PHYLLIS BIRNBAUM teaches at Brandeis University. Her essays, reviews, and articles have appeared in many publications, in the United States and abroad. For her work, she has won awards from the National Endowment for the Arts and the Translation Center. She is author of a novel, *An Eastern Tradition,* and translator of *Rabbits, Crabs, etc.* Her translation of the complete novel, *Confessions of Love,* is forthcoming.

CHANA BLOCH is Head of the English Department at Mills College. Her books include *The Secrets of the Tribe, A Dress of Fire: Selected Poetry of Dahlia Ravokovitch,* and *Spelling the World: George Herbert and the Bible.*

ALAIN BOSQUET, born in Russia, has long lived in France. He has served as editor of *La Voix de France,* and has taught French literature at Brandeis University, as well as American literature at the University of Lyon. He is author of novels and poetry, is literary critic for *Le Monde.* His books include *Une Mère russe,* which won Grand Prize for Fiction from the French Academy.

DANIEL BOURNE has recently returned from a Fulbright in Poland; he is editor of *Artful Dodge*. He has published his Polish translations in *Salmagundi, Chariton Review, Greenfield Review, Poetry Now,* and elsewhere.

STEVEN FORD BROWN is editor of The American Poets Profile Series and Ford-Brown & Co., publishers in Houston, Texas. He has published criticism, poetry and translations in many American, Argentine, Canadian and English literary journals. He is currently editing a book of interviews with contemporary women writers.

LENNART BRUCE, born in Sweden, is now a poet and translator in San Francisco. In 1977 he was awarded the Poetry Translation Prize of the Swedish Academy of Letters. He has published twelve volumes of poetry; another collection of his poems is forthcoming.

EDITH BRUCK was born in Hungary, survived a concentration camp as a child, and moved to Italy, where she became a journalist for *Il Messaggero*. She is author of many books of poetry, novels, short stories and plays; she is now a film director in Rome. Her books include *Chi Ti Ama Così, In Difesa del Padre, Andremo in Città,* and *Due Stanze Vuote,* a prize-winning novel.

THOMAS C. CARLSON is a specialist in American literature at Memphis State University. Previously, he was Senior Fulbright Fellow at the University of Bucharest. He has published widely on Poe and Melville; his translations of Rumanian poets have appeared in journals in the United States, England and Canada.

NINA CASSIAN is a leading Rumanian writer and translator. Her honors include a Writers' Union Award, a Writers' Association of Bucharest Award and a State Prize. She has written more than fifty books; her books in the United States include *Blue Apple, Lady of Miracles* and *The Lion and the Unicorn.*

GU CHENG was a carpenter in Beijing during the Cultural Revolution. He has since published *Selected Poems by Shu Ting and Gu Cheng* and *Selected Poems by Bei Dao and Gu Cheng.* He is a member of the Chinese Writers Association.

RAMAPADA CHOWDHURY lives in Calcutta, India. He is joint editor of *Ananda Bazaar Patrika*, the largest Bengali newspaper published in Calcutta. He was recently awarded the Tagore Prize from India.

RAE DALVEN was born in Greece, grew up in New York. She is the first translator from the Greek to introduce modern Greek literature to the United States. Her many books of translation include *Poems, Modern Greek Poetry, The Complete Poems of Cavafy, Anna Comnena, Fourth Dimension* and

Selected Poems of Yannis Ritsos. She was recently awarded a grant from the National Endowment for the Arts, and is currently working on a book of translations, *Daughters of Sappho*.

BEI DAO is editor of a magazine in Beijing. He has published *Selected Lyrics by Bei Dao and Gu Cheng*. He has also translated *Selected Modern Poetry of Northern Europe* into Chinese.

IVAN DAVIDKOV, a Bulgarian poet, holds the title of National Artist, one of the highest cultural distinctions in Bulgaria; he is also a gifted painter, with widely exhibited work. Davidkov is a privately-lyrical poet, and a retired rather than a public person. He has published nearly twenty volumes of poetry and several novels.

VAHAKN DAVTIAN is one of Armenia's two leading poets; he has been publishing his work since 1947. Deeply rooted in Armenian soil, his work had been compared to the poetry of Yeats and also to that of Seamus Heaney.

EUGENIO DE ANDRADE is Portugal's leading contemporary poet. He has published twenty-three volumes of poetry, two of prose, two children's books, and a number of anthologies. He has also published translations of Yannis Ritsos and Garcia Lorca into Portugese. His work has appeared in more than twenty foreign languages, with books published in Italy, France, Luxembourg, Spain, Mexico, and the United States.

DIANA DER HOVANESSIAN lives in Cambridge, Massachusetts. She is author of eight books of poetry and translations, which have won many national and international awards. Her new book is *About Time*.

DENNIS DING is instructor of English at Guizhou Normal University, in China. He has translated from English to Chinese more than 100 works by T. S. Eliot, H. D., Frost, Pound, W. C. Williams, Roethke, Bellow, Hemingway and Peter Benchley; many of his translations have appeared in leading Chinese magazines. He was recently a visiting scholar at Oakland University in Michigan.

EUGENE DUBNOV is a Russian author who is currently Writer in Residence at Carmel College in Oxfordshire. His poems in Russian have been published in the USSR, France, Canada, the United States, Germany and Israel; his books in Russian include *Kontinent, Grani* and *Ryzhiye monety*. His poems and short stories translated into English have also been published in many countries. For his work, he has won awards from the Public Council for Emigre Artists and Russian Writers in Exile, among others. He is currently compiling an anthology of Russian poetry, translated in collaboration with John Heath-Stubbs.

CHARLES EDWARD EATON, an American poet, won the 1984 Hollins Critic Poetry Award; he was also awarded the Zoe Kincaid Brockman Memorial Award for his eighth collection, *The Thing King.* He is also author of three volumes of short stories and a book of art criticism. His most recent book is *New and Selected Poems.*

ROGER ELKIN is one of England's leading poets; his work has been published in many reviews and anthologies. He won nine poetry awards in 1986, including the Sylvia Plath Award, Douglas Gibson Memorial Award and the Open University Award. Recent books include *Greenhouse* and *Pricking Out.*

ODYSSEUS ELYTIS is one of Greece's most esteemed poets. His poems have appeared in *Modern European Poetry, Six Poets of Modern Greece, Four Greek Poets, Penguin Book of Greek Poetry,* and many other periodicals and anthologies. His books include *Six and One Regrets for the Sky.* He was awarded the National Prize in Poetry in 1960, and the Nobel Prize for Literature in 1979.

D. L. EMBLEN has published his translations in *Modern Poetry in Translation, Mundus Artium, Northwest Review, An Anthology of Swedish Literature,* and elsewhere. His collection of Werner Aspenström's poems is forthcoming from Clamshell Press.

GEVORG EMIN is a Soviet Armenian poet. He has published more than thirty books of poetry, as well as twelve books of translations, and two of prose; he has also written two film scripts. His poetry has been translated into more than a dozen other languages, and he has won many Soviet literary awards, including the State Prize and the Lenin Prize. His new book of poems in English translation, translated by Diana Der-Hovanessian, is *For You on New Year's Day.*

RICARDO FEIERSTEIN is an Argentine poet. His books of poetry include *Letras en equilibrio, Inventadiario,* and *La Balada del sol.* He also wrote a trilogy, *Sinfonía inocente,* which was recently cited for excellence in the Buenos Aires Literary Competition.

RUTH FELDMAN's poetry and translations have appeared in many magazines and anthologies, and include a volume of Primo Levi's short stories, *Moments of Reprieve.* She has won several awards for her work, including the Sotheby International Prize, and awards from the New England Poetry Club and the Poetry Society of America. She frequently spends summers in Italy, where she recently read her work at the University of Urbino.

WILLIAM FIELDER, a translator, lives in the Martha's Vineyard area. For many years, he lived and worked in Turkey.

488 Literary Olympians II

H. E. FRANCIS is Professor of English at the University of Alabama. His books include Naming Things and A Disturbance of Gulls.

FRANCES FRENAYE is a well-known translator of French, Italian and German authors. She lives in New York.

PETROS GLEZOS is a Greek author living in Athens. His principal published books are Greek Themes, Spiritual Freedom, The First Acquaintance, The House with the Pigeons, and Journey to the Past. His volume of short stories, Clouded Eyes, was awarded the Literary Prize from the Academy of Athens. His most recent book is Memoirs of a Gentleman.

ANGEL GONZALEZ is a leading Spanish writer. He has published seven volumes of poetry, including Muestra and Prosemas O Menos. His book, Grado Elemental, was awarded the Antonio Machado Prize for Poetry in Spain. Harsh World and Other Poems was translated into English by Donald Walsh. Gonzalez has taught at the University of New Mexico since 1976.

OLAV GRINDE was born in Haugesund, Norway. He lived for twelve years in the United States, but then returned to his native land. He now lives in Bergen; he makes wood and ceramic sculptures, and translates Norwegian literature into English. He has also published a book, Breathing Exercise: Poems of Rolf Jacobsen.

MARGHERITA GUIDACCI is a leading Italian poet; she teaches English Literature at the Vatican's College of Maria Assunta. Her work has been translated into nine languages and has won many Italian literary prizes. Her major works include Neurosuite, Taccuino Slavo, Inno Alla Gioia and Liber Fulguralis.

FERREIRA GULLAR is a leading Brazilian poet, as well as a journalist, art critic, essayist and playwright. His books include Por Você, Por Mim, Antologia Poética, Toda Poesia and Barulhos. In English translation, his poems have appeared in Brazilian Poetry, 1950–1980, Anthology of 20th Century Brazilian Poetry, Translation and American Poetry Review.

OSCAR HAHN, born in Chile, teaches Spanish at the University of Iowa. Enrique Lihn has called him "the top poet of his generation." Hahn's most recent books are Arte de Morir and Mal de Amor.

SAMUEL HAZO is Professor of English at Duquesne University and Director of the International Poetry Forum. His work has appeared in the Atlantic Monthly, Harper's, Yale Review, Kenyon Review, Sewanee Review, Malahat Review, and many other publications and anthologies. His most recent books include Thank a Bored Angel and The Color of Reluctance.

ROBERT HEDIN teaches at Wake Forest University in North Carolina. He is a well known translator, and is author of *Snow Country, At the Home Altar* and *Country O.*

JUAN JOSE HERNANDEZ is correspondent for the Buenos Aires newspaper *La Nacion.* He has published many stories, several collections, a novel and numerous volumes of poetry. He is most famous for his collection, *Il Innocente.*

JOHN V. HICKS is one of Canada's leading poets; he is currently an Honorary Fellow of the University of Emmanual College. For his literary achievement he has recently been awarded the honorary degree of Doctor of Laws by the University of Saskatchewan. His poetry collections include *Now Is a Far Country, Winter Your Sleep, Silence Like the Sun, Rootless Tree,* and *Fives and Sixes.*

JAMES HOGGARD teaches English at Midwestern State University. He has published translations of poems by Oscar Hahn and Salvador Díaz Miron. He has also published several collections of his own poetry, and two novels, *Trotter Ross* and *Elevator Man.*

SYED SHAMSUL HUQ is a professional writer in Dhaka, Bangladesh. For his work, he has been awarded the Bengali Academy Prize, the Adamjee Literary Prize and the Writer's Circle Prize.

KOICHI IIJIMA is a prominent poet and critic in Japan. His many volumes of poetry include *My Vowel, Microcosm, Goya's First Name, Barcelona, Miyako,* and *Wander Up and Down in Ueno and Penetrate Ou.* He has also written many critical studies of French and Japanese writers and also works on art and cinema. A most recent book is *Stranger's Sky: Selected Poems of Iijima Koichi.*

JOSEPHINE JACOBSEN is a Canadian born poet, short story writer, lecturer and essayist. Recent awards include the Prairie Schooner Award for Fiction and an O. Henry Award. Her work has been anthologized in *Best American Short Stories,* in many volumes of *The O. Henry Prize Stories,* and in *Fifty Years of the American Short Story.* Her most recent book is a collection of short fiction, *Adios, Mr. Moxley.*

ROLF JACOBSEN, a Norwegian poet, is credited for introducing modern poetry into Norwegian literature. His first book, *Earth and Iron,* was published in 1933. His literary career spans over half a century; his work has been translated into more than two dozen languages. He has published twelve collections, including *Think About Something Else;* most recent is *Night Open.*

J. KATES' translations and other work have appeared in *Massachusetts Review, Kansas Quarterly, Tendril, Greenfield Review, Cyphers, Florida Review, Shirim* and elsewhere.

EDMUND KEELEY teaches in the creative writing department at Princeton University. His work has appeared in *Antaeus, Triquarterly* and *Pacific Review*. For his work, he has won the Harold Morton Landon Award from the Academy of American Poets; he has recently translated a collection of Ritsos poems since 1969.

MARY KEELEY is a noted translator of Greek writers; she has translated Greek novels by V. Vassilikos and poems by several contemporary Greek poets.

THOMAS E. KENNEDY is a Danish writer and translator. In the United States, his fiction and criticism are recent or forthcoming in *North American Review, Kenyon Review, Literary Review, Black Warrior Review, Writers Forum, Sewanee Review*, and elsewhere. He served as guest editor of the Nordic literary supplement recently appearing in *Frank: An International Journal* in Paris. His book on the short fiction of Andre Dubus will soon be released by the G. K. Hall/Twayne Series of Short Fiction Studies.

JASCHA KESSLER is a Professor of English at UCLA. Among his awards are a Shirley Collier Award, PEN Club's Memorial Medal, and two Senior Fulbright Awards to Italy. He is an eminent translator, and has published four collections of his own stories and three collections of poetry, as well as several plays.

YUSUF al-KHAL is a Lebanese publisher and owner of Gallery One in Beirut. He has published many volumes of poetry and prose, as well as works of criticism and translation; his books include *Herodiat, Al Bi'r al Mahjourat* and *Qasa'id fil Arba'yn*.

BYONG MOK KIM, born in Seoul, educated at UCLA and Columbia University, is a practicing physician in San Diego who continues his lifelong interest in literature.

NAM CHO KIM, a Korean poet, is Professor at Sook Myong Women's University in Seoul; for her work, she won the 25th Independence Day Literary Award in 1984 and also a Korean Poetry Award. Her books include *Tree and Wind, Soul and Bread* and *Selected Poems*.

SARAH KIRSCH was born in the Harz Mountains of Germany; she now lives in Schleswig-Holstein, West Germany. She is author of some thirty-three books, including *Katzenkopfpflaster*; she has won many prizes in both East and West Germany, including the Heinrich Heine Prize, the Petrarch Prize and the Holderlin Prize.

SANG KOO, a Korean poet, is Professor at Chung-ang University in Seoul and served as Chairman of the Asian Poetry Conference there in 1986. His works have won several awards, including the Cultural Literary Award and the National Literary Award.

MARIA KÖRÖSY, a Hungarian translator, is English Secretary to the Hungarian P.E.N. Club. For her work, she has been awarded a British Council Grant.

YU KUAN-CHUNG, Professor at the Chinese University in Hong Kong, is one of the most prolific and celebrated poets of contemporary China; he is also a translator, essayist and literary critic.

CAHIT KULEBI is a Turkish educator, and is one of Turkey's most published poets. Also active in politics and government, he has represented Turkey abroad and in Parliament.

MAXINE KUMIN is an American poet, novelist and author of books for children. For her work, she was awarded an honorary doctorate from Radcliffe University. Her many books include *The Privilege, Halfway, The Passions of Uxport* and *Through Dooms of Love.*

NAOMI LAZARD is the author of four books of poetry. She has won the Robert Payne Translation Award from the Translation Center at Columbia University, and also two fellowships from the National Endowment for the Arts. Her translations from the Urdu of Faiz Ahmed Faiz, *The True Subject,* is new from Princeton University Press.

ALEXIS LEVITIN has published translations of Brazilian and Portuguese short story writers and poets in more than 100 magazines and in numerous anthologies. His translations of contemporary Brazilian short fiction, predominantly by Luiz Vilela and Clarice Lispector, have appeared in magazines such as *Fiction, Latin American Literary Review, Translation* and many others. He is currently completing work on a translation of a collection of short stories by the Brazilian author, Clarice Lispector.

YANG LIAN was born in Beijing and settled in the countryside during the Cultural Revolution. His poems have since appeared in many national magazines, and he is a member of the Chinese Writers Association.

JULIA C. LIN was born in Shanghai, but has long lived in the United States; she is Professor of English at Ohio University. Her books include *Modern Chinese Poetry: An Introduction* and *Essays on Contemporary Chinese Poetry.*

TAN A. LIN is pursuing his Ph.D. in English from Columbia University. He won first prize in *Mademoiselle's* 16th Annual College Poetry Competition in 1979. He is presently working with his mother, Julia C. Lin, in translating the poetry of Li Shang-yin, a late Tang poet.

ARTUR LUNDKVIST is one of Sweden's foremost writers. He has published nearly fifty books of poetry, prose, essays and critical works. He is a member of the Swedish Academy of Arts and Letters, and he has not only influenced Swedish literature, but has worked for the understanding of African and North and South American literature in Sweden.

JAYANTA MAHAPATRA is a leading Indian poet. He is also editor of the literary magazine, *Chandrabhaga*, in Orissa. His work has been published and translated widely; in the United States, it has appeared in *Poetry*, *New York Quarterly*, in *Crictial Quarterly* and elsewhere. His many honors and awards include a Rockefeller Foundation Fellowship, a Jacob Glatstein Memorial Prize and a Bisuva Milana Award. His books include *Tales from Fakir Mohan* and *Folk Lores of Ancient India*.

ISSAM MAHFOUZ is a Lebanese journalist who has published plays as well as his poetry.

BRONISŁAW MAJ, a Polish poet, teaches at a university in Krakow; he is founding editor of *Na Głos*, a living journal that holds monthly readings, and is sponsored by the Catholic Intellectual Club. For his work, he has won the international Koscielski Prize.

GIORGIO MANGANELLI is an Italian writer known both for his books and for his role in the avant-garde "Group 63." His books include: *Hilarotragedy, China and Various Other Orients, Pinocchio: A Parallel Text*, and many others. His book *Centuria* won the Viareggio Prize.

EUGENE J. McCARTHY is former Senator from Minnesota and a Presidential Candidate in 1968. His books include *Frontiers in American Democracy, The Year of the People, Other Things and the Aardvark* and *Minnesota*.

STEIN MEHREN has published many volumes of poetry, essays and novels; his poetry, in particular, is known throughout the Scandanavian countries.

CHOU MENG-TIEH, a Chinese poet, lives in Taiwan. He is a Buddhist, and his poetry has been much admired for its Zen-inspired themes, diction and imagery. He has published two volumes of his work.

CZESLAW MILOSZ, Polish poet, essayist and novelist, was born in Lithuania; he has lived in the United States for decades. Until his retirement he taught in the Department of Slavic Languages and Literatures at the University of California, Berkeley. His work has appeared in many periodicals, including the *New Yorker, Partisan Review* and *Saturday Review*; translations of his work also appear in *Polish Post-War Poetry* and *Selected Poems*. For his work, he was awarded the Neustadt International Prize in 1978 and the Nobel Prize for Literature in 1980.

KIYOKO MIURA, a translator, is also known as a forerunner of free verse in Japan.

EDWARD MORIN is a professor at Wayne State University. His translations from French and modern Greek have appeared in *New Letters, Chariton Review, Confrontation, Berkeley Poetry Review, Stylus* and *Webster Review*. His own poems have been published in *Hudson Review, Ploughshares, Poetry Northwest*, and elsewhere. He has also published a collection of his poems; another collection is forthcoming.

KIYOKO NAGASE, a Japanese writer, has published more than twenty volumes of her own poems; she has received several awards for her work. She is also publisher of *Yellow Roses* and *Women's Essays*.

HENRIKAS NAGYS, a Lithuanian poet, was one of the founders of the *Zeme* (Earth) group of Lithuanian emigre writers during the post-World War II years. His books include *Eilerasciai, Lapkricio naktys, Saules laikrodziai, Melynas sniegas, Broliai balti aitvarai* and *Prisijaukinsiu sakala*.

LEONARD NATHAN teaches in the Department of Rhetoric at the University of California, Berkeley. His work has been published widely; his many awards include a National Institute of Arts and Letters Award for Creative Literature and a Guggenheim Foundation Fellowship. He has published many books; most recent is *Carrying On: New and Selected Poems*.

CHRIS NEWMAN, an English writer, is a noted translator of Russian into English.

CEES NOOTEBOOM, from Holland, has written short stories, travel books, poems and four novels; his books include *Vuurtijd ijstijd: Gedichten, 1955–1983*. He has won the Pegasus Prize for Literature in the Netherlands; this award was given his book, *Rituals*, honored as the best Dutch novel of its decade. With Leonard Nathan, he is now translating a selection of his poems for English publication.

MAREK NOWAKOWSKI is a prolific Polish author of novels and short stories. Since martial law he has published only in Western and underground presses. His book of short stories about martial law, *The Canary*, was recently released.

NAOMI SHIHAB NYE lives in San Antonio, Texas. She won a National Poetry Series Award in 1982 for her book, *Hugging the Juke Box*. She has also published *Different Ways to Pray* and *Yellow Glove*.

JOYCE CAROL OATES teaches creative writing at Princeton University. She is a prolific author of novels, short stories, poems, essays, reviews, articles and plays. With her husband, Raymond Smith, she edits and copublishes

Ontario Review and Ontario Review Press. She is recipient of many honors and awards, including a Guggenheim Foundation Fellowship and a National Book Award for *Them*. Her work has been widely anthologized, including regular selections in the award collections. She was selected for a Special Continuing Achievement Award from the O. Henry Awards. Recent books are *Mysteries of Winterthurn* and *You Must Remember This*.

SHOKO OKAZAKI is a Japanese national, a promising scholar who has presented her work before many audiences in the United States.

TOMMY OLOFSSON is one of Sweden's leading younger poets. He has published five volumes of poetry; he is also a well known literary critic for *Svenska Dagbladet*.

EWALD OSERS is a Fellow of the Royal Society of Literature. He's also a Fellow of the Institute of Linguists and of International P.E.N., among other organizations. He has translated more than eighty books, and more than 1000 poems. He is recipient of many medals, honors and awards, and has lectured at numerous American universities, congresses and symposia.

ALICIA OSTRIKER is Professor of English at Rutgers University. She is author of six volumes of poetry, most recently *A Woman Under the Surface*. Among her awards are the William Carlos William Award from the Poetry Society of America and a Guggenheim Foundation Fellowship. She is also a critic, author of *Vision and Verse in William Blake*.

TU-JIN PARK is Professor at Yun-sae University in Seoul; he has served as past Chairman of the Academy of Korean Arts and Letters. He has published many books, including *Love on Earth* and *The Masses*.

LINDA PASTAN is an American poet. Her awards include the DiCastagnola Award and the Maurice English Award. Her books include *A Perfect Circle of Sun, Aspects of Eve, Waiting for My Life* and *AM/PM*; most recent is *A Fraction of Darkness*.

LEFTERIS PAVLIDES, born on the island of Lesbos, educated in Athens, also studied at Yale and the University of Pennsylvania. He has published his translations in *New Letters, Confrontation, Chariton Review, Webster Review, Berkeley Poetry Review, Wayne Review*, and elsewhere.

OCTAVIO PAZ is a leading Mexican poet, philosopher and literary critic. His many books include *Eagle or Sun?, Conjunctions* and *Selected Poems*. Forthcoming is *Collected Poems 1957–1987*.

JEAN PEARSON is a free-lance writer and translator in Pennsylvania. She has published her translations of Swedish and German poets in *Stone Country, Poet Lore, American Poetry Review*, and in many other journals. Her own poems have been widely published also. She has also served as editor for *Mickle Street Review*, the annual literary journal of the Walt Whitman Association.

C. DENIS PEGGE is an English writer living in the Canary Islands. His work has appeared in many periodicals and anthologies, including *Blackwood's Magazine, Poetry Review*, the *Times Literary Supplement* and *Fear No More*. His honors include the Crabbe Memorial Poetry Prize; his books include *Tribute* and *Night View*.

VASILE POENARU is a promising young Rumanian poet; he is editor of the English Page of *Tribuna României*, a multi-lingual cultural journal published in Bucharest. His books include *Jungla Marina* and *Investigatii*. His work has appeared in translation in Greece, Turkey and Bulgaria.

LI QI is a college teacher, as well as a poet, in China.

AI QING is a leading Chinese poet. He has also served as editor of *Poetry* and of *People's Literature*, although he disappeared from the literary scene through twenty years of political upheaval. He has resumed publishing his work in recent years; he has published more than fourteen books of his poetry.

JAMES RAGAN is Director of the Professional Writing Program at the University of Southern California. Recent publications include *Denver Quarterly, Windsor Review* and *Ohio Review*, among others. His books include *In the Talking Hours* and *Neighborings*.

PEDRO GUTIERREZ REVUELTA, born in Madrid, Spain, is an Assistant Professor of Spanish at the University of Houston. He is the managing editor of *Americas Review*, and Arte Publico Press. He has published criticism, poetry and translations in American, Latin-American and Spanish literary journals. He has also published two collections of poetry, *Nosotros* and *Del Amor Presente*.

FOU'AD RIFQAH was born in Syria but is now a Lebanese citizen. He has published poetry, translations and philosophical essays.

DIONIS COFFIN RIGGS is a poet and translator from the Martha's Vineyard area. Her poems have been published for more than fifty years.

YANNIS RITSOS is an esteemed Greek poet; he has published eighty-two volumes of poetry. He has received many national and international awards, including the State Prize Award for Poetry, the International Prize and the Lenin Prize. His books include *Chronicle of Exile* and *the Fourth Dimension: Selected Poems*.

M. J. ROBERTS is an American poet, short story writer and award winning playwright. Her work has appeared in journals and anthologies such as *Electrum, A Door Ajar* and *End to End*. Her plays, *Reflections* and *Match Point*, have been widely staged and cited for excellence. She is also author of the novel, *Tangled Vines*.

NORBERTO LUIS ROMERO is an Argentine, now a citizen of Spain. He is an advertising specialist and commercial filmmaker, specialist in animated cartoons. His work has been widely published in the United States and Canada, as well as, in Spanish, in South America. He won the First Noega Award for Short Fiction in 1983 for *Transgressions*.

LARRY RUBIN is a well-known Southern writer. His honors include a Reynolds Lyric Award from the Poetry Society of America, the Smith-Mundt Award and the Sidney Lanier Award. His books include *All My Mirrors Lie*.

ROBERT SABATIER is a French novelist, memoirist, critic and poet. His books include *Les Années secrètes d'une vie d'un Homme, Fêtes solaires, Icare et autres poèmes,* and *Les Poisons délectables.*

STEVEN SADOW is Associate Professor of Spanish at Northeastern University in Boston. He teaches Spanish Language, Latin American Literature and Culture, as well as Inter-Cultural Communications. In 1982 he was awarded an Excellence in Teaching Award. His work includes studies of Ricardo Guiraldes and Manueles Rojas; his books include the textbook *Idea Bank* and forthcoming, *Fantástico.*

JOHN SATRIANO's translations have appeared in *Harper's, Salmagundi, Monthly Review,* and elsewhere. He has also translated works by a number of Italian writers, including two books by Ennio Flaiano and a volume of essays by Alberto Moravia.

CLINTON B. SEELY is Associate Professor of Bengali at the University of Chicago. He is also author of many articles, books and translations; his awards include a Fulbright-Hays Faculty Research Abroad Fellowship and an American Institute of Indian Studies Senior Research Fellowship. His books include *Grace and Mercy in Her Wild Hair: Selected Poems to the Mother Goddess* (co-author, Leonard Nathan) and *Intermediate Bengali.*

ERIC SELLIN is Professor of French at Temple University. His translations of French, Swedish, Italian, Maghrebian, and African poets have appeared in many journals. He is also a poet in English and in French. His books include *Night Voyage, Trees at First Light, Borne kilométrique* and *Crepuscule prolongé à El Biar.*

LEI SHU-YAN, a Chinese poet, works for Workers Press. He has published nine books of his poems; his awards include a National Prize for Poetry. His books have been translated into four continental European languages; his books include *The Little Glass Is Singing*.

KIRSTI SIMONSUURI, a Finnish writer, is Senior Researcher at the Academy of Finland, and Docent in Literary History and the Classical Tradition, Universities of Helsinki and Turku. For her poetry, she has won the J. H. Erkko Prize in Finland. Her books include *Ivy Balustrade, The Rape of Europa* and *The Northern Noctuary*.

WILLIAM STAFFORD recently retired from Lewis and Clark College; he is a former Consultant in Poetry to the Library of Congress. His many awards for poetry include a Shelley Award, a Guggenheim Foundation Fellowship and a National Book Award. His new books are *You Must Revise Your Life, You and Some Other Characters* and *An Oregon Message*.

VENO TAUFER is a Yugoslavian poet, essayist, translator; he has also served as writer, editor and critic for RTV. He is on leave as Distinguished Artist-in-Residence at the University of Maryland, under the Senior Fulbright Program. His work has been awarded the Preseren Award for Literature and the Sovre Award for Translation. His nine books of poetry include *Lead Stars, Straightening the Nails, Sonnets* and *Selected Poems*.

DALTON TREVISAN is a leading Brazilian writer. Since 1959 he has published a score of volumes of short tales dealing with love and death set in the microcosm of Curitiba, a provincial capital in the South of Brazil. His collections include *The Vampire of Curitiba, The Mysteries of Curitiba* and *The King of the Earth*.

GEORGE UBA is Assistant Professor of English at California State University, Northridge; he is past winner of the Academy of American Poets Prize. Recent and forthcoming publications of his own poetry and of his translations include *Seattle Review, Bridge, Jacaranda Review,*

CHIYO UNO is one of Japan's most eminent writers. Now a *grande dame* of Japanese letters, Uno has gathered media attention during recent years; her life story was serialized on television and recent movies have been made from her books. Previously, she won the Noma Prize, Japan's highest literary award. Of her many books, *Confessions of Love*, is considered her best work.

RUBEN VELA is an Argentine author, currently Ambassador of Argentina to Zaire. His work has been included in twenty-five anthologies in the Americas and Europe. He has won many Argentine and Latin American Poetry prizes. His books include *American Poems, Secrets* and *The Armed World*.

CINTIO VITIER is a Cuban poet. His books include *Poemas, Sedienta Cita, Extrañeza de Estar, De mi Provincia, El Hogar y el Ovido, Víspera* and *Vanto Illano*.

ANDREI VOZNESENSKY is one of Russia's leading poets. This year he was instrumental in establishing the first official Pasternak festival and reading in Moscow. He has won many honors and awards, including the State Award in Literature, as well as awards from the American Academy of Arts and Letters and the French Poetry Academy. His works include *Juno and Perchan* and *Unaccountable*; his most recent collection is *Arrow in the Wall*.

ANTHONY WATTS is an English poet who has published his work in magazines and anthologies, including *New Poetry, Orbis* and *The Pen*. For his work, he has been awarded the Arvon Foundation Prize, the Michael Johnson Memorial Prize and the Lake Aske Memorial Award. Two collections are forthcoming.

ELIOT WEINBERGER is editor and translator of many books of Latin American poetry and prose, most recently, *The Collected Poems of Octavio Paz 1959–1987*. He is also author of a collection of essays, *Works on Paper*.

SANDOR WEÖRES is Hungary's greatest living poet; he is a prolific translator as well. His books in English include *Sandor Weöres—Selected Poems, Overhearing, Collected Works, Collected Translations, Thirty-five Poems* and *Mail from Abroad*.

MERRYN WILLIAMS is an English poet. She has published work on Thomas Hardy and other Victorian novelists; she has also published a biography of Margaret Oliphant.

OZCAN YALIM is a Turkish educator and an authority on Contemporary Turkish poetry.

YEVGENY YEVTUSHENKO is Russia's most well known poet; he also works in prose and with film. He has won many honors and awards, including the USSR Peace Award. His works include *Under the Skin* and *Ivan the Terrible*; his most recent book is *Almost at the End*, which features a foreword by John Ashberry.

YAN YI, a Chinese poet, works for a film studio in Sichuan. He has published thirty books of poetry, plays, movie scripts, criticism, and other prose.

JONAS ZDANYS is director of communications and publications for the Office of University Development at Yale University, where he also teaches a seminar on the theory and practice of poetic translation. For his work, he has been awarded grants from the Connecticut Commission on the Arts and the National Endowment for the Arts. He has published nine books, including both translations and his own work. He has two books forthcoming: *Water Light* and *Blue Snow: Selected Poems of Henrikas Nagys*.

RICHARD ZENITH's poems and translations have appeared in *Atlantic Monthly, Partisan, Paris Review, Georgia Review,* and in many other periodicals. Last year he won a National Endowment for the Humanities Fellowship for translation, and he has just been awarded a Guggenheim Foundation Fellowship. He has also just been awarded a grant from the Vogelstein Foundation to produce a bilingual anthology of Gullar's work.

MUSEUM ACKNOWLEDGMENTS

The editors wish to extend special thanks to those museum curators and other personnel who allowed photographs of pieces from their permanent collections to be included in Literary Olympians II. And personal thanks are offered to those who so graciously assisted in selections and permissions: at Hearst Castle, to Bill Clawson and Bob Latson; at Korean Cultural Service, to Jiwon Suh; at Los Angeles County Museum of Art, to Anna Graham and Pamela Jenkinson; at Museum of Photographic Arts, to Bobbie Gilbert and Jean Wilder; at San Diego Museum of Art, to Lisa Davis and Carmen Lacey; at Santa Barbara Museum of Art, to Virginia Cochran and Lesley King-Wrightson; at Norton Simon Museum of Art, to Cheryl Barton and Sara Campbell.

HEARST CASTLE: Front cover, *Mars with Cupid,* by Marcellini. Back cover, *The Three Graces,* by Boyer.

LOS ANGELES COUNTY MUSEUM OF ART, PERMANENT COLLECTION: page 22, *Memory,* Elihu Vedder; page 90, *Anger,* Heister; page 212, *Seated Harlequin,* Juan Gris; page 278, *Horses and Cranes,* Soga Shohaku; page 360, *Flight,* Hans Hofman; page 388, *Sunlight,* Max Herman Pechstein; page 406, *Flowers,* Ma Yuan.

MUSEUM OF PHOTOGRAPHIC ARTS, PERMANENT COLLECTION: page 52, *Aspens, Northern New Mexico,* Ansel Adams; page 120, Untitled, Elliott Erwitt; page 128, *Golden Gate Bridge,* Peter Stackpole; page 182, *Le Menège de Monsieur Barré,* Robert Doisneau; page 318, Untitled, Arthur Rothstein.

NATIONAL MUSEUM OF KOREA: page 204, Gilt Bronze, *Maitrea,* Old Silla Dynasty.

NATIONAL MUSEUM OF MODERN ART: page 170, *The Echo of a Bow,* Yun Hyo-jung.

SAN DIEGO MUSEUM OF ART, PERMANENT COLLECTION: page 224, *The Young Shepherdess,* Julian Dupre; page 306, *Three-Headed Deity,* Anonymous (India); page 324, *Two Herons in Reeds,* Seiko; page 458, *A Bend in the River with Houses and Poplars,* Camille Corot.

SANTA BARBARA MUSEUM OF ART, PERMANENT COLLECTION: page 256, *Timber Brig, Sandwich Bay,* Sir Frank Brangwyn, Gift of Mary and Will Richeson, Jr.; page 292, *Seat Supported by Figure of Kneeling Female,* Luba Tribe, Gift of Mrs. Max Schott; page 332, *Woman Playing Shakuhachi,* Utagawa Toyokuni, Gift of O. S. Southworth; page 412, *Siddhartha, Cutting His Hair,* Anonymous, Gift of Mrs. Wilbur L. Cummings, Senior, in memory of her son, Wilbur L. Cummings, Jr.; page 432, *Le Pardon de Ste. Anne-La-Palud,* Henri Riviere, Gift of Mr. and Mrs. T. Frame Thomson; facing title page, *Head of Griffin,* page 268, *Statuette of Hermes,* page 298, *Head of Aphrodite,* Anonymous, Gifts of Wright S. Ludington.

NORTON SIMON ART MUSEUM, PERMANENT COLLECTION: page 34, *Françoise on Grey,* Pablo Picasso, c. 1950, lithograph, Norton Simon Foundation; page 62, *Dancers in Pink,* Edgar Degas, c. 1883, pastel on cardboard, Norton Simon Foundation; page 80, *Library Interior with Still Life,* Jan van der Hayden, oil on canvas, Norton Simon Foundation; page 106, *Red-Headed Woman in the Garden of Monsieur Forêt,* Henri Raymond de Toulouse-Lautrec, oil on cardboard, Norton Simon Foundation; page 152, *Life and Death,* Alexei Jawlensky, 1923, oil on cardboard, The Blue Four Galka Scheyer Collection, Norton Simon Museum; page 246, *Tulips in a Vase,* Paul Cezanne, c. 1890–92, oil/pp. mounted board, Norton Simon Art Foundation.